Anacostia

Anacostia

The Death & Life of an American River

JOHN R. WENNERSTEN

THE CHESAPEAKE BOOK COMPANY
BALTIMORE, MARYLAND
2008

Library of Congress Cataloging-in-Publication Data

Wennersten, John R., 1941-
Anacostia : the death and life of an American river / John R. Wennersten.
    p. cm.
Includes bibliographical references and index.
ISBN-13: 978-0-9635159-6-4 (alk. paper)
ISBN-10: 0-9635159-6-9 (alk. paper)
    1. Anacostia River (Md. and Washington, D.C.)--History. 2. Anacostia River
(Md. and Washington, D.C.)--Environmental conditions. 3. Anacostia River
Watershed (Md. and Washington, D.C.)--History. 4. Anacostia River Water-
shed (Md. and Washington, D.C.)--Environmental conditions. 5. Anacostia
River Region (Md. and Washington, D.C.)--Politics and government. 6. Wash-
ington Region--Politics and government. 7. Conservation of natural resources-
-Political aspects--Anacostia River Region (Md. and Washington, D.C.) 8.
Conservation of natural resources--Moral and ethical aspects--Anacostia River
Region (Md. and Washington, D.C.) 9. Environmental protection--Political
aspects--Anacostia River Region (Md. and Washington, D.C.) 10. Environmental protection--Moral and ethical aspects--Anacostia River Region (Md.
and Washington, D.C.) I. Title.
 F202.A5W46 2008
 333.7309753--dc22

                              2008029284

Manufactured in the United States of America on paper containing 30 perccent
post-consumer waste. The paper used in this publication meets the minimum
requirements of the American National Standard for Information Sciences
Permanence of Paper for Printed Library Materials ANSI Z39.48-1984.

Available wherever fine books are sold. Distributed by Alan C. Hood & Co.,
Inc., P.O. Box 775, Chambersburg, PA 17201. (Phone: 717-267-0867; Toll-free
Fax for orders, 888-844-9433; www.hoodbooks.com.)

For Ruth Ellen

Contents

List of Illustrations
(following page 136)

Early tracts of land in the District of Columbia

Map of the District, 1792, made by Pierre L'Enfant

"City of Washington from Beyond the Navy Yard," 1833

Shad fisherman near the Washington Navy Yard

The Sixth Street wharf in the antebellum pierod

George Washington House in Bladensburg

The 11th Street Bridge in 1862 (Mathew Brady)

Frederick Douglass

Cows grazing in the Anacostia Marsh, 1882

Storefronts along Nichols Avenue in 1915

The Anacostia Bank on Nichols Avenue

Map of Washington, 1892

Maj. Gen. Peter C. Haines of the Army Corps of Engineers

Dredge boat on the Anacostia, 1910

"Seventh Street, Washington, D.C., Under the Flood," 1889

Washington Navy Yard during the great flood of 1936

Camp of the Bonus Expeditionary Force, July 1932

Aerial photograph of the engineered Anacostia, 1930s

Map of the Anacostia Watershed

Accumulated refuse on the river

Party of canoeists on a scenic section of the Anacostia

Robert Boone in his kayak

The Northeast Branch in winter

Acknowledgments

My work on the Anacostia River changed over time from a magazine assignment to a full-blown environmental history that took several years to finish. I owe its completion to the support and patience of my wife, Ruth Ellen, who probably learned more about the Anacostia than she wanted to know, and the unflagging optimism of John Lyon and the volunteers and staff at the Anacostia Watershed Society. Jeffrey Stine at the Smithsonian National Museum of American History became a valued colleague and mentor of all things Anacostia while I was a Senior Research Fellow at the Smithsonian. A grant from the Summit Fund has facilitated the publication of this book. The author extends his thanks.

Once there was a time when the Anacostia was a forgotten and broken river with few defenders. Most people thought it little more than a sewer. Fortunately, today that is not the case. In recent times, many men and women in the Washington metropolitan area have rallied to the cause of the Anacostia. For friendship, advice, and support during this project I would especially like to thank Jack Greer and Merrill Leffler of Sea Grant at the University of Maryland, Cameron Wiegand, watershed manager, Montgomery County Department of Environmental Protection, Tom Arrasmith, Chair of the Anacostia Citizens Advisory Committee, Professor Margaret Palmer, stream ecologist, University of Maryland, Dave Velinsky, Academy of Natural Science, Philadelphia, Jim Collier, Anacostia gadfly, Jim Cummins, the "shad man" of the Interstate Commission on the Potomac River Basin, Nick DiNardo, Anacostia Watershed Toxics Alliance, Neil Weinstein, Low Impact Development Center, Larry Coffman, hydrologist, Stacey

Underwood, U.S. Army Corps of Engineers, Dave Baron, Earth Justice, Ned Chalker, Potomac River Pilots Association, Doug Siglin, Chesapeake Bay Foundation, and Hamid Karimi of the D.C. Department of the Environment. Stephen Syphax of the National Park Service provided much needed perspective on the river as an "engineered system." Steve McKinley-Ward introduced me to the problems of stream bank stabilization in the Anacostia watershed. Robert E. Hyman deserves a word of praise as well. He has brought attention to the watershed with "No Dumping" signs that he and school children have affixed to the sewers of Washington. Thanks furthermore to Professor Brett Williams of American University, who angrily called attention to the Anacostia through her scholarship.

I would like to thank especially all those citizens of DC who live "East of the River" in Wards 7 and 8 who befriended me and patiently answered my questions. Further, I benefited from the insights of Joseph Glover, a civic leader in Ward 7, and Alberta Paul of the Washington East Foundation. Herbert Harris of Citizens in the Afro-American Community in the District deserves special mention. His organization successfully fought government policies that would have turned Anacostia neighborhoods and parklands into amusement parks and parking lots. One man at River Terrace, George Gurley, showed that raising hell on occasion brings results.

Jim Connolly, Carl Cole, and the men and women of the Seafarers Yacht Club over the years have shown an enduring commitment to the Anacostia. The have rowed it, sailed it, swum it, and championed it.

Robert Boone, the Anacostia Watershed Society's own stormy petrel, has always defended the water, its heritage, and community—even when hope had flown and others had given up. The Anacostia River runs through him.

Introduction

The story of the Anacostia illustrates how impaired river systems become contested regions of class and race. Anacostia's waters flow through Washington, D.C., the nation's capital, and after a heavy rain the river becomes a garbage and trash-laden waterway. Our political leaders have only to gaze through their windows to observe the tragedy of our rivers and watersheds. The fact that a polluted, junk-strewn river runs through one of the world's wealthiest capitals and coincidentally through the underprivileged black neighborhoods in the region, only adds to the poignancy of the Anacostia's impairment. From the colonial period to the present the river has been a manipulated environment, one altered, transformed, or planned by agricultural and corporate elites, politicians, and real estate developers. Historically the Anacostia has also been a dumping ground for dispossessed populations, rubbish, sewage, and toxins. It has not figured largely in the public thinking of either the United States Congress or the State of Maryland, and in the District of Columbia the Anacostia has always been a problematic afterthought. Yet the river gives us a point of entry for thinking about Washington, the watershed and regional and local networks of power. It also enables us to think about the environmental and cultural facts that help people make sense out of the place in which they live.

This is a river story of colonial and federal power that involves people still waiting for political and environmental redemption. It links the river with the plantation culture of antebellum Maryland and Virginia and to the creation of Washington. Rivers provide a sense of place that shapes a city's social and economic life. They are also political markers. The Ohio was a marker for anti-slavery during the antebellum period and the Mississippi demarcated the westward march of Americans into the territories. Painters and mapmakers used rivers as more than decorative objects. They were powerful symbols that often depicted the boundaries between civilization and frontier, between settlement and empire. And so has it been with the Anacostia and the capital—a marker for power and poverty, racial supremacy and racial oppression.

Washington, D.C. is a special place, outside the direct control of a single state or administrative unit. At once a federal city and an international city, it is controlled by the U.S. Congress, yet its citizens lack full political representation even though they pay federal taxes. It came into existence as a river city, and its landscape has been freighted with a host of symbolic meanings, not all of which are understood by the local populace. As a socially constructed entity, the Anacostia River, in particular, is differently construed and interpreted by whites and blacks. In the early days of capital-building, for example, it figured largely in Pierre L'Enfant's vision of Washington as a political and commercial center. The Civil War transformed the Anacostia into an urban river and sewage conduit whose problems continued into the modern era. The river also became a metaphor for regional racial problems that extended from slavery through the public housing controversies and urban discontent of the twentieth century.

Since the 1980s the river has been much in the news because of its high levels of fecal coliform bacteria and dangerous toxic waste. While environmental groups try to rescue the river, city planners and developers hope to transform the Anacostia waterfront into a pleasant locale of parks, shopping centers, offices, and residences. Meanwhile racial issues connected with the river and urban transformation scarcely enter the public discourse. It remains to be seen if urban progress can take place without the social and economic uplift of the city's African American population. Sadly, one can argue that at this writing, L'Enfant's plan for the active development of the Anacostia River as a center of democracy, commerce, and culture continues only as the cant of development.

Part of the vast tributary system of the Potomac Basin, the Anacostia courses through the capital's Maryland suburbs to its mouth at the Potomac River near downtown Washington. The Anacostia is a tidal river, and its watershed is home to 1,113,802 residents.[1] Forty-nine percent of its 178 square miles is in Prince George's County, 34 percent in Montgomery County and 17 percent in the District of Columbia. Its riverhead is just outside the District in the vicinity of Bladensburg in Prince George's County. The Anacostia in its tidal component is 8.5 miles in length, and it is hardly a major river in the sense of the Mississippi or the Ohio. But then, neither was Thoreau's Walden Pond a great lake. The Anacostia at its best has been a sanctuary for bird lovers like John Burroughs and the cradle of the Audubon Society. It has nurtured fishermen, free blacks and unfettered capitalism. It represents in microcosm the conflicted spirit of the American union.

The region's topography has been created out of swamps, marshes, and waterfronts continuously destroyed and remade. Land speculators and modern developers have paid little heed to the values of architecture and history, or to neighborhood traditions. In Washington real estate investors and public officials have been far more dominant creators and shapers of landscape than conservationists and community residents. Ecologist Richard Brewer observes that in the modern age, "government as a bureaucratic entity is no more likely to be on the side of conservation as on the side of the despoiler." Until recently the concern for the aesthetic quality and health of the Anacostia watershed was a concern limited to black leaders who lived in the region and a small group of conservationists. Most citizens passively accepted the deterioration of the region into what historian Joel Tarr has referred to as an "ultimate sink." The way we have treated our rivers and waterfronts, adds Wilbur Zelinsky, is "a classic lesson in the dictates of capitalist economics."[2]

The notion that the current social and environmental problems of urban areas might be examined through the history of rivers is a recent one. Until a few years ago, scholars used a land-focused thesis of urbanization and industrialization to explain the causes of social disruption in the United States. They did not factor in the role that rivers played in this process. Now historians are looking at rivers in new ways. Libby Hill and Blake Gumbrecht, for example, have used the Chicago and Los Angeles rivers as settings for the study of the interplay of environmental and social problems that befell urban regions.[3] Adding rivers to this frame of historical reference gives the urbanization-industrialization model a sharper focus. The Anacostia River, I contend, has shaped the social identity of metropolitan Washington and is at the center of its historical development. Similarly, political and economic events over time in Washington have shaped the Anacostia's destiny.

Until now the Anacostia River has been relatively unstudied. The literature on the Anacostia is slim, confined mostly to engineering reports, planning documents, scientific studies, and the community story of Anacostia by Louise Hutchinson.[4] Most books about American rivers are written by non-historians and are impressionistic and romanticized. Using local data, these writers focus on the tourist dimension of rivers—what makes a river aesthetically attractive rather than how a river connects to a city in terms of an environmental and community symbiosis.[5] This book explores the historical connection in Washington, D.C., between the forces of urban development, sanitation, race, and the Anacostia River.

Further, the history of the Anacostia demonstrates that environmental burdens like pollution and resource depletion are not shared equally, and there are compelling ethical grounds for remedying this river's environmental problems. As ethicist David Schlosberg points out, the mainstream middle-class environmental model itself must be rethought because it often does not include protection for unrepresented minorities.[6]

Washington is also in many respects a small tidewater town. Until recently, Washington was a city defined by plans and monuments, one that sought to affirm democracy even while keeping its people in slavery and poverty. It cared more for its architecture than its residents, headily turning its back on its own history and environment. But the Anacostia flows through Washington, D.C., and the story of this river is a social and environmental chronicle of our time.

Anacostia

CHAPTER ONE

Genesis

The Anacostia River is a product of geological and historical processes that have created a unique environmental setting in the mid-Atlantic zone of North America. The bedrock and waterways that became the Anacostia watershed took shape over the course of thousands of years as Appalachian mountain floods cut through ridges of sandstone and limestone that are now covered with parks, houses, apartment complexes, malls, and a new baseball stadium. The floods deposited sediment, creating a flat coastal plain to which aboriginal populations came and eventually settled. Archaeological remains suggest that by the end of the seventeenth century they had developed a social organization and considerable technical skills. But then came the English, and with them commodity trading in fur and the development of a prosperous tobacco industry. The aboriginals soon disappeared, their place taken by a wave of Africans bound to hard labor. The European colonial encounter with the Anacostia transformed a beautiful river into a ballast dump and an artery of commerce and trade, tempered by the dynamics of racial slavery.

From Prehistory to European Settlement by 1690

The Anacostia is a crucible where people of various races—aboriginal, African, and European—have commingled and altered the natural environment. As they sought to utilize the Anacostia, it became a metaphor for racial oppression and economic transformation.

To understand how it happened, we must reach far into the past.

Movement and change have been persistent themes of the mid-Atlantic's ecology since the dawn of time. Scientists examining the Chesapeake coastal plain have found that the region originated as a part of East Africa that approximately two hundred million years ago split off and drifted westward. The outer edge of this new land mass became the coastal plain and the Atlantic continental shelf. The lands and waters of the region evolved at different rates over time. That which we know as the Anacostia is a fairly recent development. Once covered with tropical rain forests, swamps, grasslands, and pine forests, it later became a cold and bleak tundra. Roughly three thousand years ago, when the great glaciers melted and retreated and sea levels rose, the Anacostia River came into existence as an eastern branch of what is now known as the Potomac River.

Close by the Anacostia, scientists have discovered dinosaur and crocodile bones. Perhaps the most interesting of the prehistoric animals that once flourished here was the plant-feeding *dinosaurm genuse Pleurocoelus*,[1] a creature that attained a length of seventy feet or more. In the 1850s scientists discovered prehistoric shark teeth and teeth of *Priconodon Crassus*, an unusual armored dinosaur. In 1898 workers installing a sewer at 1st and F Streets, NW, found the bones of a large, carnivorous dinosaur. Several more dinosaur bones were found along the Anacostia when the city in 1900 began to excavate a sewer line forty-five feet beneath the surface at 1st and 2nd Streets, SE.[2]

Washington continues to yield up fossilized remains. In 1942 workers building a water filtration plant at 1st and Channing Streets, NW, uncovered the hip bones of a sauropod, ten feet high and sixty feet long, that had become trapped in a mud hole and perished.[3] All dinosaur remains discovered in the District of Columbia are approximately one hundred million years old, from a time when this region more closely resembled in topography and climate the bayou country of southern Louisiana. Recently, near Beltsville, Dr. Peter Kranz uncovered the tooth of a juvenile *tenontosaur*, possibly the only one ever found in North America.[4] These fleet-footed carnivorous dinosaurs grew up to thirty feet long and weighed between six and seven tons. Extinctions are the rule of nature—more than 99 percent of all the species that ever lived are now extinct—and about sixty-five million years ago the dinosaurs disappeared.

People arrived at the end of the most recent Ice Age, about eleven thousand years ago, though descendants of the Anacostans and Piscataways argue that their ancestors have always been here. Scientific evidence suggests that the first human inhabitants might have migrated from the south or west. Scholars speculate that they traveled great distances on foot, which would mean that those aboriginals were nearly as migratory as the metropolitan nomads of our own age. Unfortunately, while we know a little about Paleo-Indian tools, we know practically nothing about their housing and settlement patterns. Excavations of Paleo-Indian artifacts at Thunderbird National Historic Landmark near Front Royal, Virginia, suggest that the aboriginals lived in small post stockades with grass mat dwellings.

As recently as nine thousand years ago, Anacostia's climate and local flora were much like today's northern Canada. Using sediment bores obtained from the flood paths, scientist Grace S. Brush found the region to have been covered with spruce forests 13,000 to 2,500 years ago. After a slight warming over five centuries, the climate came to resemble the Anacostia of today but with much colder winters.[5] "The longest continuous history of postglacial vegetation in the mid-Atlantic region," she noted, "is contained in sediments deposited in the floodplain of Indian Creek, a tributary of the Anacostia."

The Chesapeake reached well up the Potomac, and estuarine waters reached the Anacostia. Meanwhile, dramatic shifts in the forest took place prior to European settlement. White pine, hemlock, birch, fir, ash, hemlock, and oak gradually replaced the boreal forest.[6] By that time, shellfish could be found in the Chesapeake Bay, and large quantities of freshwater mussels and fish were probably important aboriginal foods. The watershed also provided an abundance of tubers, wild rice, and waterfowl. In winter, deer meat and hickory nuts became staples. Because of the dense forest cover, the Indians early on took to setting the forests ablaze to create small meadows where they could grow corn and build their stockaded settlements. In wastefully altering the environment, the Indians revealed a human characteristic that has not changed over time.

The presence of ground stone tools for woodworking indicates that the Indians used wood for fishing weirs, bowls, and baskets. By 1000 BCE, or the Early Woodland period, they began to use ceramics and clay bowls, signs of a more sedentary or storage culture. Corn and stewpot cooking improved the diet and increased longevity in this estuarine community. The Anacostans regularly harvested chestnuts, pumpkins, squash, beans, and maize. Wild rye, called *mattoume* by the Indians, was a grass used in making bread. Indians also harvested raspberries, blackberries, huckleberries, persimmons, and wild grapes—fruits that grew in profusion.

According to Richard J. Dent, archeological remains also suggest that the Anacostans had flourishing trade networks with Native Americans as far west as Indiana and Ohio. In excavating mortuary complexes, archeologists discovered fire-clay implements and shales and slates that came from Ohio.[7] Evidence also shows that improved hunting weaponry, in the form of spears and arrows, allowed the Anacostans to feast on all sorts of meat, from deer to bobcat, and extraordinary amounts of fish.

The Indians used the Anacostia watershed, the Potomac, and the Chesapeake as avenues of commerce and communication. Indians usually built towns at the confluence of navigable streams or directly on the river. Their villages consisted of long houses covered with straw or reed mats, encircled by post palisades with the posts placed vertically into the ground eight to ten inches apart. Gaps in the palisades were covered with a wooden latticework daubed in clay. Experts on early

Indian demographics assert that the Indian tribes in the Anacostia watershed were of Algonquin stock and seldom numbered more than two hundred souls.[8]

In the last two centuries before the European arrival, the Indians of the Anacostia left a rich and intriguing archeological trail. According to archeologist Wayne Clark, Indians in the Potomac region established "horticultural base camps that were occupied throughout the year by part of the populace. Their economy was based on slash and burn agriculture with extensive deer hunting for the procurement of meat." Besides meat, deer provided an "elaborate bone industry" of tools and decorative items.[9] Agriculture and growing social complexity are the hallmarks of this final non-white era in the watershed. Discoveries of above-ground granaries, warehouses, and refuse middens indicate the Indians tended to stay in place. The extensive use of ceramics and a storage infrastructure show a high level of social organization and social stratification. Shellfish harvesting took on new importance, and projectile points highlight the presence of bow and arrow weaponry.

Archeological investigations of Algonquin funeral sites in the Potomac region have uncovered ossuaries that held ancestral bones. Burial pits also reveal food deposits that reveal a carbohydrate-rich diet of wild rice, amaranth, and maize. Amaranth, especially, produced nutritious seeds that the aboriginals made into baking flour. (Today amaranth flour is highly prized in organic cooking circles.) Significant numbers of aboriginal skulls show a greater frequency of dental caries than more nomadic hunting Indians. In the final centuries before the arrival of Europeans, Indian tools were increasingly more sophisticated, and the food base was adequate to support an expanding population.

The Indians' cultural values remain largely unknown to us. Changes in pottery design may indicate a greater reliance upon agriculture. One thing is certain: Archeological investigation reveals an aboriginal culture that began with the chipped stone implements of hunter-gatherers and evolved into a settled life dependent upon small-scale, maize-squash-bean agriculture and the resources of the rivers and Chesapeake Bay. Yet, though indirect evidence is abundant, the mosaic of Indian culture nevertheless remains as incomplete and elusive as the pottery shards found in ancient burial pits.

Perhaps the best view we have of local Indian culture on the eve of European settlement is contained at the Accokeek Creek National Landmark in Prince George's County, Maryland. There, archeologists have found evidence of a densely occupied settlement in which farming was the paramount activity. The site contains ossuaries as well as clusters of food storage pits, hearths, and several levels of household refuse. Located on the shores of the Potomac, it was protected by a circular stockade wall. Plants from local marshes provided material for sleeping mats and roofing. Cattail roots and tuckahoe tubers from the marsh were readily available to be ground into flour for various breads. Inhabitants gathered eggs from bird and turtle nests, plundered beehives, and trapped fish in weirs. The town was on a major travel route and was high enough on terraced banks to avoid flooding and the worst of insects during summer and the rainy season.

Anaquash-a-tan

The word "Anacostia" has an interesting etymology. According to historian Thomas Cantwell, it "evolved from the name of the tribe of Indians who lived in the area, the Nacochtank," who were of Algonquin linguistic stock.[10] While on a trading voyage up the Potomac in 1632, Captain Henry Fleet recorded in his journal that he encountered a tribe he called "Nacostines." Jesuit missionaries arriving with Lord Baltimore a few years later Latinized "Nacochtank" to "Anacostan," whence we get "Anacostia." Other scholars have speculated that "Anacostia" is an anglicized corruption of the Algonquin word *anaquash-a-tan*, or village trading center. Throughout its history the word "Anacostia" has been used to describe a people, a river, a region, a town and a post office.[11]

At the moment of European contact, the Anacostia watershed was a thriving center of Indian culture. Calling themselves Nacotchtanks, these coastal Indians lived a semi-agricultural life at the confluence of the Potomac and Anacostia Rivers at what is now the Washington Navy Yard. Food was in ample supply.[12] The Anacostans pursued their own personal and material interests, often in partnership with other tribes like the Susquehannocks and Piscataways. Trade flourished.

This wholly Indian world of the Anacostia changed forever with the coming of the Europeans. In the first quarter of the sixteenth century, the Chesapeake Bay and its tributaries were "cartographically known" in Europe and are included on Spanish maps of the time. By the end of that century, English reconnoitering expeditions had entered the mouth of the Chesapeake and were taking the full measure of the landscape and its inhabitants. Based on their reports, investors and adventurers concluded that the Chesapeake Bay was a hospitable environment. The Virginia Company sent a three-vessel expedition in 1607 and established Jamestown colony on a river the English named for King James I. From there Captain John Smith set sail in 1608 to explore the estuary and eventually sail up the Potomac River.

Perhaps the most crucial piece of intelligence that Smith and his English contemporaries gathered was the extent to which the Indians everywhere around the bay and up into the Anacostia engaged in sophisticated corn or maize agriculture. Smith reported Indian warehouses brimming with the staple. Thus when the first settlers arrived in the Anacostia watershed and in the Potomac basin generally, they encountered a people who were hardly savages inhabiting an impenetrable wilderness. Historian Timothy Silver writes that despite extensive Indian agriculture there was little soil erosion. "Many of the first Europeans," he writes, "were amazed at the clarity of the various streams and rivers which seemed to carry very little sediment even during high water."[13] Indian agriculture probably did not involve massive deforestation.

For Thomas Harriott, perhaps the most perceptive reporter on indigenous Chesapeake culture at the beginning of the Contact Period, the Indians were a remarkable, waterborne people. "Doubtless it is a pleasant sight," Harriot wrote with a touch of romanticism in 1588, "to see the people sometimes wading and going, sometimes sailing in those rivers, which are shallow and not deep, free from all care of heaping up riches for their posterity, content with their state, and living friendly together of those things which God of his bounty hath given unto them." Additionally he noticed that the Indians were very sober in their eating and drinking and subsequently very long-lived because "they did not oppress nature."[14] Unlike the Indians, Europeans did not understand the formative powers of nature, nor did they understand the interdependence of flora, fauna, and waterscape. Nature for the first English settlers was something to be bought, sold, traded, and developed—ideas that would remain in force in the Anacostia watershed long after the English colonists had vanished into history.

Captain John Smith sailed the waters of the Potomac and Anacostia in 1608 and informed Jamestown that the Indians already were caught up in European commodity culture. "Many hatchets, peeces of iron and brasse we saw among them, which they reported to have from the Sasquesahanocks."[15] These goods had filtered southward from places where French and Dutch traders operated. During his 1608–9 reconnaissance of the Potomac, Smith the soldier observed a people who enjoyed ample supplies of corn, venison, and fish. Ever concerned about the strength and numbers of possible adversaries, he made a careful count of native warriors.

His crude seventeenth-century demographic suggests that the number of Indians was relatively small. He counted only eighty "Nacotchanke" braves or "Anacostans" living at the confluence of the Anacostia and Potomac and up the Anacostia at the village at Indian Creek.[16] Smith also found they were organized in small chiefdoms. These chiefs, or *werowances*, formed a loose-knit community of Algonquin groups like the Piscataways and Mattawomans.

To the north were larger, more warlike nations like the Iroquois and the Susquehannocks. Often the Anacostan people were caught in the middle of hostilities between the Susquehannocks and the Powhatan tribes to the south, near the James River. Perhaps that explains the edginess of the Anacostans with regard to foreign intruders into their river and the fact that they were quick to take hostages for their own protection. In trying to protect themselves, they resorted to an alternating pattern of resistance and collaboration with the English, both of which worked to the detriment of the Indians. Though they feared the newcomers, they soon grew to depend upon European trade goods, which made continued resistance difficult.[17]

The beginning of a major white presence in the region dates from the entrance of that merchant adventurer, Captain Henry Fleet, who first sailed into the Anacostia in the 1620s. Fleet came from a family of successful London merchants who had invested in the Jamestown colony, and as a young man of twenty he took ship for Jamestown aboard the *Tigris* in 1620. He later took command of the *Tigris* and sailed up the Potomac in 1621 as part of a trade and food-gathering expedition. The expedition ended badly when the Yawaccomoo Indians attacked the *Tigris* on the Potomac, taking Fleet and his crew of twenty-one captive. Only Fleet survived; the crewmen were all murdered. The young English trader remained in captivity until 1627, when his family ransomed him with a large quantity of trade goods. Yet to judge from his subsequent experiences in the Anacostia and elsewhere in the Chesapeake, Fleet's captivity may have been more enjoyable than onerous. Upon his release, he returned to Jamestown and thence to London, where he obtained a commission to serve as an agent for Cloberry and Company dealing in beaver skins. With the exception of John Smith, Henry Fleet, and a few others, most of the English settlers in the seventeenth century "never acquired even a superficial knowledge of Indian languages or culture."[18]

Fleet's adventures were part of an English fur-trading enterprise that extended from a post on Kent Island founded by Virginia adven-

turer William Claiborne to the Jamestown entrepreneurs. In his journal
Henry Fleet recorded how English beaver traders plied the tributaries
in search of skins, and claimed that nearly five thousand Indians along
the Potomac were in engaged in the beaver trade.[19] Beaver pelts rose to
fifteen shillings a pound in the 1630s, a very high price compared to
tobacco, which traded at a penny a pound. Moreover, profits from the
beaver trade were shared by a much smaller group of people than were
the profits from tobacco. With fortunes in beaver fur at stake, conflicts
arose over what came to be called the bay trade. When Maryland became involved in the fur trade after 1634, Governor Leonard Calvert
found an antagonist in William Claiborne, a Kent Island fur trader
with political power in the Virginia colony.

It is surprising, given the immensity of the Chesapeake Bay country,
how quickly the Indians were drawn into various forms of commodity
culture. John Rolfe, whose early tobacco cultivation greatly influenced
Chesapeake culture and world trade, observed in 1616 that when Indians came to buy tools and piece goods "they seek to sell their skins from
their shoulders." Soon, Rolfe predicted, they would be mortgaging their
furs and lands to buy colonial trinkets and hatchets.[20] By 1640 the trade
in Dutch cloth was well established along the Potomac River and its
tributaries, and Indians had become sophisticated consumers.

The beaver trade in the Anacostia was fairly depleted in the 1640s,
and the expansion southward of militaristic Indian tribes like the
Susquehannocks disrupted the fragile stability of this first phase of the
bay trade. By 1660, English settlers had begun to establish farms and
fledgling communities in the Anacostia, impinging on lands Indians
used for hunting and gathering. Nor did the English acknowledge Indian claims to the land, even though groups like the Anacostans had
been in the watershed for thousands of years.

English colonists may have taken the land with relative ease, but
they were ill-equipped for living there. For example, despite the fact
that the Anacostia was blessed with a productive and valuable fishery,

Europeans were slow to take advantage of it. In 1676 Swiss traveler Louis Michel wrote of the fishery, "the abundance is so great and they are so easily caught that I was surprised." Colonist Thomas Glover of the Virginia settlement reported in his travels "that fish in the Rivers are plentifully stored, with Sturgeon, Porpasse, Bass, Carp shad, herring . . . All of which I have seen great quantities taken." Sturgeon, the largest fish to enter fresh water in the Chesapeake region, was in ample supply in the Anacostia, but their size—many were over six feet long—tended to intimidate the English. They were, however, familiar with the valuable sturgeon roe or caviar imported from Baltic countries by the English gentry, and since the Indians often considered it a romp to catch a sturgeon in a fishing weir and with a rope try to drag it by the tail to shore, the English traded with them for it. Captain John Smith relates how they caught sturgeon with nets that the fish altogether destroyed in the tumult.[*]

Through unremitting demographic and military pressure, the English gradually drove the Indians from the tributaries. One of the last legal records of the Anacostia Indians can be found in the *Proceedings of the County Courts of Charles County* for the year 1666.[21] A brave named Misapacka complained that whites trading for food and weapons had cheated him. The court records mention "The Old Indian Fields of St. Isadore's Creek," an early name for the Anacostia River given by Jesuit missionaries. The court's use of the past tense signified that the Indians had ceased to have a viable presence in the watershed. By the time Prince George's County was founded in 1693, the few hundred Anacostans had moved on, blended into other tribal groups, or intermarried with black and white colonials.

Indians of the region had no immunity to Old World diseases, which had more to do with English success in pushing the Indians

---

[*] Folklorists still tell the tale of how, during the Revolutionary War, an American soldier rowing across the Potomac toward the mouth of the Anacostia was killed when a giant sturgeon leaped out of the water and landed in his boat.

out of the Anacostia and Potomac River systems than military might or political accommodation. In addition to smallpox, the Indians had to contend with venereal disease, measles, diphtheria, chicken pox, bubonic plague, yellow fever, and influenza. The hold of every pinnace or schooner that came upriver brought pathogens that decimated tribes and destroyed aboriginal culture. In "virgin soil epidemics no one is immune so everyone gets sick at once," explains historian Alfred Crosby. "Whether the Europeans or Africans came to Native Americans in war or peace, they always brought death with them."[22]

Between 1660 and 1690 the European population in the Maryland colony increased from 2,500 to 20,000. It was a mix of jailhouse rabble and impecunious free men anxious to make their fortunes in the New World. The several hundred whites who lived in the Anacostia began to make the transition from beaver trapping and deer hunting to tobacco planting. For the most part their cabins or farmhouses were rudimentary huts, a far cry from the mansions that would ultimately spring up along the Potomac and Patuxent Rivers. The first dwellings the English constructed in the Anacostia region also reflected their environmental outlook. Whether they were home to people of social rank or those of a lesser sort, they "had yards strewn with garbage and dumps flanking every doorway." From the first, the English used the Anacostia as their waste receptacle.[23]

Present at the creation of colonial society in the new world of the Anacostia were all of the driving cultural and economic forces and racial attitudes that helped to lay the foundation of what would become a manipulated and problematic river. By 1690 the Anacostia was part of a world market economy. The river would now work as a menial in the service of others. Anacostia would forfeit its resources and its people would be dispossessed. The defeat of the river would be implicit in the victory of the tobacco planters and slaveholders as they successfully turned the environment into capital.

Looking at the Anacostia and its surrounding wetlands, woods, and communities today, it is fairly easy to detect the pulse of modernism. Unemployed black men gather at storefronts. Automobiles rust along the river. Deserted factories, ruined wharves, and hulks of boats rot among modern buildings, frenzied construction sites, shopping malls, parklands, and sprawling suburbs. The constant rumble of traffic on nearby highways attests to the automobile's dominance of our spatial world in recent times. Cynical urban analysts comment that the statistics of growth may wear a smile but the people still get taken.[24] The changes we perceive in our midst often frighten and confound us— much as the depredations of the first settlers frightened the Indians when the English expropriated the lands and river of the Anaquash.

CHAPTER TWO

The Anacostia in Plantation's Shadow, 1690–1776

". . . the most pleasant and healthful place in all this country."
— Sir Henry Fleet

The Chesapeake in the seventeenth and eighteenth centuries was an empire built upon smoke. Tobacco, the first profitable cash crop of the New World, and the slave trade soon became the ruling British economic deities. To a great extent they shaped the labor system, the culture, and the landscape of the Anacostia watershed. Ultimately, tobacco defined every aspect of life, from sustenance to social identity and political power. The region's utility and beauty doomed the Anacostia and its aboriginal populations. Its forests and waters offered an abundance of products, and its navigable river, which remained free of ice in winter, served as a commercial highway to the Chesapeake Bay and beyond. A moderate climate and an attractive landscape lured hundreds of colonists, who in turn made the region uninhabitable for its former residents. The Anacostia soon became an environmental metaphor for patriarchy, slavery, and poverty. The plantation's long historical shadow is still visible today.

A Cash Crop Culture

In the late seventeenth century the Anacostia maintained its frontier quality, dominated by trees and water. "This place without all question

16

is the most pleasant and healthful place in all this country," remarked Sir Henry Fleet, who by this time knew the river well. "It aboundeth with all manner of fish. And as for deer, buffaloes, bears, turkeys, the woods do swarm with them and the soil is exceedingly fertile."[1]

To the fisher, trapper or hunter, the river and its shores was a paradise. The water was alive with shad, pike, perch, bass, and herring; its surface swarmed with gulls, swans, and varieties of ducks. Herds of deer ranged in the forest. Maryland colonist George Alsop thought them numerous as "London cuckolds." The bird life was so remarkable as to attract serious naturalists and market game hunters. The birds seemed to float through the air like small kites. Plumed clouds provided a wind-driven tapestry of white. The tides carried Fleet's boats forward on a river that seemed to lead into the very heart of creation. In the upper Anacostia, where the tributaries were still navigable, cattail and reed tidal marshes were home to kingfishers, herons, muskrat, beaver, and turtles. Sturgeon could be harvested from the depths, and canvasback ducks, who flourished in extensive shoreline plots of wild rice, were easily shot for an impromptu dinner.

In 1695 an inexperienced traveler in a shallop would have seen little but an unending wilderness along the banks, with small clearings of tobacco and sturdy wharves here and there jutting out into the water. To the English, accustomed to the swift-flowing Thames, the river was sluggish. Its currents ran with the cycle of the tides. Nevertheless, the Anacostia was a natural highway of communication and commerce with England and was navigable for ocean-going vessels all the way to today's Bladensburg.

Forests and rivers dissected the terrain and helped to shape the environmental consciousness of the small groups of settlers, traders, and military men who were its first European inhabitants. In the Anacostia-Potomac region they found cold, though not severe, winters and excruciatingly hot summers. The climate was moist, a product of abundant forest, marshes and wetlands. Their reports and correspondence were interspersed with references to the humors of heat and cold and phlegm and ague. These bodily perceptions extended outward into the social world. For them the term "body politic" had a precise and profound meaning. Just as "humors" affected individual health, so too did humors or natural forces shape political consciousness.[2]

Certain things remained remarkably stable. The English lived on corn as a staple and hunted much like the Anacostans who preceded them. Their approach to clearing new land followed the aboriginal tradition of slash and burn. Small colonial settlements were scattered and isolated in the vast woodland. Whenever possible, the plantations had to be economically self-sufficient. The Anacostia, Potomac, and Patuxent waterways therefore became vital links for travel, communication, and commerce.

Newer to the region was a European ecology of extraction that went far beyond anything seen in the mid-Atlantic during several millennia of Indian activity. As the English population expanded, beaver, bear, and deer quickly became over-hunted. Unlike the Indians, the colonists identified wild game as a commodity from which to derive profit. Traders were eager to buy all the deer hides they could in order to satisfy a market for soft leather gloves in London. So great was the damage that in 1729 the Maryland legislature found it necessary to pass an act regulating the killing of deer for purposes other than subsistence.[3]

When John Smith and Henry Fleet sailed into the Anacostia in the seventeenth century, they reported a region rich in animal and marine life, but by the middle of the eighteenth century, those riches had largely vanished. Buffalo, which had once grazed on wild marsh grass in the Anacostia, were gone, leaving only their name on parts of the landscape to testify to their former presence.[4] Tobacco had replaced furs and animal skins as the premier commodity.

The Anacostia and other tributaries of Chesapeake Bay gave planters the means to avoid cumbersome land routes and trade directly with their factors, or agents, in England. Unlike the settlers of New England

(or their Anacostan predecessors), Maryland colonials did not live together in towns and villages. The great water highway system of the
Chesapeake encouraged the dispersion of the population. As Lord Baltimore wrote in 1678: "The people there not affecting to build nere each
other, but soe as to have their houses nere the Watters for conveniencye
of trade and their Lands on each syde of and behynde their houses by
which it happens that in most places there are not fifty houses in the
space of Thirty Myles." Port cities and harbor towns were as yet unnecessary and nonexistent. Ships from England called at all the local landings to collect furs and tobacco and deliver orders of goods from home.
The largest town in seventeenth-century Maryland was the provincial
capital, Saint Mary's City, and it was a mere village.

Tobacco or "The Royal Weed," as it was called by those who did not
use the still more vulgar "sotweed," became popular as early as 1614 at
the court of James I, who despised smoking himself. As a status symbol
it soon became another in the flow of commodities like gold, silver, and
furs between North America and Europe. Earlier attempts at lumbering
and silk production had been restricted by climate, bulk, or lack of ex-
pertise, but tobacco flourished in the humid, almost subtropical, climate
of the Chesapeake country. Along the Anacostia farmers could count
on hot summers, two hundred frost-free days, and relatively benign
winters with ample rainfall. Tobacco brought such handsome profits
that it became a medium of exchange. It was standard lore that some
Chesapeake planters purchased their brides with tobacco and imported
them to the New World. Soon the old system of small land grants to
pioneers and their sponsors gave way to larger grants that were better
suited to a labor-intensive tobacco farm. Throughout the early seventeenth century tobacco prices remained high in England, and planters
and farmers in the Maryland colony prospered.

The real tobacco "boom" arrived in the Anacostia sometime around
1688 and made tobacco the linchpin in the complex relationship between ecosystem and human settlement. In many respects tobacco was

an excellent staple for the early Anacostia settlers because it was what scholars have called an "ideal beginners crop."[5] Planters could set themselves up with a hoe, an axe, a few rudimentary tools and nails, and lumber for a tobacco shed. Though it required intensive care, tobacco could return large and dependable profits provided there was an ample supply of freshly cleared fertile land. Had it been a more difficult crop like flax or silkweed, the region might have had a much different destiny. Tobacco, though, harmonized with the fertile soil. A long growing season and careful tending did the rest. A planter made decent money from tobacco during boom periods with as few as two laborers, often as much as ten or fifteen pounds sterling, a comfortable income by contemporary English standards. Although it did not return the 20 percent profits obtained from more heavily capitalized rice and sugar plantations, planters along the Chesapeake tributaries could assume a steady 5 to 10 percent annual return on their investment in land and labor.

In 1696 the newly created Prince George's County comprised the entire western part of the Maryland colony. In the next eighty years the county's wealth grew dramatically, and Prince George's became one of the premier tobacco-producing counties in the British empire. When high tobacco prices brought flush times to the Anacostia, small freeholders as well as middling planters increased their wealth, status, and power.

The Calvert family had provided speculative land grants to friends and relatives in the 1660s, some of them bearing colorful names. A survey of Maryland land patents around what would become Washington, D.C., shows tracts named Rome, New Troy, Scotland Yard, Widow's Mite, and Cuckold's Delight.[6] The best tobacco lands along the Patuxent, Anacostia, and Potomac Rivers were quickly claimed by men of standing in the colony who were close to Lord Baltimore. Eighteenth-century observers would report the rich and fertile land along the Anacostia to be "partly cleared of woods." The clearings held tobacco fields that became the economic prime mover of colonial life.

Because tobacco constantly demanded new soil if it was to flourish, tobacco land came to mean new land. Farmers left behind older, less productive fields and assaulted the forest cover to clear fresh ground. A tobacco field could only produce four years of good yields before it drained the soil of nitrogen and potassium. In less than a decade, land went from forest to tobacco fields to broom sedge and little pines. Usually, "old fields" required a twenty-year fallow to recover their vitality. Thomas Johnson, a successful farmer from Frederick County and a commissioner for the new federal city of Washington, wrote insightfully on what the empire of tobacco had done to the landscape around the Potomac and Anacostia. To him it was a classic case of land misuse. "Two years in tobacco, a third in Indian corn and then sowed in wheat. After this destructive course the land is again planted in Indian corn and sowed down with wheat and rye without any assistance. The crops accordingly lessen and the land becomes so exhausted as scarcely to pay for ploughing." In the space of seventy years the Anacostia region, which had been thickly forested with islands of Indian clearings, had lost nearly half its woodlands.[7]

Around 1695, when improving economic conditions in England dried up the flow of white indentured servants to Maryland and the rest of the mid-Atlantic, planters resorted to African slave labor. The first slaves appeared in the Anacostia less than a year later. Unlike the limited terms of their white counterparts, black servitude was for life. In the eighteenth century, the importation of black slaves enabled tobacco planters to produce large crops, which they converted into wealth, leisure, and power. By 1750 over half the white male population of Prince George's County owned slaves.[8]

The hillside plantations of the Anacostia shaped every aspect of what became the sub-regional Potomac River economy. The Bealls, Notleys, Youngs, and Addisons, for example, were tidewater autocrats, speculators, social operators, cardsharps, and drunks whose politics and manner of living determined the Anacostia's destiny. Admittedly they behaved no differently from the Washingtons, Lees, Byrds, Carters,

Pacas, and Lloyds of Virginia and Maryland's Eastern Shore, though the shadows they cast over the countryside were smaller than those of their wealthier tidewater cousins.

The Anacostia the Planters Made

A brief look at these regional planters and slaveholders is instructive. Most got their start because they married into or were related by blood to the Notley family. By the high point of the tobacco economy in the mid-eighteenth century, there were in the Anacostia region about a dozen estates of between ten and twenty thousand acres that rivaled any manor in the tidewater South. By the eve of the American Revolution, ten families, all linked through marriage, controlled most of the arable land and river frontage of the Anacostia watershed.*

In 1639, Walter Notley, an Irish gentleman, received from Lord Baltimore twenty thousand acres of land for transporting or promising to transport one hundred men into the colony. His son, Thomas Notley, patented eighteen hundred acres on the Anacostia in 1671 and later became governor from 1676 to 1679. Notley was allied politically with Benjamin Young, a land commissioner for Lord Baltimore, who in the late seventeenth century acquired most of the land on the north side of the Anacostia from what is now Bladensburg to the river's mouth. Young's widow married into the Notley family, whose offspring married into just about every wealthy family in the region, among them the Roziers, Digges, and Carrolls.[9]

In the seventeenth century women married young, especially those who were in good health or came from families with assets. Some girls in Maryland married as early as age twelve, and most were married by

---

* Addison (north Anacostia riverfront); Beall (most of what is now New Carrollton and Cheverly); Carroll (large acreage on Capitol Hill); Digges (Southwest Anacostia); Calvert (Bladensburg to Greenbelt); Notley (Capitol Hill and Southeast); Thompson (Blue Plains); Rozier and Young (most of southwest Washington); Berry (Anacostia to Oxon Hill).

the time they reached sixteen. Young men inherited their estates at the legal age of eighteen. Marriage among youth of the upper classes was more social and economic than romantic.[10]

Despite the large estates, the Anacostia still had room for newcomers. In 1662, George Thompson patented two tracts, Blue Plains and Duddington, the latter comprising fourteen hundred acres on the north side of the river, including much of what is now Capitol Hill. Thompson had been a soldier of fortune and entrepreneur who had thrown in his lot with William Claiborne and those who temporarily overthrew the Calvert family in Maryland during the Puritan Revolution. In those uncertain times Thompson established himself as a lawyer in Charles County and used his rapidly accumulating wealth to buy tobacco land along the Anacostia. During the Puritan Commonwealth, from 1642 to 1660, Thompson served as chairman of the Admiralty Committee and exercised considerable influence over shipments of tobacco to England. Shortly thereafter, Thompson purchased the Geisborough Tract, which is today Congress Heights in the District. On the eve of his death around 1669, Thompson was heavily involved with other similarly situated men in investing in cargoes for the West Indies and speculating in land.[11]

Colonel John Addison was also part of the early Anacostia gentry. A colonel in the Maryland militia known for being both a good negotiator and a determined opponent of the local Indian tribes, Addison established large holdings along the Anacostia. He did so largely through family connections and a fortuitous marriage to the widow of Thomas Dent, the heir to the Thompson family's Geisborough Tract. By 1688 the Addisons were one of the most important and well-connected families in the Potomac region. According to historian Louise Hutchinson, "Addison's descendants owned much of Anacostia for the next 150 years."[12] In 1775 the plantation and chattels of Thomas Addison of Oxon Hill were valued at 5,275 pounds in Maryland money, a fortune that included more than 130 slaves.[13]

Today's multimillionaires can only dream of having the power and the lifestyle that Addison and his wealthy contemporaries enjoyed. The Digges family of Prince George's County navigated the same social circles as George Washington and was part of the Roman Catholic community of Maryland. Mary Digges married Thomas Sim Lee, another local planter of great wealth, who became a governor of Maryland. Estates like the Lee house at Blenheim or the Digges estate at Mellwood Park were in the tradition of the English country gentry. Other planters like Notley Young, who owned most of the land that became the capital were rough around the edges but came from money and good ancestry. John Meekes, an ambitious, social-climbing physician, completed the oligarchy of prominent landowners in the Anacostia when he patented Chicester grant, which would ultimately become a large part of modern-day downtown Anacostia. Some were grandees like Jeremiah Berry, owner of more than four thousand acres when he died in 1769. Berry flourished in the same milieu as Notley Young, who owned 265 slaves and large portions of waterfront property along the Anacostia, and the Addison family, whose estates conferred millionaire status on their offspring. Through business and marital alliances the Berry and Addison families came to own in the early nineteenth century most of the land on the north side of the Anacostia River. Land engrossment occurred at a rate that can only be deemed astonishing.

Not all who became planters in the Anacostia watershed were descended from families of rank. Ninian Beall, a Scotsman, who came to the Chesapeake in 1666 as an indentured servant, earned his liberty eleven years later. His freedom dues included a parcel of swampy land known as Terrapin Thicket for the large number of turtles that roamed its marshes. (Much of this area is today New Carrollton.) By the time of his death at the age of ninety-two in 1717, Ninian Beall had expanded his holdings through real estate speculation and mercantile pursuits to thousands of acres extending from Upper Marlboro through Bladensburg to Georgetown. The mansion he built and called "Dumbarton" on

Georgetown Heights reflected the ambitious rise of a former servant in a competitive Chesapeake world.[14]

By 1785 mercantile wealth along the two rivers at Georgetown and Bladensburg began to assert its influence in the plantation world.[15] Although the Anacostia planters invested principally in land, they also kept an eye out for the main chance, especially if it involved commerce on the Potomac and Anacostia Rivers. Anacostia planters were comparable to landholders of social class in Virginia, but very few were in the same league with aristocrats like David Ross of Richmond, who owned a hundred thousand acres in several counties, or the several members of the Carter family, Virginia's richest men, with more than 170,000 acres and significant capital. Though land-rich, many of the Anacostia planters were capital poor like their Virginia counterparts, and wealth on both sides of the Potomac declined when tobacco prices began to fall.

Early on the Anacostia would be identified with the development of a hereditary plantation squirearchy that raised tobacco, sued regularly in the courts, owned significant numbers of slaves, and did pretty much what it pleased. Planters loved woodcraft and dogs and wagering on practically anything. Most made their money in merchant trade, law, and real estate speculation, but their financial accounts were often overdrawn, and simple interest, if imposed, would have ruined them. Spirited horsemen and such hard drinkers that sometimes they had to take to their beds for several days to assuage hangovers, they survived the ravages of strong drink with bowls of a weak toddy of gin or brandy mixed with tea and spices and occasional drops of opiates from their planter-physician friends. When drunk they humorously created signs advertising for "runaway masters," supposedly circulated by the slaves who dominated their lives and ate them out of house and home. Planters were accustomed to having sex with their "Negro wenches" in the quarters and occasionally tried to give their mulatto offspring their freedom in the wills they wrote. More often than not, property-conscious family members, attributing their deceased relative's decision to the influence of liquor, halted the manumissions in court.[16] The most conscientious of this class sought to provide for their illegitimate white children as well. Unlike black slave offspring, planters' white bastards had legal standing in the Prince George's County Orphans Court during probate.

A plantation in the colonial Chesapeake seldom resembled an English country estate. Most were small agricultural units or land grants of between 150 and 250 acres. Of course, at times even the wealthiest planters refused to refer to their holdings as plantations. James Madison referred to his three-thousand-acre estate as "the farm." There is, though, a critical difference between a "farm" and a "plantation." Farms were primarily subsistence units, whereas plantations were larger acreages with a division of labor and management handled by an owner and overseer. For the most part plantations specialized in a single money crop like tobacco and used involuntary or forced labor. Farms were rough-hewn cabin-in-the-woods affairs that involved all members of the family in subsistence.

Regional plantation architecture was ordinary only by the standards of the British gentry, but it is easy to infer a more luxurious plantation culture in the Anacostia and Potomac than actually existed. True, there were great manor houses like those of Robert Carter and George Washington, but most plantation houses seldom contained more than three sleeping rooms. Guests were often accommodated three or four to a room, with strangers sharing the bed. The steady and inevitable diet of ham and home-distilled liquor like persimmon brandy repelled fastidious visitors from abroad. A planter's china seldom matched, and broken windows were not repaired for months because glass, always in short supply, had to be imported from England at considerable cost. Plantation life produced fine horsemen, for planters loved to race. It also whetted appetites for marriages among cousins and uncles and nieces that would be considered incestuous by today's standard.[17]

The plantation system defined labor along caste or racial lines with negative social consequences. Thomas Anburey, an English traveler in

1787, wrote of the Potomac area, "it would seem as if the poor white man here would rather starve than work, because the Negro works."[18] In the years after 1720 the region was organized around the core values of white racial supremacy, patriarchy, localism, and hierarchy. It was not open to ideas of political equality, liberation, or notions of change in class and caste. The rise of a penniless Scotsman like Ninian Beall would be extremely difficult in the Anacostia after 1730, when class lines hardened. Gentlemen held all the local and provincial offices, and their families intermarried.[19]

The Slaves' Anacostia

In 1664 the Maryland colonial assembly passed a statute that established hereditary slavery, thereby legalizing what often had been the practice since 1639. Slave laws reflected the attitudes of society and the manner in which it attempted to ignore social and economic problems. Colonial court records shed light on a labor system that evolved from white and black indentured servitude to enslavement of the African. Nearly eleven thousand Africans came in chains to various parts of the Chesapeake between 1695 and 1709, and servitude took on a racial cast.

Until recently, historians seeking to determine the extent to which Africans were brought to the Potomac have been misled by incomplete or unreliable information that fostered the idea that the Chesapeake was not a major importer of slaves. New data suggest that nearly twice as many slaves were sold in the Potomac than had previously been estimated. Altogether, more than eight thousand Africans were imported to the Potomac from 1727 to 1769. Many came on ships owned by Foster Cunliffe, a Liverpool-based company with slaving enterprises in the Gambia region of West Africa.[20]

The health of black newcomers was in most circumstances better than that of white laborers. Only the hardiest survived the Middle Passage across the Atlantic, and Africans, who had been exposed to it at home, were better able to withstand malaria. Those who did not die in transit were dispersed to river plantations where, in a disorienting wilderness, they suffered from loneliness and homesickness.

The shock encountered by white servants imported from England to the region was as nothing compared to that experienced by Africans, whose language, culture, and political systems were profoundly different. Not until well into the eighteenth century did a native-born "creole" African American population begin to emerge along the shores of the Potomac. Although the slave population grew at an extraordinary rate in the four counties of Prince George's, Calvert, Charles, and St. Mary's, it was a community of imports. Men consistently outnumbered women on the slave ships by more than three to one, and this gender imbalance created social and demographic disruptions that deeply affected the formation of black community life. "The skewed sex ratio," wrote one demographer, "apparently reflect[ed] the preferences of planters as well as the structure of the immigrant population."

Planters did not provide wives for all of their slaves, and we are too quick to assume that slaveowners recognized the advantages of a self-perpetuating labor force. Few children appeared in slave inventories during the mid-eighteenth century, when slave traffic on the Potomac was at its height. "The small proportion of children reinforces the impression of a stunted family life for most blacks in early colonial Maryland." Adult slave reproductive rates remained low. It would not be until nearly the eve of the American Revolution that occupational mobility, cultural assimilation, and growing opportunity for a family life added a modicum of stability to slave life along the Potomac. By that time the slave population in the four counties had grown from 3,500 in 1710 to more than 15,000 in 1755. More than half the inhabitants of Prince George's County were slaves, and they accounted for about two-thirds of the personal property of free whites.[21] The development of Chesapeake tobacco agriculture into a labor system based on caste, race, and severe social control encouraged the development of a patriarchy in which white planters controlled or sought to control nearly every aspect of agrarian life—from work to diet to social relations, religion, and sexual activity.

Despite those efforts, slaves were never without power. Early in the eighteenth century, when the frontier abutted the tidewater, Africans attempted to run away as soon as they landed. Some formed communities of their own in the wilderness. Others made their way to Indian villages where they were favorably received. That may explain why the Maryland assembly launched several punitive expeditions against the Piscataway tribe along the Anacostia and Patuxent Rivers. Slaves sometimes destroyed crops and animals, were truant, escaped, and occasionally murdered their masters when they felt they could stand the system no more.

A well-documented slave conspiracy took shape in Prince George's County in 1739–40. Whites along the Anacostia, Patuxent, and Potomac Rivers believed that two hundred slaves planned to kill all the white men, marry the white women, and seize the colony. Though Jack Ransom, the slave leader, was captured, tried, and executed, fear of rebellion prompted white planters to thwart African attempts to establish an independent social life. "Running to the woods, founding outlying communities, or meeting in large groups challenged work discipline and cost planters profits. Nevertheless, substantial numbers of Africans probably participated in activities away from the plantation."[22] Later, as slaves acquired Christian piety and skills important to plantation life like carpentry, blacksmithing, cooperage, and bricklaying, they occasionally enjoyed better treatment from their masters.

Some blacks were born to free status; others were manumitted out of charitable, or parental, interest. Most free blacks worked in small shipyards or as stevedores loading the great tobacco ships for the fall voyage to England. From the outset free men of color could be found on the waters of the Anacostia and Potomac, where they harvested herring and shad that planters like Robert Carter and George Washington pickled and exported to the Caribbean sugar colonies.[23]

Fishing in the Anacostia remained excellent throughout the colonial period. Along with stressing the enormous spring runs of herring and shad and the abundance of sturgeon, contemporary local accounts of the fishery usually mention the presence of blacks in the fish trade. Fish was a staple of poor white and slave diets, and even the upper classes turned to bass, catfish, herring, and planked shad to break the monotony of cured salt ham. Significantly, black fishermen took over the harvesting of sturgeon from white watermen. These big, muscular prehistoric fish were considered too difficult to handle for the small profits they offered when compared to the vast spawning runs of herring and shad. Shallops in the Anacostia, ferrying tobacco and other commodities from one wharf to another, had mixed black and white crews. Historian Philip Morgan has remarked that "the readiness of masters to place Africans aboard boats suggests the post did not convey great prestige."[24] But working on the water fostered self-reliance and a more personal dignity than the routine drudgery of plantation life.

Nevertheless, the labor system to the last remained what it was in the beginning, a violent, arbitrary, and oppressive way of extracting wealth from agricultural commodities via human misery. Unlike their white counterparts on the eve of the American Revolution, Anacostia blacks could not migrate to Kentucky in search of cheap land and a new life. Violence, isolation, exhaustion, and alienation led Africans to depression and suicide.

The Port Town of Bladensburg

In 1742 a town was established on the upper reaches of the Anacostia. Named after Thomas Bladen, who became provincial governor of Maryland the year of the town's founding, it would serve as a tobacco warehouse and commercial entrepôt for the eastern portion of Prince George's County. The imperial government appointed commissioners to build sixty-one houses on one-acre lots. Each new owner was to erect a house four hundred feet square, with a brick or stone chimney. Aiding Bladensburg's growth and development was the passage of the Tobacco Inspection Act of 1747, which set up tobacco inspection stations throughout the colony. When a station was established at the warehouse of Bladensburg tobacco trader David Ross, business quickly sprang up around it. Blacksmiths and carpenters did a flourishing trade, and retail stores owned by British "factors" imported cloth, implements, and luxury goods unavailable elsewhere in the region. The stores were helpful to small Anacostia planters and farmers who could not afford to buy in bulk from factors in London.

Soon, Christopher Lowndes, a maritime store merchant, settled in Bladensburg and started a rope business. High quality rope was much in demand for ships and wharves, and Lowndes made a fortune. His ropewalk became central to maritime commerce on the Anacostia and the Potomac and was a major reason for improving the primitive rolling road that extended to Bladensburg from Georgetown. The newly enriched Lowndes built a mansion he called Bostwick overlooking the Anacostia, and his business lured sail and boat makers to the small but prosperous river town. William Wirt, a resident of pre-revolutionary Bladensburg, described it as "a thrifty, business-driving, little seaport profitably devoted to the tobacco trade." With its London connections, flour mills, tobacco warehouses, and merchants, Bladensburg "communicated a certain show of opulence."[25] The town also attracted gardeners and apothecaries who served the planter class, and bakers and hemp makers who helped fuel the regional economy. The town prided itself on its shipyard, tannery, stores, and taverns. Bladensburg even became popular as a spa, whose mineral springs made it a favorite with visitors seeking cures for various maladies.[26] The springs were located on what is now 46th Street between Pusher Street and Windom Road. Bladensburg's development as a tobacco inspection port demonstrates how the staple could generate economic growth along the river through a number of collateral activities.[27]

A smallpox epidemic in 1759 was so severe that business leaders contemplated evacuating the town, but by then blacksmiths with access to cheap iron from local furnaces had turned Bladensburg into a metal fabrication center. Among the more important things these "smithy" shops produced were iron manacles for slaves, for by the 1750s Bladensburg had also developed into a significant port of entry for the Chesapeake slave trade. Outside his tobacco warehouse Dr. John Ross sold cargoes of convict servants and slaves who had become too troublesome for their masters.

Slavery and tobacco had built a flourishing town.

A Revolutionary Age

The years leading up to 1776 witnessed a growing disaffection among the tobacco gentry and their mercantile allies in New England. Even when planters turned to wheat farming, another plague of agricultural inspectors came to judge, regulate, and tax their staple in much the same way they did tobacco. Along the Anacostia and the tributaries of the Chesapeake's Tobacco Coast, a new sentiment emerged, one that equated economic freedom with political independence. Although a host of political and cultural developments influenced a population of nearly a million in Virginia and Maryland to entertain notions of independence, certainly the profit motive was one of the more important reasons the tobacco gentry turned into revolutionaries.

Yet the Revolution—and the British navy—brought disaster to the tobacco trade. Bladensburg was forced to rely on a small boat building industry and corn and wheat trading to sustain itself. Even after the war ended, ships bound for the Caribbean from the Anacostia and Potomac were at risk because the British continued to seize cargo and force American sailors into His Majesty's service.

The economy of the Anacostia watershed languished for a decade. Planters' hopes for free and unfettered prosperity with a revived tobacco trade went unrealized. Not until the Napoleonic Wars of the 1790s would the local economy emerge from depression. This time, prosperity was not founded upon smoke, but upon wheat and flour. Businessmen, real estate promoters, and military men like General George Washington, saw economic expansion linked to a vast trans-Appalachian empire that was just coming into settlement. The future of the Chesapeake Bay and its tributaries would be determined by a hardy generation of pioneers pouring across the mountains into the Ohio Valley. These settlers, George Washington argued, would provide food to be shipped at a profit to Europe along a network of middlemen and manufacturers from Georgetown to Cape Charles, Virginia.[28]

Environmental Problems

In an age of opportunity, upper Anacostia planters and shippers confronted an unexpected difficulty—the increasing sedimentation of their river. This was a direct result of soil erosion and the human tendency to treat the upper Anacostia as a dump for ship ballast, construction debris, and animal carcasses. As the upper watershed gathered silt, little thought was given to the ramifications downstream.

When it was founded, Bladensburg had a river depth of forty feet, and ocean-going vessels could easily make their way upriver to Dr. Ross's tobacco warehouse. Second only to Yorktown, Virginia, in the amount of tonnage shipped from its wharves, it was also located at the convergence of two busy highways, the Annapolis Road and the Georgetown Pike. Those traveling between those cities usually found themselves in Bladensburg. This ideal arrangement of land and river should have spurred fantastic economic growth, but twenty years later in 1762, docks were so heavily silted that the town advertised a lottery to raise money "for removing the shoals in the Eastern Branch from the wharf at Bladensburg down, and from there to the bridge upwards."[29]

Flooding also became a problem. "Freshets" turned the Anacostia into a muddy torrent that flooded tobacco houses and caused merchants and residents no end of grief. In 1724 and 1738 floods tore out wharves and damaged shipping. The worst floods in the colonial period occurred in 1771, when all the rivers of the bay country seemed to rampage after heavy rainstorms. Numerous buildings were swept away and thousands of hogsheads of tobacco ruined. For a lengthy period the ship channel in the Anacostia was clogged. To historian Arthur Middleton, the reason for such intense flooding was clear: "a result of the rapid settlement and deforestation" of the countryside.[30]

The constant planting of tobacco and corn also loosened the soil and weakened its binding capacity. Thousands of tons of topsoil could be carried away in a single rainstorm. Such destructive washing harmed the landscape of the Chesapeake tidewater and made waterways shallower. By the late colonial period, a vessel of only three tons had difficulty making the journey upriver to Bladensburg. The silting may have contributed to the construction of a new public wharf at Georgetown at the foot of Water Street, now Wisconsin Avenue, where ships, shallops, and sloops engaged in the coastal trade could easily navigate. Merchants then transshipped goods by oxcart and wagon along the Bladensburg Road. Deforestation continued, as farmers turned to timbering to supplement their income and supply an expanding, small-boat building industry along the Anacostia.

On the eve of the American Revolution, the Chesapeake country had reached the point at which its population had the ability to alter the region's natural cycles in much the same manner that ecological transformations are taking place in Third World societies today.[31] Although ducks and other waterfowl were still plentiful and allowed for a market hunting industry in meat and feathers that lasted well into the modern era, local species like black bear, beaver, and white-tailed deer disappeared from the Anacostia.

What emerges from a study of the Anacostia during the early plantation period is a paradigm for understanding the subsequent history of the river system, in which changes in the region's social ecology paralleled deteriorations in the natural environment. Early on the Anacostia became a two-tiered social and environmental system. Those who grew powerful through family and political connection appropriated the landscape and the river. The dispossessed lived and worked there. A number of things combined to produce this undesirable result. An excessive reliance upon tobacco and racial slavery brought about the concentration of landownership and limited the opportunity for whites and free blacks of limited means to find a toehold in the regional economy. Slavery gave a negative connotation to the idea of work and forced many of the laboring classes to emigrate from the region in search of new opportunities beyond the Appalachians. Through displays of wealth and spending patterns, the planter class in the Anacostia established a hegemony that would be unchallenged commercially and politically until after the creation of the national capital at Washington. As anthropologist Brett Williams has observed of the Anacostia, "linked transformations in environment and social processes created unsettled, contradictory, and unjust relations between the people and the natural and built environments."[32]

If the development of family ties is one of the most important milestones in the social ecology of a community, then slavery profoundly hindered that natural course by preventing the formation of black kinship networks during the early colonial period. The significance of that cultural fact continues to provoke debate in our own time.

This overview of local plantation society in the colonial period underscores one central fact about the early social ecology of the Anacostia. As early as the colonial period the river was being shaped economically by tobacco and culturally by the political ideas and social behavior of local elites. Bladensburg never recovered from the deforestation and silting. Today the river at this historic and once dynamic port town is only inches deep at low tide. The rich Anacostia environment that Sir Henry Fleet described in 1623 had by 1776 produced some very strange and dangerous fruit—racial hegemony and dispossession—that over time poisoned local community life.

CHAPTER THREE

L'Enfant and the Failed Vision of an Anacostia Waterfront, 1790–1820

"The Eastern Branch is one of the safest and most commodious harbors in America."
— George Walker, 1789

"The city can only be made by the Eastern Branch."
— Thomas Law, 1795

The birth of the nation's capital can be attributed to three factors. The idea of citing the capital city on the Potomac sprang Athena-like out of General George Washington's brow, fully armored with a political, economic, and environmental vision born of revolution and nation-building. It was also a cynical attempt to mollify southern slaveholders by giving Virginia immense power in configuring the economic development of the trans-Appalachian West. Finally, the city that became Washington, D.C., began as a cluster of waterfront warehouses at the junction of two rivers, a place where speculators participated in ambitious real estate schemes that rivaled in their audacity the development zones of today's entrepreneurs in the District. Unfortunately, between 1790 and 1820, the original vision for the Anacostia waterfront emerged far less successfully. Had it developed as Pierre L'Enfant intended and businessmen and investors hoped, the capital would have looked to the Anacostia as the center of commerce and residential development. But that plan foundered in the machinations of local landholders and the froth of real estate speculation.

The Anacostia Factor

Had it not been for developments in Philadelphia, Washington's passion for creating a national capital might not have come to pass at all. In the 1780s the United States lacked a permanent seat of government. Congress and the president resembled a wandering medieval court more than a national government. Following the Revolution, the capital of the new nation was moved from New York to Philadelphia. No sooner had the Congress unpacked than it was besieged by hordes of Pennsylvania petitioners and office-seekers, who gave congressional leaders little rest or privacy. Even more troubling was the Pennsylvania legislature's attempt to dictate to the national government as if the two bodies were reversed in status and power. Furthermore, Pennsylvania law stipulated that any slave who remained in the state more than six months became free, a policy that greatly vexed southern planters.

Seeking a less problematic site for the capital, General Washington turned southward. Since his days as a young surveyor he had been enamored of the place where the Anacostia met the Potomac. Between 1770 and 1774 he made careful studies of the two rivers and saw them as arteries of tidewater commerce between his Virginia home and the West. In 1772, Washington joined with other investors in forming the Potomac Company to make that river navigable from Fort Cumberland to the tidewater. Thomas Jefferson, James Madison, and Maryland's Thomas Johnson were similarly river-struck, but they emphasized commerce as a way of binding northern and southern states together with common interests that transcended slavery.[1] One of his earliest backers was planter Daniel Carroll of Maryland. Carroll's Duddington Plantation bordered a sizeable piece of the Anacostia waterfront, and his family had laid out a community along the river called Carrollsburg in the hope that it would become the shipping and commercial center of the new capital.

In the spring of 1792 a well-dressed man on horseback descended Jenkins Hill* on a narrow path down to the Anacostia near the present site of the Washington Navy Yard.[2] Thirty years old and of late the secretary and plantation business manager of President Washington, Tobias Lear was charged with reconnoitering the Anacostia and Potomac riverfronts to ascertain whether they were the right setting for the capital of the American republic. The president wanted at once a political capital and a maritime center that would connect the rich Ohio Valley with the tobacco coast of Chesapeake Bay and European markets. Did soundings of the rivers provide accurate knowledge of their channels? Could a new capital emerge as a large commercial port? Was the Potomac on the Virginia side navigable for ocean-going vessels? How navigable was the Anacostia? If the proposed new capital were to become a maritime center, the Potomac and Anacostia first had to be thoroughly understood.

Washington envisioned a mercantile center and a federal enclave that would link the existing port of Georgetown with what he thought was the more promising future port on the Anacostia. Lear's report, *Observations on the River Potomak and the Country Adjacent, and the City of Washington,* provided important intelligence for maritime development and complemented Pierre L'Enfant's plan for the city. Navigating the three hundred miles up the Potomac from the Chesapeake Bay to the new city was "easy and perfectly safe," Lear reported. A vessel carrying twelve hundred hogsheads of tobacco could easily sail as far as the port of Alexandria, and one carrying seven hundred hogsheads could unload at the wharf at Georgetown on the mouth of Rock Creek. Of

*Jenkins Hill is now Capitol Hill. The name Jenkins Hill is confusing, since it bears no relation to early land patents. One historian suggested that it received its appellation from a Thomas Jenkins, who leased a cow pasture on the tract from the Carroll family.

particular interest to Lear was the fact that the site for the new capital was well suited for boat-yards.

Lear noted that the Anacostia River or the Eastern Branch that flowed into the Potomac "affords one of the finest harbors imaginable for ships." Its channel lay next to the proposed city and was thirty feet deep. The river at this point was over a mile wide, and the land on each side was "sufficiently high to secure shipping from any wind that blows." Furthermore the Anacostia, unlike the Potomac, did not freeze easily in winter and was less troublesome to navigate during spring freshets.[3]

Early maps illustrate the importance of the Anacostia to the development of the new city. From an aesthetic standpoint, the bluffs that gently spilled down to the water and its forested slopes seemed an ideal place for the new capital. As historian Carl Abbott has written, the early maps of the District show a city "embraced by rivers."[4] The plan for the federal city had its origin in a 1790 map produced by John Frederick Prigs, a Prince George's County surveyor. It clearly shows the enormous commercial and aesthetic possibilities of the Anacostia as well as the environmental and navigational advantages of what was then referred to as "the Eastern Branch of the Potomac River." The map shows a safe and ample harbor with detailed markings of the river's depth upstream toward Bladensburg. As students of this map have pointed out, "the delineation of roads, the ferry, and the river surroundings suggest that whoever commissioned this map must have had serious business ventures in mind."[5] That investors were greatly interested in the region is beyond question; the map was created prior to L'Enfant's plan for the capital. A second map, by Thackara and Vallance in 1792, in which the Anacostia emerges at the map's right edge, supplies additional evidence that harbor facilities were intended to be a prominent feature of the capital. The entire shoreline of the proposed city—from Georgetown to Buzzard Point to the ferry located well beyond the navy yard—is sketched with wharves.[6]

In 1790 the Washington riverscape was vastly different from what it is today. The contemporary waterfront is largely the creation of dredging and filling operations commenced in the 1880s and carried over into the twentieth century. As one historian put it, "In 1792 the city of Washington had a long shoreline, lined with bluffs since leveled, overlooked by a succession of plateaus affording picturesque vistas."[7] In the 1790s tobacco and cornfields covered much of the adjacent countryside. Most of the area below Jenkins Hill was marsh and forest with "tall and umbrageous forest trees" along the riverbanks.[8] When General Washington looked at the topography of his new capital, he preferred the land along the Anacostia with its bluffs and sharp geographic distinctions. The general had a shrewd estimate of natural landscape. As a surveyor, he studied trees and woodlands, and his early notes showed a seasoned acquaintance with Piedmont and Appalachian forests that lent itself to an informed ecological view of the region.[9]

L'Enfant and the New Capital

To plan the new city, President Washington retained the services of Pierre L'Enfant, an expatriate French engineer who had joined Washington's revolutionary army, fought courageously, and been wounded in battle. L'Enfant or "Lanfang," as Washington called him, had already acquired fame as a budding urban designer with his work on Federal Hall in New York City right after the Revolution. One thing L'Enfant and Washington shared—their vision of the new capital began at the water's edge. On his return to France in 1783, L'Enfant was impressed by Paris and Bordeaux, cities experimenting in public architecture that had episodic interplay with their rivers.

Landscape nomenclature probably had some influence with the surveying team. The portion of Jenkins Hill that would be the site of L'Enfant's capitol was part of a plantation called "the New Troy tract" and was originally part of a 1,500-acre parcel of land given to planter George Thompson by Lord Baltimore in 1663. At the bottom of the hill, where today the statue of General Grant looks toward the Mall, was "Rome," patented by a Thompson neighbor, Francis Pope, with the "Tiber River" running through it. As early as the seventeenth century what would become the capital already had its share of lofty classical allusions. Only the most ignorant of Frenchmen would have failed to link Rome with the new seat of government, even if it gave the proposed city a pronounced imperial connection. L'Enfant hoped his new capital would rival Paris with its half-million people and London, the largest city in Europe at the time with 800,000.

Given the precarious state of national finances, Washington and Alexander Hamilton devised a scheme to finance public buildings and principal streets and avenues through the sale of lots and assumed that Americans would flock to the sale. The land was platted into double parcels or squares. The city received some of the land free of charge to sell as it chose for the construction of public buildings and streets, and to create reservations (L'Enfant's term for parks). The original proprietors retained half of the lots in each square for sale at auction at very high prices. As people settled in the new capital, the proprietors expected to make a killing, anticipating as much as $265 for a 40-by-100-foot lot on land that had been valued at less than fifty dollars an acre.

Most of the six thousand acres that would become the national capital was in the hands of three groups comprising fewer than twenty individuals: the old Anacostia group led by Daniel Carroll and Notley Young; the Georgetown merchant group led by Uriah Forest; and speculators with lines of credit to foreign banks like Robert Morris and James Greenleaf of Pennsylvania and Massachusetts. The Anacostia group* were part of a circle of Catholic cousins dominated by the Carroll patriarchs. Strong-willed and conservative, this band was part of a family network that extended as far south as Richmond and sought to preserve and protect the Catholic planter way of life. The church was

---

* They claimed L'Enfant as one of their own. In his last poverty-stricken years, the Frenchman found refuge in the Catholic Digges family plantation on the heights of Anacostia overlooking his beloved city.

their faith, Georgetown College their school, and the Anacostia their stronghold.[10] Interestingly, Daniel Carroll of Rock Creek, one of the first commissioners of Washington, was the brother of the Reverend John Carroll, the first Catholic bishop in the United States. Robert Brent, a relative of the Carrolls and descended from the first group of Catholic families that landed in Maryland on the *Ark* and *Dove*, became the new capital's first mayor.[11]

Daniel Carroll of Duddington and Notley Young owned most of what is now Capitol Hill and the Anacostia shoreline on the city side of the river. Carroll also owned a brick kiln and would make far more money from the capital project by selling bricks and timber from his plantation than he would in land sales. Smaller freeholders like William Prout, a merchant and Anacostia backer, also owned land on the river that they hoped to sell at a profit. Prout, an immigrant from Bristol, had arrived in Baltimore in 1790 and opened a store. A shrewd entrepreneur, Prout used his profits to buy five hundred acres, mostly near Capitol Hill, and wound up being one of the few speculators to make money in those early days. From his holdings near the navy yard on the Anacostia, he ventured into a host of businesses, the most lasting of which would be the Eastern Market.[12]

The Georgetown group consisted of Uriah Forest, who had a manor house in Georgetown Heights, Robert Peter, George Walker, and Benjamin Stoddert. Together they owned several parcels of land that now make up Georgetown and most of northwest Washington. Perhaps the most tenacious was David Burns, a canny Scot who owned the land on which the White House is currently situated. Of all the landholders, Burns gave President Washington the most trouble and got the best price for his holdings from the government.[13]

When President Washington signed the Seat of Government Bill creating the new capital in July 1790, it was a ten-mile square tract of land donated by the states of Virginia and Maryland. Critics pointed out that the Virginia and Maryland planters had made out handsomely.

Their real estate would grow in value and they would be influential in the federal government's decision-making process. George Mason, for example, owned two thousand acres of Potomac shoreline on the Virginia side, from Georgetown to Little Falls. Washington himself owned 1,200 acres of Potomac riverfront near Four Mile Run, and his wife's grandson, George Custis, owned a 950-acre Potomac plantation that came to be known as Arlington House. Though most Americans refused to attribute personal motive to Washington's plan for a seat of government on the Potomac, John Adams believed that the Virginians were not averse to lining their pockets at national expense.[14]

Notley Young, perhaps the most patriarchal Anacostia landlord, owned land along both the Potomac and the Anacostia vital for the capital's development as a port. He and his fellow patricians hoped to make a real estate killing in the new capital once the architect L'Enfant completed a city plan. The landowners would receive half the lots platted as well as $66.67 an acre for as much land as Washington wanted for reservations and public buildings. After the survey, the government's share amounted to 10,153 lots at no cost to itself. Land for streets and public reservations the Capital Commission purchased for $36,099. In turn the landowners were left with an equal number of lots, which stood to appreciate greatly once the construction of the new capital began.

Speculators hoped that when the government developed its share of the city a real estate boom would make the land sell for about ten times what the original acreage could have brought as plantation land. As it happened, the first subscription sold only thirty-five out of 10,000 lots and raised only $2,000, indicating that more energy was required to build the capital than many had anticipated.* Some of the landowners took out their frustration on L'Enfant, who had wanted a slower,

---

* The only similar exercise in capital-building in an undeveloped country in our own time in the western hemisphere is Brasilia, built mainly by involuntary, low-wage peasant labor. Brazilian politicos did not have to deal with well-connected local planters, only defenseless campesinos and Indians.

government-controlled approach to capital building. Daniel Carroll and Notley Young, unwilling to be ordered about by some French mercenary, built houses on land expressly marked in L'Enfant's plan for avenues and streets because it suited them.

In a fit of pique, L'Enfant ordered a portion of Daniel Carroll of Duddington's house torn down, though he saved the bricks for Carroll's future use. The outraged planter appealed to his family and the commission to do something about L'Enfant's highhandedness. When L'Enfant refused to adopt a more moderate course in dealing with the sensibilities of the landowners, President Washington sacked him.[15] The landed gentry of the new capital proved to be more than a match for an ambitious French urban planner.

Real Estate Speculation and the Anacostia

From the outset, speculators have played an important and often nefarious role in Washington's economic and environmental development. The creation of our national capital rode a tide of avarice that shaped its development, but in the end, real estate speculation led to the Anacostia's underdevelopment rather than to growth and prosperity.

With lagging real estate sales came the rapid depletion of the $192,000 in seed money Virginia and Maryland had provided to cover the start-up costs of surveying the city and establishing the new seat of government along the waterfront. Prospects seemed dismal. If the city were to evolve in accordance with L'Enfant's plan and Washington's ambitions, the commissioners would have to make a large sale. A second auction of lots in 1792 raised little more than in the previous year, and hopes were dim that the city could raise the $800,000 it needed to embark on ambitious construction plans. In 1793, with the ailing capital project still mired in the real estate morass, frustrated landowners and stagnant sales provided an opportune moment for sharp businessmen with long lines of credit who could buy up large blocks of land at prices far less than advertised. James Greenleaf and Robert Morris, two veteran businessmen, were drawn to the city by the scent of a lucrative deal. Both were respectable financiers with ample credit. Greenleaf, a Bostonian who had made a fortune speculating in American continental currency while residing in Amsterdam, had the backing of Dutch banks. Robert Morris, the esteemed financier of the American Revolution, had the Philadelphia financial community in his pocket.

Greenleaf entered the Washington financial waters modestly by agreeing to underwrite the finances of Tobias Lear, whose mercantile and warehouse operation had failed to obtain European financing. Next, Greenleaf courted President Washington, who was anxious to sell his western lands to underwrite his impending retirement from government service. The good will of Lear and Washington provided Greenleaf with entrée to the small community of Washington property owners who were frustrated that they had not made a large profit during the initial sale of lots. He opened negotiations with the city commissioners by offering to buy three thousand lots for $66 each with the proviso that he had seven years to pay for them. He also agreed to build brick houses on the lots and to lend the commissioners $2,660 a month. When Robert Morris learned that Greenleaf had a $1 million line of credit in Amsterdam, he immediately joined him in a financial alliance. On December 1, 1793, Greenleaf, Morris, and John Nicholson, another prominent investor, formed the North American Land Company. In modern parlance, they intended to "flip" the real estate and make a fast profit.

Greenleaf now set out to acquire a controlling position in Washington real estate. First he bought all the parcels of land owned by the local squire, Notley Young. Counting what he purchased from the city, Young, and Daniel Carroll of Duddington, Greenleaf controlled 7,234 lots. Along with his backers, Morris and Nicholson, he hoped to double his investment, but at a critical moment his Dutch investors bowed out, perhaps fearing the economic instability the French Revolution was stirring in Europe. Now undercapitalized and over-extended, Greenleaf and Morris found themselves reduced to near penury. The Washington lots failed to appreciate significantly, and both Greenleaf and the city commissioners were left with real estate that was undeveloped and encumbered in bankruptcy and financial confusion.

More stagnation ensued. One of the favorite comments around Washington in the late nineteenth century was that most of those lots ended up costing more in property taxes than they ever realized in profit. Wilhelmus Bogart Bryan, an historian of early Washington, wrote that there were times when a calculated gamble as large as that which Greenleaf, Robert Morris, and their backers took could have earned them a reputation as saviors of the new capital. "As it is," he wrote, "the actors in these opening years . . . have come under the shadow of the cloud of disaster and failure which marks this period, and their achievements, as well as the manner of men they were, have been so obscured as to be almost impossible to revive even in faint outline."[16]

George Walker, a Georgetown developer, invested $25,000 in a 358-acre tract on the Anacostia on the east side of the federal city. His money was much needed. Walker had a reputation for business acumen that made it highly unlikely he would be relegated to the dim pages of historical obscurity. A flamboyant Scot, Walker sought his fortune in the Potomac tidewater sometime in the 1780s and built a prosperous business as a commercial representative for a Scottish tobacco and wheat trading firm. Walker quickly established himself as one of Georgetown's leading business figures, and when the plan to establish a capital on the Potomac unfolded, he became an enthusiastic investor. Historian Kenneth Bowling finds that Walker was extolling the virtues of establishing a political and commercial metropolis on the Potomac at a very early date. On January 23, 1789, Walker published a broadside in the *Maryland Journal and Baltimore Advertiser* that heralded the advantages of establishing a political capital between Georgetown and the Anacostia. A close ally of L'Enfant after 1790, Walker invested heavily in city lots near the Anacostia, firm in his belief that "the Eastern

Branch is one of the safest and most commodious harbours in America." It was "sufficiently deep for the largest ships for about four miles above its mouth; while the channel lies close along the edge of the city, and is abundantly capacious."[17] Walker promoted his 358 acres in what was then known on Capitol Hill as the "Houpyard." It extended from the District boundary at G Street, NE, through what today is Lincoln Park and on down to the Anacostia River.

Walker was eventually thwarted by his fellow merchants in Georgetown, who relentlessly angled to move most of the construction to the western part of the District, near themselves. These men well knew the port of Georgetown was already heavily silted, Walker asserted, and despite that fact strove to make it the navigational centerpiece of the new capital. Out of moral conviction and determination to protect his investments, Walker argued that the Anacostia was better and deeper. Whether or not his enemies in Georgetown were responsible for the stagnation of his Capitol Hill lots, his investments did not bring a profit, and by 1804, George Walker's adventure had ended in bankruptcy.

Nevertheless, no one worked harder to develop the Anacostia than George Walker.[18] Ultimately he quarreled with the city commission and went to England to find backers to defend his investment, but, like Greenleaf, he failed to win the support of cautious bankers. When Congress finally moved to Washington and all hope of recouping his investment was mired in a bureaucratic tangle, Walker returned permanently to Scotland. One of the new capital's most fervent supporters disappeared from the pages of history as well. That he failed points to the dangerous shoals of Washington real estate speculation that continue to this day. The banks of the Anacostia and capital real estate have ruined many otherwise sensible investors, for whom the euphoria of building the new District of Columbia turned into a fool's errand.

Developing the Anacostia Waterfront

The one man to come out of the Washington real estate market with his reputation intact was Thomas Law, who materialized on the Anacostia waterfront in 1795 with a store of Asian tales to regale travelers in the taverns and boarding houses of the still half-civilized Capitol Hill. A thirty-seven-year-old investor who had spent nearly half his life in the East India trade, Law had a fortune of $250,000 when he arrived from England. He was an intriguing man, who had used political connections to amass a fortune as a tax collector in the Indian capital of Bahar and acquire an Indian concubine. When his benefactor in London, Lord Hastings, became involved in a financial scandal, Law departed for America with his three half-caste sons.

Shortly after his arrival in Washington, Law purchased lots with cash and offered the city commissioners a lofty vision of the future. The one way the capital could successfully develop, he argued, was to become a major port. Law purchased lots along the Anacostia and announced that he would build an agency house and waterfront operation for trade with India and the Orient. Annoyed by the financial fecklessness of city commissioners who purchased lots near Georgetown, Law declared, "The City can only be made by the Eastern Branch." Several other investors followed his lead and built wharves and warehouses on the Anacostia. The most notable were Lewis Deblois and the ever opportunistic Notley Young, who commenced operations in the vicinity of what is now 11th and 12th Streets, SE.[19] From 1795 onward, wharf and warehouse-building along the Anacostia and Potomac steadily increased. James Barry, an Irish businessman from New York, built Barry Wharf at the foot of New Jersey Avenue in 1795 and engaged in the East India Trade. Notley Young constructed his wharf at the foot of 7th Street, and the city commissioners also had a wharf at the foot of New Jersey Avenue.[20] Thomas Law became the acknowledged leader of Anacostia shippers and used his money to help finance a fleet of vessels laden with articles for the markets of the world. On April 22, 1797, the Law-backed *Maryland*, a commercial ship of four hundred tons laden with bread and flour, sailed from Barry's wharf on the Anacostia bound for Greece.[21]

Law eventually married the granddaughter of Martha Washington and joined the ranks of Virginia squires. An expert on local currency and land, he survived the real estate debacle, became a planter in Maryland, and served as president of the Prince George's Agricultural Society. In his last years he remained financially solvent, though not so rich as formerly. For Thomas Law, the Eastern Branch was always the key to Washington's future as a river port. His imposing three-story brick mansion on N and 6th Streets still looks out on the river he loved.[22]

Given the depth of the river and the attractiveness of its harbor, Anacostia did become a wharf and shipping zone. Bladensburg had long been silted in and Georgetown was suffering from an increasingly shallow channel. The harbor was at the foot of South Capitol Street and provided the shortest and most direct land route to the Capitol's construction site. From the wharf, stone and lumber were hauled uphill to the site in horse-drawn sleds. Boat builders, too, established themselves along the Potomac and Anacostia waterfronts. As late as 1826 perceptive visitors like Ann Royall were speaking of the swelling hills and the Anacostia with "lordly ships" to stir the imagination.[23] The waterfront's growth did not come soon enough to rescue the investors who had banked on L'Enfant's vision.

In these formative years, three areas of settlement arose, with chandlers, hotels, and boarding houses: Greenleaf Point, Capitol Hill, and the area along the Anacostia that is now M Street. Additionally, a small diplomatic community of foreign ministries opened their offices in the vicinity of what is now the Washington Navy Yard. Merchants clamored for a customs house to be located at the confluence of the Anacostia and Potomac, and for pilots to help ship captains avoid the Potomac's shallows en route to Georgetown.[24] Before he was fired, L'Enfant planned to make 8th Street, SE, the great commercial street of the new capital and home to its proposed Commercial and Financial Exchange, reasoning that the Anacostia would have to be the main waterfront to serve international trade.

But the waterfront between the Anacostia and Georgetown just did not develop as rapidly as Washington, Pierre L'Enfant, and Anacostia investors like Thomas Law had hoped. Commercial life failed to grow into anything resembling the central financial exchange the city's founders so eagerly anticipated. After L'Enfant's dismissal, Congress scaled back its financial commitment to the waterfront. By 1798 public interest in waterfront real estate had evaporated. Development west of the navy yard on the Anacostia would be a limited private enterprise affair. Unfortunately for history, the agitation of Georgetown landowners, who were fearful that the new city would come under the sway of Capitol Hill and diminish their own port, has obscured the mercantile vision of waterfront development on the Anacostia in the early years of the republic.

The Capital Canal

The Washington Canal, chartered by Congress and completed in 1815, was a trench, one and a half miles long, cut out of Tiber Creek, a stream that flowed through what is now the national Mall along Constitution Avenue. The Washington Canal Company commissioned a successful architect and engineer, Benjamin Henry Latrobe, to route the canal in a straight line along the north side of the Mall. It would then take an abrupt bend in front of the Capitol and meet the Anacostia River at Buzzard Point. Though Latrobe used L'Enfant's plans for a grand canal in the Mall, many of the elegant features he proposed, including a water cascade down Capitol Hill and a majestic turning basin, were abandoned because of expense. Yet the canal did live up to L'Enfant's intentions by providing a waterway at the north end of the Mall that connected the Potomac and Georgetown with the Anacostia River. It was also part of a larger plan that included a future canal along the Potomac into the western hinterland.[25]

Had the plan been completed, the capital and its superior port on the Anacostia would have become a strong commercial entrepôt with access to the Ohio Valley, capable of diverting trade away from Balti-more.[26] Noah Webster, a New Englander who championed Washing-ton, believed the canal trade would bring draymen and boatmen who would build houses or rent them. "No sooner is a canal formed through a town or city than stores etc. are erected on its banks," he noted.[27] George Washington and the generation of leaders that followed fore-saw an America tamed and disciplined by canals, locks, and dams. Thus did the ideal of the canal add its weight to plans for the capital.[28]

The Washington Canal proceeded sluggishly from design to real-ity. Gangs of Irish laborers imported for the purpose labored on it after 1810, dredging out the Tiber River and James Creek and extending the canal through the city between Capitol Hill and Georgetown. When it opened for traffic in 1815 only barges drawing three feet of water or less could pass. It could carry scows supplying coal and firewood to stores and homes on Pennsylvania Avenue, and one branch connected with James Creek, which allowed small barges access to lower Capitol Hill and the Anacostia. By 1850 coal dominated the Washington Canal trade because of insatiable demands by homeowners and factories at the Washington Navy Yard.[29] But the waterway was poorly maintained. Its locks and wooden walls suffered damage in storms and easily rotted. Mud flowed back into the canal, rendering it too shallow for commer-cial navigation. Congress was forced, grudgingly at times, to provide additional appropriations for repairs.

The Washington Navy Yard

Yet not everyone was disappointed with the lack of development along the Anacostia. The collapse of real estate speculation made the waterfront ripe for military and federal use, and the young U.S. Navy had its eye on the deep water harbor just off Buzzard Point.

The Washington Navy Yard came into existence in 1799. Prior to that, naval shipbuilding had depended upon private yards. But the navy's decision to build large frigates of forty-four guns taxed many private yards, which suddenly became too small and logistically too expensive. Secretary of the Navy Benjamin Stoddert, who saw the need for even larger ships, told President Washington the new nation required a strategically located federal facility capable of building warships of seventy-four guns. Deep and wide, the Anacostia was an excellent site. Stoddert recruited Captain Thomas Tingay, "an officer of great merit in our service," as the superintendent for the new yard. Tingay recruited workers and began building warships during the tense years of deteriorating relations between the United States and Great Britain. Soon the navy yard had a channel marked by buoys in the Anacostia and a pilot to bring ships up from the mouth of the river. By 1804 the yard had store clerks, boatswains, sail makers, a block maker and crew, a carpenter and sailing master, and a hundred seamen. In a short time it became both a shipyard and the repair facility for the entire fleet. The navy, it turned out, became the one entity to profit from L'Enfant's vision of a busy waterfront.

During Thomas Jefferson's presidency, the federal government constructed one of the largest military wharves in North America, a structure some eight hundred feet long and parallel to the Anacostia, with a large storage facility for ships' timber. It was here at the navy yard that Jefferson and architect Latrobe experimented with a mammoth dry dock as a way of storing naval vessels not in use. Construction of warships continued until the facility was burned in 1814 to prevent its falling into British hands.

After peace was restored, the federal government rebuilt the facility, and between the end of the War of 1812 and the Civil War, the navy yard built twenty-two vessels, including four gunboats, four sloops-of-war, four frigates, five schooners, one ship-of-the-line, and the screw frigate *Minnesota*. Between 1844 and the 1870s the yard constructed paddle-wheel and screw propeller gunboats.[30] Later it manufactured ordnance. From its inception, the navy yard was the most significant employer on the Washington waterfront, and it had a major impact along the Anacostia River.

The Black Seamen and Other Skilled African American Labor

African Americans were prominent in the early history of the Anacostia waterfront. Like Philadelphia, Boston, Charleston, and New York, the capital had a substantial black population. Washington's resulted from its location between Virginia and Maryland, the states with the largest black populations in the country in 1800. Visitors remarked upon the nature of those who were building the capital, for slaves erected the buildings, dug the piers, and built the wharves. In 1804, Irish poet Thomas Moore, his pen dripping acid, wrote:

> Even here beside the grand Potomac's streams
> The medley mass of pride and misery
> Of whips and charters, manacles and rights
> Of slaving blacks and democratic whites.[31]

In 1800 the Federal District had a population of 11,093, of whom 1,025 were African Americans clustered mainly near the mouth of the Anacostia and in a small settlement near the mouth of Rock Creek.[32] It is perhaps one of the great ironies of local history that, long after the land was devastated by tobacco monoculture and the planters had squandered their immense wealth, their black servants remained at the water's edge, having survived slavery and its oppressive political economy. By 1820 blacks numbered 3,531, about 27 percent of the city's 13,000 inhabitants. More than half were classified as "free Negroes."[33]

The terms "free" and "slave" were kept remarkably fluid by the avarice of white employers, and the condition of blacks was often determined by the nature of the slave-master and the employer-employee relationship. For example, Michael Shiner, who worked his way out of slavery and purchased his freedom, was part of a community of free blacks and slaves that gravitated toward the District's waterfront. Literate and active in the community, Shiner worked as a mechanic in the navy yard, owned a house on 8th and D Streets, SE, and kept a diary that is currently deposited at the Library of Congress. He was one of the few Washingtonians who actually saw the British troops arrive in the city on August 24, 1814, after President Madison and his government had fled. Shiner was a free man, but his wife and children were not. He worked heroically and successfully to redeem them from slavery and in time succeeded.[34]

Black crewmen could usually be found on schooners laden with flour bound down the coast for distant ports of call like Barbados.[35] On long voyages they sometimes were treated harshly. One white Virginia sailor reported that his officers often threatened crewmen, and if a sailor disobeyed they would "cut him and staple him and use him like a Negro, or rather like a dog." Blacks and whites alike agreed that the tobacco colonies were "one of worst countries in the Universe for Sailors."[36]

Although many black sailors and workers had freedom papers or "near freedom" by virtue of their ability to hire out their labor, they had a profoundly different view of what it meant to "follow" the water than did whites. Blacks saw in just about any kind of maritime work economic opportunity and a means of self-determination rather than the drudgery that many whites deemed it to be. Nearly every public works project in the District involved "Negro labor." This was particularly evident in the construction of wharves and smaller docks in the city.

Travelers from Europe remarked in 1800 that "only the Negroes work." Working conditions at the Capitol were dangerous, and blacks occasionally suffered broken limbs, severe cuts, and exposure to the weather. In 1797, for example, ninety slaves worked on the Capitol building and received medical care and probably some of the money that was supposed to be allotted to their masters.[37] Slave carpenters hired out for $55 a year. Four of them are documented as part of the work force that built the White House, and upwards of forty slaves worked for contractors on public buildings.

The presence of a skilled black labor force in the new capital had a number of important ramifications. Many built houses in the growing Anacostia River community near what is 8th and M Streets, SE, today. They also established a precedent for working independently. Living in shacks and small houses along the Anacostia they interacted with Irish immigrants who were beginning to settle in as well. Thus along 8th Street, SE, evolved an interesting racially and socially diverse community known for its independence and for miscegenation.[38] Along the Anacostia much of the river trade fell to African Americans who handled flatboats and small craft on the rivers or worked as teamsters carrying flour and other goods from Bladensburg to Baltimore.

Skills as a carpenter, bricklayer, blacksmith, or able seaman were often the tickets to freedom, and black master craftsmen were common on the Anacostia. Benjamin Banneker, a free black man and later a famous creator of almanacs, was employed by the surveyor of the Federal District. Significantly, he stayed at inns and ate at the table with his white contemporaries, for such was his talent and intellect that little thought was given to his race. Along the waterfront William Winters, a ship carpenter, and John Woodland, a rope master, provided the skill necessary to repair ships like the *Porpoise* and the *Brandywine*, which were routinely outfitted in the Washington Navy Yard. Richard Brooks, the "Negro messenger" to the yard's commander, Captain Thomas Tingay, kept the black community informed of employment opportunities and white thinking about local blacks. The contributions of blacks who worked on the ropewalks or in the navy yard's sail-making lofts helped to foster belief among local blacks that they could overcome latent public hostility to their race by being "useful law-abiding members of a biracial community."

What historian Constance McLaughlin Green called "a self-reliant Negro community" grew up with the nation's new capital. As long as free blacks did not constitute more than 15 percent of the population of Washington and Georgetown they suffered from only minimal harassment. Free blacks of all occupations, including restaurant owners, barbers, messengers, and clergymen, used the wealth they gleaned from the Anacostia River economy to build schools. In the new national capital slavery displayed, according to one historian, a "steadily diminishing vitality."[39] The Washington waterfront provided blacks with opportunities that let them find ways out of slavery, to become either quasi-free by occupation or legally free through manumission. In that unanticipated way, George Washington's riparian dream helped to build a small free black community along the Anacostia River.[40]

Ultimately, Pierre L'Enfant's vision of a city with a deep harbor and commodious port on the banks of the Anacostia River went unrealized. Speculators failed to develop lands along the river into a mercantile and residential center that would be home to both a bourse and foreign embassies. The Anacostia, planned as part of a vibrant river port, could not shake its plantation heritage. The Washington Navy Yard and the Washington Canal were the only elements of L'Enfant's planned city that completely matured. The navy yard would play an important role in Washington's military and economic life. The Washington Canal ultimately became a sewage problem. And the black community on the Anacostia would come to know economic deprivation and oppression.

CHAPTER FOUR

The Anacostia and the Civil War

"The citizens were often at the mercy of malaria, dysentery, and cholera epidemics."
— Margaret Leech, *Reveille in Washington*

From 1812 to 1860, Washington experienced growth and the accompanying problems of urban development that it was ill-equipped to solve. With its southern social values and tradition of plantation leadership, it felt less urban than rural, a collection of individuals, many of them aristocratic, rather than a community. The Civil War forced the capital to develop a new understanding of its rivers and water resources and gave rise to debates about public health, sewage, and the environment that would profoundly affect the city for the rest of the century.

The Capital Environment, 1812–1860

In the years between the British invasion and the outbreak of the Civil War, the Anacostia River played a complex role in shaping the environment and the concept of nature in the capital. The Anacostia and Potomac tidal flats, with their summer and autumn miasmas, generated public complaint and discussion. Though still considered primarily in commercial and military terms, both rivers began to be viewed as threats to public health. Sewage had become an issue almost as soon as the new capital organized itself, and the term "public nuisance" came to be associated with waste of all kinds. Fresh air, abundant unfouled land, and clear water gave way to slops in the streets, offal shoveled from slaughterhouses, and a general climate of urban squalor. In 1810 the District began building sewers to drain wastewater into the river wetlands, but most of what passed for sewers were little more than open drains. Fumes nauseated District residents, and rats infested everything, including the White House.

In all matters relating to the city's sanitary infrastructure, Congress ruled. Under Article One, Section 8 of the U.S. Constitution, virtually any law in the District had to receive congressional approval before it could be enacted. In Washington, Congress was the supreme power, and the right of the people to choose their own political representatives in the form of a mayor or council depended on congressional whim. When it came to public health matters, on which Congress was largely silent, private citizens had to take the initiative.

Following the War of 1812, Dr. Henry Hunt became the Superintendent of Public Health, the city's highest public health official, and for twenty years distinguished himself as a clinician and public health leader. He organized the first board of health in the District and served as President Andrew Jackson's personal physician during Old Hickory's numerous medical crises. A native of Calvert County and a Maryland navy veteran of the War of 1812, Hunt's major contribution was his campaign to require the District of Columbia to keep accurate and verifiable medical statistics.[1]

But Hunt had a crucial flaw in his thinking: He rejected the idea that fevers came from the low grounds of the Anacostia, the Potomac, and Tiber Creek and crusaded against the notion that Washington's rivers and wetlands fostered disease. As Washington's unpaid medical and health officer from 1819 to 1822, Hunt conceded that cases of scarlatina, aginosa, cholera infantum, dysentery, and bilious fevers were numerous, but he maintained that Washington was no more sickly than other cities in the nation.

A recent study by Betty Plummer found that indeed "Washington had no special health conditions setting it apart from other areas," so that Hunt was at least right about that much. Fevers and illnesses did not affect government operations, nor did the so-called sickly season of the summer months prevent the District from functioning. People in Washington were just as likely to be as well or as unhealthy as citizens elsewhere.[2] Like most American cities, Washington suffered from smallpox scares and other epidemics, but most of the time the principal cause of death was consumption and summer flux (typhoid). Both were familiar diseases that provoked little concern or fear. Under Hunt's direction the city began to vaccinate against smallpox, though the procedure was not popular with blacks and the white laboring classes. Washington, like other contemporary cities, was largely inured to the kind of disease and contagion that American cities would find intolerable by 1900.

Civic authorities panicked from time to time over the prospects of yellow fever or cholera coming to the District. In 1832 a deadly strain of Asiatic cholera, part of a cholera pandemic that swept across Europe and came to the United States via Great Britain, struck the capital. Unsanitary water systems and the working and living conditions of workers on the Washington Canal and near the navy yard provided a ripe environment for pestilence. Cholera is an intestinal infection caused by contaminated water or food. Its symptoms are watery diarrhea, muscle cramps, and severe dehydration. Cholera lurks in sewage and makes a host of the human intestinal tract. Unfortunately, public health officials believed that cholera was not contagious but caused by change in the atmosphere or some unknown miasma that "corrupted the natural humors." To combat the Asiatic cholera, doctors forbade their patients from eating ripe fruit and misguidedly administered calomel and other purgatives to drive out "noxious substances."

By July 7, 1832, the cholera had reached Baltimore and was slowly making its way up the Potomac. In the first week of August, District health officials sought to put restrictions on slaughterhouses and fruit stalls and ordered that all pools of stagnant water be eliminated. As

Plummer noted, "by the second week of August, rumors about the presence of Asiatic cholera were widespread, causing considerable fear among residents." Local officials, unsure of themselves, placed a broadside in the local newspapers blaming "intemperance" in the consumption of alcoholic beverages as a cause of the disease. Irish workers were counseled to be moderate in their consumption of potatoes. The actions of the mayor's office and local officials indicate they had no idea how to handle the outbreak, and that terrified them. It was not easy for survivors to forget a cholera epidemic. Marked by severe vomiting, painful cramps and dehydration, and cyanosis or blue discoloration of the face caused by loss of oxygen in the blood, a victim could die within a day of being stricken.[3]

The dying began that August, and when it was over an estimated 432 Washingtonians had perished. The "Dead Wagon" became a familiar sight along streets near canals and watercourses. Its driver called out, "Bring out the dead!" and the bodies were loaded and carted off to a cemetery outside the city. Newspapers published accounts of people who had fallen ill after eating watermelon or drinking bad whiskey. As the number of casualties increased, newspapers became more reluctant to report bad news. Instead they campaigned for the removal of hog sties, which were classified as "public nuisances." Fear gripped the city. One thing became clear during the crisis: Most of the victims were blacks, the poor, and recent immigrants.

Meanwhile, everyday life continued, and citizens grew resentful of the municipal government's public cleanliness campaigns as well as its use of police to quarantine neighborhoods near the navy yard and the Washington Canal. To the poorer classes the issue of controlling public health had become a question of personal liberty. One physician, Dr. Thomas Henderson, joined the chorus of criticism directed against the city and the board of health. Henderson believed the moderate use of wine and spirits was perfectly acceptable and argued that city officials applied their policies inconsistently. In an essay entitled *Observations on the Epidemic Cholera as it Appeared in the City of Washington,* Henderson admitted he did not know what caused Asiatic cholera but charged that the District was doing little to halt its spread.[4]

By September 28 the scourge had disappeared as quickly as it had appeared. While the city government and its citizenry continued the debate over cholera and whiskey and watermelons, the real everyday diseases of Washington went on taking their toll. The fact that consumption, typhoid, malaria, and dysentery caused far more deaths than cholera seemed not to influence the thinking of District authorities. This suggests that only when exotic diseases came to Washington did physicians and laymen discuss a vigorous regimen of public health controls.

Disease accompanied growth in the antebellum period. By 1850 the population had reached fifty thousand, with more than eight thousand free blacks and four thousand immigrants in residence. This increase strained housing facilities and contributed to the overloading of privies and the contamination of wells and springs. The Washington Canal remained an open sewer. The sanitarian Charles Force claimed it was a "great cesspool for the filth and washings of about one half of the city." Child mortality was high along the Anacostia and Potomac watercourses, but only a few doctors entered the discussion on its causes. Dr. Thomas Miller, a sanitarian working in Washington during the 1840s and 1850s, pointed out that many health issues resulted from poor water drainage and other sanitary problems like the cattle, hogs, and geese left to roam the streets. Miller campaigned for "scavengers" to remove the offal, garbage, and decayed vegetables that caused "stenches," but most of his suggestions fell upon deaf ears.[5]

Medical practice for the most part remained in the tradition prescribed in 1823 by Dr. Nathaniel P. Causin of the Medical Society of the District of Columbia. In his study of "Autumnal Bilious Fevers" (typhoid, malaria, yellow fever, or hepatitis), Causin relied on emetics, cathartics, and toxic drugs like mercury and antimony "to dislodge from the stomach and bowels, all irritating matter, whether of food or secretion." He believed that whenever the human system became excited by his drugs and emetics, "the disease almost always yields," and his remedies became the standard of medical care.[6]

Preventive medicine based upon the study of bacteria would not make serious inroads in public health policy until after the Civil War. It was increasingly apparent to sanitarians, though, that ground water was becoming seriously contaminated by the growing human and animal population. Landlords in the poorer sections made no attempt to provide clean drinking water to their tenants, who had to rely on the community well or cistern. The middle and upper classes had access to better water from private companies or the water brought in later via an aqueduct from the upper Potomac constructed by the Army Corps of Engineers. As the city continued to grow during the 1850s, largely in response to the rise of government as an important local industry and the expansion of the Washington Navy Yard, many more residents became concerned with the city's sanitation, or lack of it. Clearly, on the eve of the Civil War middle-class residents, at least, had come to believe in a close correlation between wealth, water, and public health. Sanitation problems, ignored during the war, would afterward shape the debates about public health and the environment.

Agriculture in the Watershed

After 1800, when tobacco prices plummeted and wheat prices sank in the face of ruinous foreign competition, planters resorted to constant single-cropping of the two commodities. Less profit compelled them to produce more to make up the slack. Little thought was given to building farms and restoring the landscape.

Most of the erosion and heavy silting that eventually choked the Anacostia's tributaries began around 1820. Visitors deplored fields littered with stumps, ragged old fields, and slovenly methods of cultivation. Northern agricultural reformers like Frederick Law Olmsted blamed slavery. Montgomery County experienced perhaps the worst effects. By 1820 boats transporting flour could no longer reach Adelphi Mill on the northwest branch of the Anacostia. By 1853 the Army Corps of Engineers had closed Bladensburg to large commercial ships because sediment had clogged the river channel. Erosion in Montgomery County was so widespread that after 1830 agricultural reformers referred to it as the "Sahara of Maryland." Farmland did not rise above eight dollars an acre until the Civil War. By comparison, an acre in Pennsylvania was worth twenty-five dollars. "The splendid and delightsome land" once described by Captain John Smith had simply vanished by the hand of man.[7]

Land stewardship found its most influential expression in the public careers of John Stuart Skinner and Charles Benedict Calvert. Both men were appalled by the ruination of local agriculture and served as well-connected spokesmen for saving the landscape. Skinner, the energetic agriculturalist and long-time editor of the *American Farmer* in Baltimore, championed land restoration by urging young farmers to study their craft seriously. Through pamphlets, speeches, and newspaper articles, Skinner waged a determined campaign to bring the land back from the brink of destruction. Unfortunately, the small farmers ignored him, and after briefly enjoying the patronage of the planter class, the *American Farmer* limped along as an obscure publication.[8]

In the 1850s, Charles Benedict Calvert was one of the most influential planters in Maryland. The heir to Riversdale plantation in the Anacostia watershed, Calvert mixed rural philanthropy with agricultural reform. Since most of his wealth was inherited, this scion of Maryland's founding family could afford to pursue his own personal interests. Fortunately for the Anacostia, Calvert had a missionary zeal for restoring agricultural lands and recapturing the beauty of a lost landscape. He read farm journals and turned his 2,200-acre plantation into a productive hay and dairy farm. Throughout the watershed he was known for his use of modern farm machinery and his experiments in

crop rotation. His lands, which extended from Bladensburg to the Beltway along what is now Route 1, were the most productive in the state.
On his journey through the seaboard slave states, Frederick Law Olmsted found him to be one of the few planters who were clear-sighted
and oriented toward the future.

Calvert also feared that his fellow planters were on the verge of
becoming nothing more than an ignorant class of clodhoppers. One
element of his vision for a renewed landscape was a revitalized planter
elite to lead the state and the nation as the country embroiled itself in
matters of nullification, states' rights, and sectionalism. Calvert was a
staunch nationalist and on the eve of the Civil War served in Congress
as a representative of slaveholding, pro-Union planters.[9] Eventually he
gave much of his land to the Maryland Agricultural College, what is
now the University of Maryland in College Park. Well into his later
years he remained interested in agricultural experimentation and preserving the land.

The Anacostia and the Civil War

In many respects the Civil War magnified the sanitary, racial, and
social problems that had intensified in Washington since its founding.
The vast number of sick and wounded housed in hospitals and clinics on
Capitol Hill and elsewhere contributed to growing problems in public
health. Increasing numbers of troops and animals strained rudimentary
sewers and privies. Garbage mounted, especially along the Washington
Canal, where many troops encamped as they waited to fight in northern
Virginia. Many suffered from dysentery caused by living in fetid camps
along the western side of the Anacostia and in what is now the Mall.
Soldiers violated the health ordinances by bathing in the effluvia-filled
Washington Canal. "They were often ignorant," wrote the *Washington
Star*, "that it was hardly more than a drain for the most populous por-
tion of the city, into which all the sewers empty."[10] Land use along the
Anacostia and Potomac was the prerogative of local government, and

the absence of effective control left most decisions about refuse disposal and shoreline development to what Chesapeake legal historian Garrett Power has called "the market mechanism." Public goals of sanitation and clean water have "not fared well in the market place."[11]

Yet, given the times, the response to sanitation problems in a town like Washington was understandable. Local government labored to control disease with the knowledge they had, and numerous individuals provided heroic service. Louisa May Alcott and Walt Whitman risked their lives to work with the wounded and sick in District hospitals. Alcott, who later became famous for writing *Little Women*, had to be taken back to her home in New England after she fell victim to typhoid fever.

Disease imposed a heavy burden on the city, one from which it would not easily recover. From the first year of the war on, the lack of adequate hygiene in the military led to the eruption of diseases that debilitated soldiers and civilians alike. Many of the troops contracted diarrhea and malaria, increasing the strain on public health facilities. To combat dysentery, which frequently caused death by fever and dehydration, doctors prescribed oil of turpentine, a remedy that proved minimally effective. Hospitals were neither heated nor well ventilated, and sanitation was both primitive and of little concern.

Military livestock were also a nuisance. To feed troops quartered in the District, the army had to bring in droves of cattle, until at times the numerous slaughterhouses made the city seem like a vast abattoir. Residents also had to contend with cattle, horse, and sheep urine and thousands of tons of manure that made local life both offensive and dangerous. A few months after the beginning of hostilities, the mayor of Washington visited general headquarters to complain about the feces and bloated carcasses of sheep and horses left haphazardly in the streets or unceremoniously flung into the Washington Canal. Secretary of War Simon Cameron was more than a little responsible for those dead horses in the streets. Through insider business deals with his cronies in

Pennsylvania, Cameron foisted hundreds of broken-down horses on the army. Many were fatally infected with glanders, a highly infectious disease that affected their jaws and mouths.[12] Not until January 1863 did military leaders give the problem their attention and collect wagon-loads of dead animals for disposal in the countryside.

By October 1861, fifty thousand soldiers had arrived in Washington, more than doubling the urban population and putting a huge strain on sewer and water resources. The soldiers seemed to be everywhere—in bars, restaurants, and hotels—and none too mindful about casually uri-nating in the crowded and chaotic streets. Not only were fighting men on the march, their pathogens marched as well. As the campaigns of 1862 lengthened, military encampments in Washington grew rife with measles, malaria, typhoid fever, and diarrhea, diseases that incapacitated as many men as did battlefield wounds. In 1863 and 1864 typhoid fever raged through the city. Young Willie Lincoln, the president's son, died in the White House in February 1863, at the age of eleven, proving that the rich and powerful were also helpless to protect their families from the dreaded maladies of battlefield and camp.[13] Adding to the huge numbers of sick were the wagons filled with corpses arriving from the battlefield. "The embalming parlors, like the hospitals, were crowded beyond capacity," writes historian Ernest B. Ferguson. "Some restau-rateurs complained that the odor of death and chemicals from nearby undertakers was ruining their business." Despite the shortage of trained doctors and nurses to care for the sick and wounded, many doctors de-serted medicine for the more financially lucrative trade of embalming the Union dead.[14]

Perhaps the most salutary environmental development during the war was the building by the Army Corps of Engineers of a new aque-duct that brought in ten thousand gallons of fresh water daily from the upper Potomac. The removal of many stockyards to the outskirts also made the city healthier.[15] Unfortunately the Anacostia and the Poto-mac, which heretofore had suffered from seasonal pollution, were now constantly rank sewers of human and animal effluvia. The stench was almost unbearable when the summers turned sultry. Affluent residents fled to the more salubrious air of summer cottages. Poorer whites and blacks had no choice but to endure.

Written reports detail the grisly, unsanitary life of Washington during the war, but photographs of the city and outlying areas tell another, equally distressing tale. The immediate vicinities of the Potomac and the Anacostia Rivers were virtually denuded of trees. In part this massive deforestation was the response to the army's voracious need for barracks, medical facilities, bridges, and animal pens. In the oppressive heat of lingering Indian summer in 1861, Union soldiers sweated with axes, picks, and shovels to construct two military necessities: fortifications and plank roads. Orchards, private dwellings, stores, and churches fell before the juggernaut. Much of the timber went into the complex of forts, trenches, and artillery redoubts that began to ring the city following the rout of Federal forces at Manassas in July. General McClellan and his officers took possession of the landscape.

The main forts were constructed one-half mile apart with earthworks nearly eighteen feet thick on the exposed side. In front of the works was the Civil War equivalent of barbed wire: sharpened stakes or felled trees with sharpened ends of their branches pointed toward the enemy. Hundreds of axe men attacked entire forests for stakes and lumber. One New York Infantryman remarked that the trees were like "the billow on the surface of the ocean, the forest would fall with a crash like mighty thunder." The once heavily forested ridge overlooking the Anacostia from the east became barren ground almost overnight as soldiers labored to build a massive artillery battery on the ridge to protect the city from invasion. Low water in the Potomac and the Anacostia in the summer prompted Union planners to build stockade fences along the riverbanks to protect the capital. Just between the Potomac and the Anacostia they built fourteen forts and three artillery batteries. Altogether the army constructed forty-eight defensive works encircling the city.

The assault on the watershed by more than a thousand soldiers, lumberjacks, and contraband slaves was catastrophic. It would be years before second growth covered the denuded hills and ridges. Moreover, it turned out to be unnecessary. The forts provided a sense of security to wartime Washington, though they never could have survived a major Confederate attack. Most of the 23,000 garrison troops were stripped away in 1864 to join General Ulysses S. Grant's Wilderness Campaign. Thereafter these elaborate creations of trees and dirt were manned mostly by boys, walking wounded, and superannuated home front soldiers. In July 1864, General Jubal A. Early's small army descended on Washington after defeating a small Union force at Monocacy Junction but withdrew after barely probing the defenses of Fort Stevens on the 7th Street Road north of the District because Union reinforcements arrived swiftly from Virginia. Despite the forts' diminished importance in the last year of the war, the army assigned seven hundred laborers to keep their lines of fire free from trees and undergrowth.

At the war's end, the Army Corps of Engineers dismantled the forts and sold the used lumber at public auction. It was one of the biggest sales of cut timber and lumber in the mid-Atlantic and netted the corps some $15,000. Although John Gross Barnard, architect of the forts, thought they surpassed anything comparable in Europe, at a cost of $1.4 million and incalculable damage to the watershed some wondered whether the forts were really worth it.[16]

The Black Community in the Civil War

The free black population of some eleven thousand in 1860 confronted a different reality in Washington than had their counterparts of 1800. By 1860 attacks by the abolitionist press and the subsequent response from slaveholding states prompted the imposition of a local Black Code that tightened restrictions on the personal liberties of free blacks, who also met with indifference or hostility from the federal government. The 1850 census, the first to give a clear picture of employment in Washington, indicates that most worked as laborers or servants and had to compete with Irish laborers for jobs on projects like the widening of the Washington Canal. Around what is now Eastern Market and the Washington Navy Yard, black venders of fruits and vegetables hawked their wares. Those with enough money to buy a hackney coach could engage in the lucrative business of transporting whites around the city.

Although the legal status of free blacks was more circumscribed in 1860, historian Dorothy Provine's study of the Washington Tax Books reveals their steadily improving economic condition late in the antebellum period. "A handful of free Negroes achieved phenomenal economic success," she notes. On Capitol Hill and along the Anacostia, for example, Francis Datcher, a free black working as a messenger in the War Department, owned over $10,000 worth of real property. More widely known is the remarkable story of James Wormley, who became the proprietor of the famous Wormley Hotel. An excellent chef and well-connected to black watermen, who supplied him with fresh fish and turtle, Wormley provided meals and accommodations for General Winfield Scott, commander of the U.S. Army in the 1850s. Scott boasted that Wormley's terrapin soup was the best in the nation. "In spite of legal disabilities and the prejudices of the white community, many blacks were able to make remarkable progress in the District."[17]

From the beginning, Washington attracted large numbers of paupers and homeless blacks. The District's legal code was not as harsh toward the poor, especially the free black poor, as were the laws in Maryland and Virginia. Most, including numbers of free blacks, came to Washington to find work on government construction projects. Benjamin Latrobe, the architect of the Capitol, wrote that the poor were "ruined in circumstances and health" and lived in "wretched huts" near the construction sites.[18] By 1840 the city government had successfully appealed to Congress for a steady flow of funds to provide medical treatment and food for the homeless. The number of transients may have been small by today's standard, but it is instructive to note that early District policy toward the poor was non-punitive.

During the war, when refugees and the poor flooded the city, this situation went from a small question of civic morality to a major institutional crisis. By 1863 the Union army estimated that more than forty thousand ex-slaves had found their way into the city.[19] One of the most urgent matters confronting the capital was that of finding housing for them. Many were forced to camp in cemeteries, crowd into abandoned warehouses, or even sleep in the streets. Inevitably race relations became strained. Many of the refugees were filthy, and genteel Washington blamed them for the spread of contagious diseases, especially smallpox. "Many Washingtonians believed that blacks suffered from a particularly virulent strain of the disorder known as the 'black smallpox,'" wrote historian Betty Plummer. "The thought of contracting this strain of illness had to be especially terrifying to those who loathed blacks and feared smallpox."[20]

The small group of affluent blacks, or "well-to-do colored people" of Washington as they called themselves, was appalled by the freedmen's condition. Led by free black Elizabeth Keckley, Mary Todd Lincoln's dressmaker, this group joined Quakers to establish the Freedmen's Relief Association to aid black refugees. One of their first tasks was to provide clean drinking water and a place to rest away from the wetlands and marshes. Blacks were ferried across the Potomac to set up camp at a place on the Anacostia known as Barry Farm. Others were sent to the refugee camp on Robert E. Lee's plantation at Arlington.[21]

BY 1865 IT WAS CLEAR to even the most ignorant observer that Washington had undergone a demographic revolution during the war. Returning visitors were shocked and surprised by the mud, stench, and swelling crowds that had overtaken a southern river town. From 61,000 in 1858, the population had swelled to 109,000, a number that did not include the thousands of soldiers tramping through the capital. Housing, water supplies, and sanitation had been strained to the limits. With the coming of peace and national reconciliation, civic officials faced rebuilding a city that from the standpoint of public infrastructure bordered on collapse.

The pressures of war, disease, refugees, and reconstruction crashed upon the city in successive waves after 1861. Increasingly the Anacostia River became caught up in the matrix of Washington urban development with all of its implications for lifestyle, race relations, and public health. For African Americans and whites alike, the city's demographic transformation ushered in a host of environmental problems that would center mainly on the Anacostia, which the war had changed almost beyond recognition.

CHAPTER FIVE

An Urban River:
Public Health, Infrastructure,
and Race, 1865–1914

"We are today among the most successful cultivators of the deadly bacilli of typhus and other diseases."
— Albert Reed, *Washington Post,* January 11, 1896

In 1865, Mary Ames wrote in her chronicle, *Ten Years in Washington,* that Capitol Hill and the Anacostia generally was an ugly, denuded region.[1] It would be many years before city and river recovered from the damage wrought by the Civil War. Postwar developments along the Anacostia showed that environmental change was more complex than people then or since have realized. A formerly sleepy waterfront town was growing into a mid-Atlantic metropolis and would soon shed its transport and social affiliation with its riverfront. Developments along the Anacostia from 1865 to 1918 show environmental changes imposed by urbanization. Public health issues as they related to African Americans would be an important part of the city's social dynamic in these years. Sewage and sewers came to the forefront in ecological and planning. By 1918 water quality, sanitation, and the condition of the Anacostia were important priorities.

The Postwar City

The army's need to feed men and livestock brought prosperity to local farmers and planters during the war. Farms above the Anacostia grew tons of tomatoes, vegetables, and melons to be eagerly consumed by the troops. This market-garden economy was part and parcel of the Anacostia until the late 1930s. But the end of the war also saw the passing of the Anacostia's large planters, who, after emancipation, sold their land to real estate developers or carved their holdings into more efficient dairy, truck, and poultry farms. The abolition of slavery coupled with the decline of the tobacco industry also made the large planters turn to leasing their lands out to tenant farmers. Land ownership was still important in the Anacostia, but the plantation gentry moved out of agriculture into more liquid forms of investment. The names of the old planter class were now to be found on different rosters of power in Washington—in the best clubs, in law firms, and in realty companies.

A different kind of market economy operated along the Anacostia and on Capitol Hill, where many of the city's 450 houses of prostitution flourished. Floating brothels called "Potomac Arks" usually anchored off the navy yard and Foggy Bottom. These flat-bottomed houseboats catered to the military and to government clerks. In the last year of the war the *Washington Star* reported that 2,300 white and 1,600 "colored" prostitutes serviced the military in the nation's capital.[2] Unfortunately, these capital doxies did not have a Toulouse-Lautrec to chronicle their *demimonde* lives.

Prostitution highlighted another important public health issue along the rivers—venereal disease. Capital police, using loitering and vagrancy laws to control prostitutes, arrested 727 in 1881. The city fathers had concluded it was the only way to rid the capital of venereal disease. History is silent on the women's subsequent fate, and newspapers did not report the racial demographics.[3]

Economic Change and the Washington Navy Yard

During the Civil War, South Capitol Street became the center of the city's industrial section, and until 1900 manufacturing assumed an important role in capital life. The navy yard continued as the city's largest single employer. The munitions industry offered employment to women who heretofore had been excluded from industrial work. (Several women had been killed during the war when a munitions factory near the navy yard exploded.) Much of the factory waste was dumped into the river near Buzzard Point.

Following the war, the navy yard turned to the manufacture of steam engines, propellers, and other types of hardware to be used for refitting the remaining ships in the fleet, until it became more a manufacturing facility than a shipyard. The last ships to be built there, in the 1870s, were small gunboats made of wood to utilize the lumber left over from wartime construction. Increasing amounts of silt in the Anacostia's ship channel influenced the navy's decision to change its use of the yard.

The rise of the German navy and the Krupp iron works in the 1880s, and increasing imperial expansion by the European powers of England, France, and Germany, prompted the War Department to embark on a policy of building a modern, armored steam-powered fleet. Strong navies were the policy instruments of imperialism, and Admiral Alfred Thayer Mahan's book on the influence of sea power on history became the bible of big-navy imperialists.[4] In response, Congress authorized the creation of a ship gun foundry at the navy yard. With its copper rolling mill, cranes, and huge factory building the navy yard became the largest single industry in Washington, known for the manufacture of heavy ordnance for battleships. Beginning in 1886 and continuing through the Spanish-American War in 1898, the yard provided six-inch and twelve-inch guns for ships of the line. By 1898, writes historian Taylor Peck, the Washington Navy Yard and Gun Factory was "the most modern ordnance plant in the world." A military behemoth had arisen on the banks of the Anacostia that would transform modern warfare while polluting the river with its industrial waste.[5]

Other industries also flourished along the Anacostia. The city's manufacturing establishment in 1880, for example, was capitalized at

$3,924,000, with major industries such as printing, flour and grist milling, foundries, and machine shops, brick and textile yards, and carriage and wagon establishments providing ample employment to the city's artisan and working classes. Although more than fifteen thousand connected their employment in one way or another to the federal government, some seven thousand working men and women held jobs in the manufacturing sectors that had relatively little to do with government.[6] Foundries, ship repair, lumber yards, and carpentry shops flourished in the southeast and southwest sections near the Anacostia.

Reconstructing Washington

Radical Republicans, who had been reconstructing the late-rebellious South, were equally intent on reconstructing the District of Columbia. Washington during the war had been a notorious nest of Confederate sympathizers. Memories of the suffrage bill fight with President Andrew Johnson in 1867 and how the Radicals overrode his veto were still fresh. Toward this end, the Radicals determined to make the capital a showcase of black enfranchisement while at the same time placing real power in the hands of bankers and real estate developers. This was in keeping with the dominant Republican philosophy that liberty and the pursuit of personal wealth were complimentary goals. The Radicals in Congress treated the District after the war as though it had been a seceded state and pledged to expand racial emancipation into the wider realm of full social and political equality. They devised a comprehensive plan to build $18 million worth of paved, tree-lined streets, gas lights, sewers, clean water—and public schools for blacks and whites. Radicals in control of the municipal government believed that the District had to shed its image of a southern town filled with former Confederates, and their push for internal improvement projects that benefited both whites and blacks grew out of that belief.

In 1870 most city streets were dirt and devolved into mud bogs in rainy weather. With the exception of the Washington Canal, the capital did not have an integrated sewer system at all, and certainly nothing worthy of the name. The District maintained night soil dumps at what are today Lincoln Park and Dupont Circle, and visitors to Washington were appalled to see the contents of thousands of privy vaults unceremoniously on display. The embarrassment of mud, garbage, and excrement was compounded by an inadequate street lighting system that made the streets more a hygienic terror than a criminal one. The city was so lacking in many of the amenities of urban life that some congressmen considered relocating the national capital westward.

Under the rationale of making the city operate more efficiently, Congress imposed a territorial government on the District in 1871, to be administered by officials selected by President Ulysses S. Grant. The territorial form of government accomplished two distinct things. First, by allowing blacks and whites to vote for a territorial legislature, the Radical Republicans could keep the old rebel sympathizers from regaining control of the city. Second, it created a new agency, the Board of Public Works. Its five-member board came to be dominated by Alexander Shepherd, an extremely bright and industrious former plumber who was a reigning figure in the city's Republican Party during the Civil War. Shepherd and the city improvers saw nothing wrong in rebuilding the capital and helping their friends at the same time.

With an urban vision that was as strong as his own ego, Shepherd took control. The territorial governor, Henry Cooke, brother of financier Jay Cooke, was more interested in financing sewers than building them. Into the void stepped Shepherd, who, because of his iron will, soon came to be known as "Boss." Unlike many of the carpetbaggers in the occupied South who used city government to enrich themselves, Shepherd was honest. He tore up the city and in three years modernized its infrastructure. Behind Shepherd's bluster was a man well-informed about urban problems. As he saw it, the city in the name of public health was compelled to implement new technologies in water supply, sewerage, and solid waste. He strongly believed that the most essential way to fight disease was to replace the thousands of privy vaults and cesspools with wastewater systems. During his tenure as head of public works, he sought the counsel of engineers, many whom had been trained at West Point, on the best way to rebuild the city's infrastructure. Under his direction streets were improved, bridges built, and a water and sewer system installed.

The costs of changing a sleepy tidewater port into an urban center were considerable. By 1874, "Boss" Shepherd and his Board of Public Works had spent $20 million. Despite angry complaints about his "rule," no one was able to prove his venality. In his private life he simply invested in Washington real estate with the hope that it would be profitable.*

Urban growth came with new challenges to a place long conditioned to following the slow-moving plantation model of agriculture and servitude. Historically, urbanization in the South has been as much a problem of public perception as an issue of economic growth. The District's southern mentality fostered a small town, rural world view even when the city was being brutally transformed. Granted, disease prevention and treatment was widely discussed and debated. But, writes, historian David Goldfield, "while civic leaders generally agreed on the best methods of street paving, there was no unanimity on the nature of epidemic disease." And in the late nineteenth century, "discussion of disease etiology involved more of intuition than science." Health planning was often less a matter of substance and more a public relations effort to maintain a favorable image of the city.[7]

Washington's sewer infrastructure in the late nineteenth century was profoundly influenced by the vagaries of the weather. In October 1870, for example, the rivers flooded and damaged bridges, took out docks and wharves, dumped silt in navigation channels, and frightened

---

* Despite Shepherd's prowess in building the city's infrastructure, his real estate investments did not pan out, and by the late 1870s he was bankrupt and on his way to Mexico to seek new fortunes in silver mining.

the populace. Freshets caused the sewers to overflow and also damaged the Washington Canal. The canal had to be eight feet deep in order to flush properly between the Anacostia and the Potomac, but constant silting reduced its depth to three feet in most places by 1870. After the freshets the canal was shallow and the water fetid, and local grocery merchants struggled to get grocery barges through to the central market and stores. In 1871, against the advice of General Montgomery Meigs of the Army Corps of Engineers, Boss Shepherd created a rump canal commission to rubber stamp his decision to fill in the Washington Canal. That, Meigs warned, would eliminate one of the best tidal flushing sewers the city had. The canal also had historical associations with L'Enfant's original city plan. Lumber and grocery merchants bitterly attacked the decision, asserting that Shepherd was out to destroy the businesses supplying the central city.

After 1890 the District built large trunk sewers with intercepting lines that eventually covered most of the heavily settled areas. They were built using the estimates of America's foremost sanitary engineer in the 1890s, Rudolph Hering. His calculations allowed the city with modest success to deal with its sewage using a combined waste and storm water system that functioned well into the 1920s.

The large trunk sewers, some of which were thirty feet wide, also solved the sewage problem by sending it somewhere else.[8] Topography ignored municipal boundaries, and the flow of sewage in late nineteenth-century river cities went far beyond a city's political limits.[9] The system was only half complete by 1901, and a sizeable portion of Capitol Hill and the navy yard still resorted to gravity-flow pipe sewers that emptied directly into the Anacostia River. Perhaps this sheds some light on the vastly different property values in the city after 1878. In northwest Washington, which was well served by sewers, property was assessed at from two dollars to three dollars a square foot. Property in the arc stretching from the Capitol to the navy yard was assessed at fifty cents to a dollar per square foot.[10]

As taxes, assessments, and city debt skyrocketed, Washington's older citizens, who had never reconciled to black participation in government, rebelled. These so-called "redeemers" forced a congressional investigation of "Boss" Shepherd and brought about the eventual downfall of the territorial government. For years after the war, blacks in the District were consistently referred to as "contrabands" or "the dangerous class." White genteel Washingtonians, true to their southern upbringing, believed that black suffrage was a dangerous misfortune that had befallen the city. Families of the old planter class had effectively worked in public and behind the scenes politically to neutralize blacks. When the Organic Act of 1878 passed Congress, white racists felt safer. Under this legislation, Congress abolished the territorial government and set up a three-man commission government under the watchful eye of southern congressmen, who became the de-facto rulers of Washington until limited home rule was established in 1973.

By 1901 the black population, which constituted one third of the capital's population, was politically voiceless. Few critics gave any thought to the anomaly of a republic's capital city lacking representative democracy, and many of the political difficulties that have beset the black communities east of the Anacostia River in the modern era can be traced back to the turn of the last century.[11]

Public Health and African Americans

Because outbreaks of cholera were common in many American cities after the Civil War, public health authorities worried that the freedmen would spread the disease by eating contaminated catfish caught in the sewage of James Creek and the Washington Canal. Mayor Richard Wallach and his administration feared the city would be laid waste by an outbreak of "catfish cholera" carried by blacks. No one at the time could see beyond race to ascertain that poverty and polluted water were responsible for disease, not black people. The suffering of freedmen from what health officials called "miasmatic effluvia" was so acute that many believed blacks would not survive into the twentieth century. White racists argued that blacks lacked stamina because they were careless of their personal hygiene.[12]

The National Freedmen's Relief Association reported great suffering among the freedmen who lived in shanties, hovels, and abandoned buildings at the Anacostia's edge and elsewhere on Capitol Hill. Many young black children suffered from whooping cough, which was fatal in most cases. The city did nothing to address tuberculosis and pneumonia, diseases that killed more in the District across the color line than any other. Typhoid continued to be a great challenge. The idea that typhoid epidemics are generally caused by contaminated water supplies was slow to take hold. Usually it is acquired by ingesting food or water contaminated by the urine or feces of infected carriers, but recognition that clean water and the sanitary disposal of human feces could prevent and control typhoid was slow in coming.[13] Infected workers who handled food transmitted typhoid, and although the public health records say little about carriers of the disease, one suspects that infected food handlers worked in more than a few restaurants and hotels.* Overall, health conditions for blacks were so bad that Sojourner Truth, the noted reformer, campaigned to have the city's freedmen transported to the West, where it was healthier. John Langston, a lawyer in the District and member of the health board, was one of the few officials to point out that blacks were victims of their environment. Langston, it should be noted, was black.

Changes in public health policy after the Civil War sometimes had unintended consequences in that they sometimes benefited blacks

---

* The most illustrious case of a typhoid carrier was that of a New York City cook named Mary Mallon, who came to be known as "Typhoid Mary." A carrier but never a victim, she worked as a food handler and managed to infect 1,300 people. Even though Mallon knew she carried typhus, she returned to cooking in 1915. She earned a good living as a cook and gave up her vocation only when the police power of the state curtailed her activities. Mallon ultimately had to be quarantined on a New York island.

more than the whites for whom they were intended. Historian Werner Troesken found that the coming of public water systems—laying mains to deliver drinking water and monitoring wells, for example—greatly increased some white neighborhoods' chances of avoiding disease, but it was even more beneficial to blacks, who formerly had died of typhoid fever at twice the rate whites did.[14] Water mains also served the important purpose of helping fire companies protect against urban conflagrations. Blacks later moving into neighborhoods that had originally been white thereby reaped another "white dividend." Because so much of Washington was integrated racially in the late nineteenth century, it could not under-serve blacks without adversely affecting service to whites.[15]

During its existence (1871–74) the territorial government appointed a five-member board of health with Dr. Thomas H. Miller as its president and engaged in real health planning rather than public relations. An outspoken and conscientious physician, Miller was the first public health official to recognize the health threats affecting the black community. In the 1870s, he undertook to inspect food to eliminate spoiled or "blown" meat from the public markets and butcher shops and lobbied for better housing for the poor as an antidote to tuberculosis.[16] The city's director of public health, Dr. Tullio Verdi, who was appointed late in 1871 by Dr. Miller and the Board of Health, argued that the health problems of the growing black community in the Anacostia and elsewhere in the District were identifiable and preventable. Verdi argued that builders and real estate speculators who threw up substandard houses and shanties to rent to blacks without any regard for sanitary regulations were exploiting black freedmen.*

The District's problem of administering health programs for the

* Tullio Verde was a remarkable nineteenth-century Italian expatriate intellectual. A soldier, revolutionary, and follower of Garibaldi, Verdi went into exile in 1856 after being proscribed by the Austrian government. He later became Professor of Modern Languages at Brown university and studied homoeopathic medicine as a hobby. In 1871, Verdi qualified as a doctor, resigned his professorship and came

poor was compounded by the near unanimous opinion that hospitals were dangerous places. Few middle-class Washingtonians would go to a hospital where they were likely to rub up against transients and members of the lower classes. Even though the city had an ample supply of physicians, the federal government had to recruit 138 doctors specifically to work with the freedmen in hospitals. Some were northerners with an abolitionist background; others were black physicians who had received their training in the North and abroad. Given the class and racial antagonisms of the times, hospitals did not fare well. Not until the 1880s, when private philanthropy began to finance hospitals and the wealthier classes supported them, did the bias against hospitals begin to wane. In the first two decades of freedom the best mechanism of public health in poor areas was the medical dispensary—a shoestring operation maintained by local doctors. Individual physicians offered their services for free, partly to gain clinical experience with unfamiliar diseases and maladies and partly out of humanitarianism.

Most respectable white citizens were unconcerned about the public health of the city, writes Betty Plummer, "except when something infringed directly upon them."[17] Until well into the 1880s people in Washington subscribed to the theory that "miasmas" or filth caused disease and were slow to embrace the germ theory and the importance of understanding bacteriology as a means of preventing disease. As environmental historian Martin Melosi has noted, the demise of the filth theory led to critical appraisals of sanitation and public health in most cities by the turn of the century.[18] In the early twentieth century cholera, for example, would become less frightening because it did not spread rapidly where improved sanitation regulations were in force. The one small but significant step the D.C. Board of Health took after 1900

---

to Washington to serve on the Board of Health of the District of Columbia. He was active on the city's sanitary commission and a crusader for black civil rights in the District. He practiced medicine until 1895, when he retired for reasons of ill-health and returned to Italy.

was the elimination of the common dipper in a public drinking barrel.[19] Drinking from a common dipper literally spread cholera from mouth to mouth.

Over the course of generations the poor, black and white alike, did build up immunities, even along the sewage-ridden lower Anacostia. The willingness of officials to provide rudimentary medical help for the poor also paid ample dividends. But success in public health often created its own obstacles, too—taxpayers were reluctant to fund assistance for people who appeared to be on the road to better health. When the District's health problems were at crisis levels, the city was anxious to fund programs to reduce disease, but as one public health historian noted, "the more successful a public health program is, the more taxpayers are inclined to feel that it is not necessary."[20]

"Corrupt Water"

Generally speaking, prior to the Civil War most Americans were not concerned with the quality of their drinking water but wanted enough water for horses, for fighting fires, and for washing clothes in that order. Increased interest in public health along with growing evidence in support of the germ theory eventually caused public health officials to pay more attention to the quality of water supplies. By the 1870s citizens in the District began to complain about the mud and debris in their drinking water and to voice concern that both the Potomac and the Anacostia were unclean. The recently created board of health reported finding dead cats, dogs, and the bodies of human babies in the water mains of the drinking supply.[21]

As early as 1870 scientists in England and the United States had begun to warn people of the increasing presence of impurities in their drinking water. They spoke of "corrupt rivers" that had become vehicles of sickness and death. By that time the Anacostia had become one. Based in the District, naturalist Fred Mather wrote that in Washington and in other cities "there is the murmur of complaint about the pollution of our creeks and rivers . . . and this pollution is allowed to go unheeded and unchecked."[22]

The District's water supply was dependent upon wells and its rivers. Privy vaults and wells were almost side by side. In low-density areas this arrangement persisted. Sanitarians warned that the ground water in much of Capitol Hill and other parts of the city was being infiltrated by sewage. Although they generally believed that the water problems of cities like Washington were caused by unhealthy concentrations of people, sanitarians in the 1870s were beginning to spell out exactly what a "corrupt" water source was. *Appleton's Journal of Literature and Science* in 1874 described "corrupt water" in terms that are remarkably clear to today's student of ruined industrial rivers in the United States. "When the deterioration of the water makes progress, the river loses its limpidity. The water becomes opaline, and this gray color resists filtration. The surface is covered with scum and the water deposits a black and fetid slime whence bubbles of gas are disengaged."[23] As sewage became an issue of national discussion, scientists gave a more precise definition to "corrupt water." Water was judged to be polluted by sewage when it contained two parts of fecal matter to 100,000 parts of liquid.[24] Concurrently, newspapers in the city carried stories of how sewage mud banks along the Anacostia and Potomac were becoming stench-ridden disease centers.[25]

The Development of the Post-Shepherd Sewer System

Underground sewers were laid parallel to the old canal, and in periods of high tide on the Potomac the central city was occasionally awash in sewage.[26] A sewer system relying on gravity had been in operation in the District since the 1870s and was well charted, but as a sewer and drainage system it was completely inadequate. In 1878 it had three main components. The Rock Creek system emptied raw sewage into Rock Creek, which was often a thin and foul smelling brook in summer. The B Street system was a network of narrow pipes from the central part of the capital that emptied into the Potomac. The Tiber Creek sewer began at the mouth of the Tiber River and continued by tunnel along the Mall and thence to James Creek, where it emptied into the Anacostia. The city also added by 1880 a trunk line, a large tunnel beginning on Capitol Hill at G Street, NE. It wound down the hill under the Botanical Garden at the base of Capitol Hill and emptied its human effluvia into the Anacostia at the James Creek Canal. No part of the system ever functioned properly.

The capital's residents got more than their share of experience with effluvia on August 5, 1878, when the Tiber sewer burst during a heavy rainstorm. Major areas around Pennsylvania Avenue, the Mall, the navy yard, and along the Anacostia riverbanks were covered in sewage and contaminated water. Lieutenant H. L. Hoxie of the Army Corps of Engineers wrote a lengthy analysis of the incident and concluded that "the present sewers will not carry off storm water." The engineers warned that it was becoming difficult to patch up a severely ailing system. Unless improvements were made, the corps predicted that heavy rains would result in the flooding of houses and cellars.[27] District officials, though, balked at the enormous cost of updating the city's sewer system. Most of the original sewer mains that flowed into the Potomac and Anacostia dated back to the city's founding.[28] The system leaked and at times created a wetland at the base of Capitol Hill.[29]

The difficulty in raising mass consciousness on water issues in the late nineteenth century capital stemmed from the fact that many of its residents were not very well educated about the benefits of cleanliness. Unlike many southern towns in the antebellum era, Washington was a "come here" town of migrants from rural hinterlands whose ideas about nature and sanitation did not fit well in an urban environment. That was especially true in regard to personal hygiene. Urban habits were conditioned by folk beliefs that it was unhealthy to bathe during the winter months, from November 1 to March 15. Many also believed bathtubs were "a luxurious, undemocratic vanity."[30] Not until the turn of the century did the public dimly begin to realize that dirt, crowding, and bad water were inevitably associated with communicable diseases and that these diseases did not restrict themselves to slum dwellers.

In the 1870s some of the most annoying sounds of the night were those of the night soil men. These scavengers had contracts with the city to operate with their dung carts between the hours of 11:00 P.M. and 5:00 A.M., and many a sleepless resident heard the clop-clop of the night soiler's horse as he made his way through the streets, emptying the contents of vaults and privy boxes. The night soil carts in the area of the navy yard and Capitol Hill often dropped as much contaminated waste in the streets as they transported. Protests against the noxious night soilers finally led the city to contract with the Odorless Evacuating Apparatus Company, which used a portable pumping machine for sucking waste out of the privies into air-tight tanks. Although this was an improvement over the scavengers, the District needed a comprehensive and more efficient system of human waste removal.

Washington also had more than its share of horse filth, dead animals and scavenging pigs. As Martin Melosi has commented, "animals resident in urban communities were a part of pre-industrial life—horses for transport, cattle, hogs and chicken for food use. Pigs and turkeys for scavenging."[31]

As late as 1880 the District continued to suffer from a host of environmental abuses. They ranged from thousands of dead animals in the streets, to hundreds of hog pens and unregulated slaughtering operations, to more than 16,500 defective and overflowing privies, to the need to truck away 7,456 tons of garbage and 22,153 barrels of night soil. At times the smell of thousands of barrels of rotting fish and oysters that authorities declared unfit for sale gave the Anacostia waterfront a nauseating stench that caused ladies to faint and drove strong men indoors.[32]

Clean public water or the "sanitary idea" of city management, while slow to take hold, nonetheless experienced a growing resonance among

District leaders in the late nineteenth century. By 1880 there was no gainsaying the ideas outlined by the influential sanitarian, Edwin Chadwick, whose influential 1842 study, *The Sanitary Condition of the Laboring Population of Great Britain,* argued that the best way to deal with unhealthy conditions in cities was to build sewers and waterworks, pave the streets, and ventilate commercial and residential buildings. Building a single water closet to spirit away "dejecta," Chadwick argued, did more good than all the self-medication a city resident could take to ward off typhoid or cholera. Soon a generation of engineers would arise who understood the importance of building a workable urban infrastructure of sewers and water mains.[33] Washington's upper classes, though, clung to the idea that diseases like typhoid and cholera attacked the poor and the ignorant, most of whom were either blacks or recent immigrants, and health statistics seemed to support their fears. That made it difficult to rationalize the expense of building and managing new sewers.

Despite his best intentions, Boss Shepherd's sewer system did not serve everyone equally. It was most effective in serving northwest Washington and the booming property developments stretching toward Connecticut Avenue and beyond. Other neighborhoods suffered from minimal sewer service. As late as 1895 little had been done in the Anacostia except to locate a sewage processing plant at the mouth of James Creek near Buzzard Point.[34] A review of Washington sewer lines in 1880 shows that most of the city's main lines emptied directly into the Anacostia.[35]

The one bright spot in Washington's dismal sewer record was D. E. McComb, who served as Superintendent of Sewers in the 1880s. Under his leadership, the city in 1883 built concrete sewers with full brick lining some ten feet in diameter, large enough to handle the city's increasing sewage flows. Concrete sewers were less expensive to build than those fully made of brick and did not leak as much. McComb was thus able to correct many of the defective sewers that had been installed during Boss Shepherd's time. Believing with other "sewer men" that flushing settled solids out of what was a gravity system lessened the chances for blockage, he popularized the use of flush tanks. Water surging through the sewers also was believed to mix air with sewage, helping to treat the effluvia before it was discharged into the Potomac or Anacostia. Not until years later did sanitarians learn that "flushing" was only effective in the first five hundred feet from the flushing point.

One of the most interesting approaches to flushing sewers in 1880s Washington was the Tiber Sewer Flushing Gate. Installed at the upper end of a one-and-a-half mile sewer line, the gates backed up the sewage flow in the Tiber Creek. Twice a day the gates were opened during low tide, and four million gallons of combined sewage and storm water from the city surged through the line to be emptied into the Anacostia.[36] These tidal gates were a source of great public complaint before World War I. The stench ruined many a scenic walk along the Anacostia River.

The sewerage issue reached a critical point in the 1890s. Most plans for sewage disposal at this time still involved privies and cesspools, pail collection systems, or sediment filtration, all of which had the end result of discharging sewage into watercourses that were also being used for public drinking water.[37] As public health officials made the connection between typhoid and sewage in the 1890s, watercourses and the waterborne diseases that traveled them received increased public scrutiny. In 1894, George Rafter, a sanitary engineer, published *Sewage Disposal in the United States*, a book that had a substantial impact on public thinking. Until Rafter, District residents had not thought much about "dejections," the delicate Victorian word for human excrement. Rafter's thesis that the introduction of clean drinking water reduced typhoid gained currency in the capital. "The drinking of water containing human excrement," he argued, "is a disgusting and dangerous practice, and we cannot hope for immunity from communicable diseases until the custom is entirely discontinued."[38] His warning came at an opportune time, for sewer failures became especially severe during the 1890s.

The 1890s, a decade of virulent storms and freshets that tested the limits of Washington's sewers, brought a "frightful mortality" from typhoid and other fevers that were attributed to sewage in the James Creek Canal. A representative of the Army Corps of Engineers who attended a meeting of District officials pointed out that in 1894 two-thirds of the residents of the navy yard were ill, and in the autumn of that year nearly everyone at the yard was stricken with malaria. Albert Reed, a community representative, pointed out that communities along the Anacostia River in that year had a death rate four times that of Brooklyn and twice that of New York City. Said Reed: "We are today among the most successful cultivators of the deadly bacilli of typhoid and other diseases. . . . When we put an end to the pollution of Rock Creek, James Creek Canal, and our entire water from Georgetown to the marshes of Anacostia with sewage, we will save twice as many from malarial fevers and other diseases."[39]

Why did notions of clean rivers and pure drinking water stagnate from the 1870s until well into the twentieth century? Because city sewers and the "sanitary idea" in Washington were often at cross-purposes. Politics, budgets and concern for the city's image discouraged a frank and rational public dialogue on the water supply. The District commissioners wanted the "rank vegetation" and effluvia of the Anacostia and Potomac marshes cleaned up first so they would no longer be a plague spot and an eyesore that brought discredit on the national capital. Sewers could come later. The appropriation, though, was delayed until 1882 and included directives for filling in the marshes and wetlands near the Washington Monument and dredging channels in the Potomac and Anacostia to improve navigation. Dredging the rivers and eliminating the mud flats had disappointing results. A special board of sanitary engineers found that the tidal backwash at James Creek still polluted the eastern portion of the capital with foul smelling waste.

The city tried to deal with this mess in 1901 by constructing a sewage pumping plant at the foot of New Jersey Avenue, SE, "to force the entire sewage of the city to the Potomac River at Magazine Point which is two miles below Alexandria."[40] Pumps would send the sewage by tunnel across the Anacostia, where it would be discharged into a gravity sewer. The District estimated the pumping station, to be located at the foot of 2nd Street, SE, would cost $835,000 and would pump 845,000,000 gallons every twenty-four hours. It would be sufficient to handle the city's sewage and storm water for twenty years. The *Washington Post* reported that emptying the sewage into a point where the Potomac is flowing very fast will result in its being "thoroughly diffused.... disposed of without offense to anyone."[41]

Up to this point, the sewage system carried both waste and storm water. Sanitarians had calculated in the 1890s that a twenty-four hour rainfall of two inches on the District's sixty-eight square miles would amount to 136 million gallons of water, much of which would have to be handled by the sewers. City authorities debated the issue of a combined sewer system versus a dual system through the 1890s.

To resolve the issue President Benjamin Harrison appointed a special commission to investigate and decide whether a combined system should be continued or new separate lines for storm water created. Out of this commission came the decision to construct large interceptor sewers that would carry both effluvia and storm water to a pumping station on the bank of the Anacostia and to a discharge point across the river at what is now Blue Plains. In 1890, Congress sponsored a blue ribbon study of Washington sewers to study the engineering and social costs of upgrading the system. Led by the great sanitarian Rudolph Hering, the study illustrated for the first time the enormous impact of storm water overflows on the system. The city was being paved and was losing its permeability. Increased water consumption and population growth put additional strains on the infrastructure. Hering and his colleagues pointed out the "absence of slope" in the river plain area of the city as a problem for gravitational systems. Upgrading the sewer trunk line at B Street and New Jersey Avenue would cost over $719,000, and an expensive sewage pumping system had to be installed city-wide. (These expenditures were deferred until 1907.) The study also pointed out that increasingly the Anacostia River would become a major sewage receptacle.[42] Clean water for the city was thus postponed in panels and commissions until the early part of the new century.

Not until 1908 did the city begin to address its sewer problem in a systematic way. Sewage now moved across the Anacostia River by tunnel and was then pumped through pipes five feet in diameter south to the Potomac. The sewers that simply emptied into the Tiber Creek and hence the Potomac and the Anacostia River's southeast section were abandoned.

This solution, intended as a twenty-year fix to improve public health in Anacostia and the rest of the city, left unmentioned the impact the massive flow of sewage would have on communities along the river.[43] Throughout the late nineteenth century and into the twentieth, the problems of sanitation, clean water, infrastructure and race relations interacted with one another in ways not completely understood by the leadership of Washington or its citizenry. All anyone knew was that the capital had a monumental problem that required tremendous outlays of public money. At issue was the great stench of the city, whose citizens feared they might soon be swimming in the "corrupt waters" of the Potomac and the Anacostia. Sewage and disease, originally believed to have emanated from impoverished African Americans on the banks of the Anacostia, increasingly became a major issue for all of Washington and beyond. By 1912 the discharge was causing serious harm to the Potomac oyster fishery. Inspectors from the federal government condemned all raw oysters in the Potomac above Blakistone Island, a matter that alarmed Governors Philip Goldsborough of Maryland and William Hodges Mann of Virginia.[44]

Garbage and Public Health

The District in the 1890s also grappled with the issue of solid waste.

The sheer logistics of having to deal with tons of city garbage each day brought residents into a new relationship with their environment. Aesthetic considerations were not lost on District officials who feared being known as the "city of bad odors" rather than the city of magnificent monuments. While genteel women's organizations launched clean-up campaigns, the garbage problem like the sewage problem remained particularly acute in working-class and poor areas like Anacostia. As a health officer argued in his 1889 report, appropriate places for dumping refuse were becoming scarce. "Already the inhabitants in proximity to the public dumps are beginning to complain."[45] Many acknowledged that their city and its rivers were being severely damaged by garbage but few grasped the ecological issues involved in this "nuisance."

Large amounts of garbage and waste were routinely dumped into the Anacostia and Potomac. According to F. H. Newell, a scientist with the U.S. Geological Survey, the waterways in the 1890s served as "a sort of sewer into which town and manufacturing establishments empty their refuse, and this factor must be borne in mind in all considerations of water supply."[46] Though solid waste and overflowing sewers grew increasingly problematic in the District, it was not until 1906 that civic and professional groups demanded a halt to river pollution. Using the findings of city sanitarians, the District found the Anacostia and Potomac to be very seriously polluted and appealed to Congress for help funding "a pure water supply."[47]

Additional money for expensive sewage and waste projects was not forthcoming immediately from a parsimonious Congress, but in 1907 the city secured the services of Marshall O. Leighton as a consulting hydrographer. Leighton was the chief hydrographer for the U.S. Geological Survey and served as an adviser on river pollution and water quality issues. He had been in the forefront of a campaign by the Survey and the federal Inland Waterways Commission to educate municipal leaders about the damage to public health from sewage and industrial pollution.

Ironically, it was not the local pollution of the Anacostia and the Potomac that stirred the city to action but the pollution of the Potomac upstream by pulp and paper mills in the region of Harpers Ferry. The chemicals these mills spilled into the river resulted in major fish kills in the Potomac and engulfed the capital in a river-borne morass of floating dead fish that was both nauseating and visually repulsive. As consulting hydrographer, Leighton found the situation to be more harmful to public health than had been realized, and the body of evidence he assembled on pulp and paper pollution served to educate the public and politicians about the many ills that affected their rivers. Leighton's report on Potomac River pollution enabled the city to launch a major lawsuit against the mills in federal court.[48]

Such developments stimulated thinking among the capital elite on water issues, but extending that thinking into the ranks of the lower, middle, and working classes was another matter entirely. Sanitarians rightly feared a season of low water or drought, when the normal flushing capacity of the rivers to carry waste downstream was seriously diminished. In that event, the fetid material would remain along the riverbeds to cause fevers and a host of other public health problems in a society that was both negligent and careless of even routine cleanliness.

CHAPTER SIX

Man, Nature and the River, 1870–1930

"I am of the opinion that the Eastern Branch of the Potomac River in the state of Maryland is not worthy of improvement by the national government."
— Lt. Col. Peter C. Haines, U.S. Army Corps of Engineers, 1888

B
etween 1870 and 1930, the upper Anacostia watershed maintained a pristine watery innocence that served as an environmental counterpoint to the urban development taking place downriver. It remained a region of "water meadows," and a hunting and fishing paradise for local sportsmen. During this period the Army Corps of Engineers became quite active on the river and assisted in the creation of Anacostia Park, Kingman Island, and the National Arboretum. Much of the Anacostia retained its small town and rural flavor. Local businessmen sought to develop the river for commercial purposes. The area developed as a racially diverse community into the 1930s.

Upper Anacostia

While parts of the lower Anacostia and the Potomac were turning into sewers and mud banks, the upper Anacostia watershed retained its splendor and productivity. Tidal rhythms worked their magical power of restoration. By 1875 many of the old black and white river men who had numbered over a thousand before the war had returned to follow the water and harvest the annual runs of some 2.5 million shad

94

and 750 million herring. Spring found dozens of coopers at work in warehouses near 8th Street, SE, making barrels to pack salted fish for downriver markets. In 1886 *Forest and Stream Magazine* reported uncommonly good striped bass fishing. Angling from the deck of an old beached Civil War gunboat, one local in October caught sixty-five fish in a single outing. One weighed six pounds. According to the magazine there was "no diminution in numbers or quality."[1]

Though the marshes made a boat necessary, the fishing on the upper Anacostia was excellent, and fathers took their children out on Sundays in search of largemouth bass, pickerel, and the "voracious and pugnacious sunfish." While the Anacostia was not quite the natural venue for the upper-class sports fisherman, it was popular with government workers who tested their angling skills every weekend when weather permitted. Naturalist Henry Talbott fished the Anacostia on sunny summer days with a fly reel. "When the water is clear and the tide runs swift, the shadows of the river were the favorite shelters for rockfish, perch, and sunfish."[2]

Others discovered a different kind of nature in the Anacostia. John Burroughs came to Washington as a young man during the Civil War to take a job as a government clerk. With the exception of a month each summer spent in the interior of New York, Burroughs lived and worked in the nation's capital. In the fall of 1863 he ventured forth into the upper Anacostia to watch birds—it was the beginning of his career as an immensely popular nature writer. Burroughs became one of the foremost environmental writers in the United States and helped to make "Natural History" a literary genre. He was best known among a score of writers who fueled the American environmental imagination with stories and articles ranging from robins to grizzlies. Nature writers became popular in America at a time when "the strenuous life," personified by Theodore Roosevelt, became a philosophy of rugged engagement with the outdoors.

Burroughs' appeal resided in the fact that the way of life he de-

scribed was immediately accessible to the man on the street. It was one
of simple means, simple ends, and simple values. On the Anacostia River he found a life in nature that exemplified those values. In the spring
of 1868, Burroughs went into the woods to observe robins and wood
thrush as they arrived on their migration north. As he noted, spring
days on the outskirts of Washington were bright and strong, and the
marsh and woods were filled with life. The woods were a constant source
of surprise. Here he found wild flowers every month of the year, from
violets in December to apricot trees in full bloom in April and apple
trees on May Day. Burroughs delighted in the waterfowl of the marsh,
the frogs and the birds singing in the cattails. In his journal he wrote
that as the sun rose out of the morning mist in the Anacostia woodlands, "a full chorus of voices arose, tender, musical, half suppressed, but
full of genuine hilarity and joy." Out of this initial wood and marshland
adventure on the Anacostia came much of the material that later went
into his commentary on birds, *Wake Robin*. The woods of the Anacostia
were an easy walk from Capitol Hill, he wrote. "The town has not yet
overflowed its limits like the great Northern commercial capitals, and
Nature, wild and unkempt, comes up to its very threshold, and even in
many places crosses it."[3]

The Anacostia's upper reaches in the last decades of the nineteenth
century offer a fleeting glimpse of a vanishing natural world in the
shadow of the nation's capital. By that time soil erosion from agriculture runoff had silted the river's channels. Bladensburg, where once the
river ran forty feet deep at high tide, was no longer navigable. "One
may hardly reach Bladensburg with a canoe at low tide," Henry Talbott
remarked in 1898. Many parts of the river were high mud banks at
low mean tide, and the approach to Bladensburg was less than a foot
in depth. The survey map of 1880 prepared by the U.S. Army Corps of
Engineers shows a thoroughly silted river with a few deep channels on
the west side after the Benning Road Bridge.

Yet the river, Henry Talbott found, had its compensations. Wild rice, cattails, and other aquatic plants covered the wide marshlands. It was a bird hunter's paradise and a painter's marshy Arcadia. Documentary evidence of this rich waterland is provided by the 1880s J. V. Glumer Map, which illustrates the upper Anacostia marshes in great detail.[4] Starting at the Baltimore and Ohio Railroad bridge and extending all the way to Bladensburg, a fabulous marshland was alive with fine reedbirds and sora. Most of these "water meadows" could be navigated only by pole skiff or small canoe.

During hunting season, the boom of shotguns was a familiar sound as hunters swarmed the marshes in pursuit of reedbirds, blackbirds, and ortolan. Because of the rash of accidents that usually attended the opening of hunting season, District police stationed ambulances at popular shooting areas.[5] The marshland, especially, from Benning Bridge upriver to Beaver Dam Run, was a bird hunter's delight. In the 1880s and 1890s reed birds were so plentiful that guides took hunters into the marsh with a guarantee that they could easily shoot a bag full.

Guides like R. D. Pollard of Bladensburg worked with skiffs, pushers, and guides in the September hunting season. Pollard leased out twenty-two boats. The round-bottomed skiffs were propelled by pushers through the tall reeds. The pusher's job was to "mark all birds as they fall, and this is no easy matter to do when there are sometimes twelve or more birds in the water." The best time to go marsh shooting was when the tide was high in the early morning. What conservationists called "the slaughter of the innocents" was simply recreation for hunters whose experience was often little above amateur status. Yet with a good shotgun, it was possible for even a novice to bag his share of reed birds and sora. The latter were fat with meat and could be cooked in stews. The feathers of reed and sora were worth seventy-five cents per dozen birds.[6]

For those returning from a day on the river, the many nearby truck farms were a happy temptation. Capital residents could shop the farms at Geisboro Point and Shepherd's Landing and find excellent cabbages, tomatoes, cantaloupes, beets and berries. Many of these farms were small cropping operations run on shares, or family-held units of three to five acres with boys and women doing most of the spade work while husbands worked in the city. Numerous dairy farms sold fresh milk and butter. Sometimes customers were swindled. One bought a "two-pound roll of butter" only to find when she arrived at home that the roll consisted of mashed potatoes with a thin coating of butter.[7] Most of the farmers were honest and hard-working and depended upon a repeat clientele. The best land for truck gardening was near Bladensburg.[8]

On May 3, 1896, the Anacostia freight yards of the B&O filled with vehicles and carriages of every description. Hundreds of people sat on blankets and sheets along the river bank while the river itself was dotted with men and women in small rented rowboats. A popular black minister, Reverend A. J. Berkley was about to baptize ten converts: six women and four men. During the preliminary ceremony the converts stood on the bank chanting hymns. Then three ushers took them down into the water, where they were totally immersed and baptized. The excitement was so intense that "two sisters on the river bank fainted from pure joy." Later the crowd listened to a powerful sermon on the need to come down to the water to find Jesus.[9] Such moments of religiosity and grace through interaction with nature were to be savored in 1896, before the city burst its bounds, and local waterways changed out of recognition.

Naturalist on the Anacostia

During his career as a naturalist and scientific administrator at the Smithsonian, Paul Bartsch was an avid bird watcher and photographer in the Anacostia. Bartsch had a long career at the Smithsonian as Curator of Mollusks (1914–46) and served on several scientific expeditions to the Caribbean to observe and collect data on the medical uses of shellfish.

Although his many photos capture brilliantly the isolation and splendor of the Anacostia marshes, Bartsch's principal contribution was to alert the emerging community of hunters, fishermen, and birdwatchers of the Anacostia River's ecological value and the perils it faced. In 1902, while still in the process of finishing his doctoral studies at the University of Iowa, Bartsch spent several weeks on the Anacostia. Often he could be found gently pushing his one-man skiff through the rice fields, intently watching and cataloging the waterfowl. Though his first love was ornithology, he concentrated on the study of mollusks because he believed the popularity of bird studies made for a crowded scientific field and would impede his career.

As an amateur ornithologist, Bartsch became an ardent and outspoken conservationist. Market hunters' guns boomed across the Anacostia marshes at the turn of the century. The meat of wild fowl had a ready market in Baltimore and New York, and songbirds' feathers were highly prized by the New York millinery industry. In his spare time, Bartsch spoke out at conservation meetings in "defense of the birds," especially the birds that were being sacrificed to ladies' hats. Well-connected in Washington society through his wife, Bartsch became active in the local chapter of the Audubon Society, formed in 1897 and led by Mrs. John Dewhurst Patten, a wealthy District matron. He contributed to *Bird-Lore* and other magazines of the Audubon Society and helped organize the annual bird count on the Potomac and Anacostia, a census of birds that were under environmental and hunting pressure. That same year Bartsch lobbied Congress to pass the first laws making interstate traffic in illegally killed birds a crime.

Nature lovers like Paul Bartsch helped turn back the commercial onslaught against the wild bird populations in the Anacostia. Mrs. Patten and her allies at the Audubon Society publicized the attack on birds for millinery use and the gathering of wild eggs by collectors seeking to sell them to museums and restaurants. In 1903 the District Audubon Society entered an agreement with the Millinery Association of New York that their importers and manufacturers would no longer buy feathers, or birds classified as gulls, terns, grebes, hummingbirds, egrets, or herons. Besides monitoring milliners, the local Audubon Society also sponsored "birding adventures" in the Anacostia and Potomac to acquaint men and women with the natural treasures of the watersheds.[10]

Early wild bird conservation was a middle- and upper-class effort. The bird watchers of the local Audubon chapter popularized hikes and outings along the banks of the Potomac and the Anacostia and raised questions about the suitability of the Washington police force to serve as game wardens for the marshes and wetlands. The police were too busy with other matters, Bartsch and the conservationists argued, to apprehend poachers along the water.

Bartsch the scientist spent a lot of his time studying water quality and marsh microorganisms for clues as to the role that they played in the ecological life of the river. In 1902 he examined two colonies of black-crowned night herons a little south of Benning Raid in northeast Washington. While focusing on their nesting habits, Bartsch became preoccupied with the larger question of how long the birds lived, their migration patterns, and the circumstances that led to their death. Even today, Bartsch's 1904 study, "Notes on the Herons of the District of Columbia," remains the pioneering work that many ornithologists consult.[11]

Out of this interest came Bartsch's proposal to band birds for scientific study. Bird banding had been known since the days of Tudor England, and John James Audubon had banded birds with silver cords to see how far from their birthplace they would travel, but this was largely an amateur pastime.* Bartsch systematized bird banding for scientific investigation, a program that soon received nationwide endorsement by

* Bird banding today is an avocation that straddles the boundary between hobby and science. Today the U.S. Fish and Wildlife Service is responsible for supplying bands and maintaining records. A famous blooper occurred when the agency was still called "the Bureau of Biological Survey." Instead of one band containing the return address "Biol.Surv.Washington, D.C.," it read "Wash,Boil,Surv."

bird watchers and conservationists. Until he went on a scientific research trip to the Philippines in 1907, Bartsch frequently was in a boat on the Potomac or the Anacostia. The manor house "Lebanon" and 485-acre estate that he and his wife rehabilitated on the Virginia banks of the Potomac twenty-five miles south of Washington became a sort of informal headquarters called "the Bartsch Botanical Club" for bird lovers, hikers, scientists, and advocates of the kind of strenuous life that Paul Bartsch loved. During his years of observation, Bartsch avidly collected plants and assembled a herbarium of some five thousand specimens that came from the forests and rivers around Washington. This collection, which his widow donated to the Smithsonian, is notable because Bartsch developed it just as many of the natural areas around Washington were giving way to real estate developments and sewage districts. One scientist summed up Paul Bartsch's contribution by pointing out that today "Bartsch's collections are valuable chiefly for the important information they add to our historical knowledge of the local flora, by giving us a better picture of the native and introduced flora around the turn of the century, when natural areas were more abundant within and around the city."[12]

An Aquatic Mecca

For the Army Corps of Engineers, transforming the natural environment of the capital had as much to do with aesthetics as it did matters of drainage, reclamation, and sewers. Navigation of the Anacostia was not a priority with the corps. In fact as early as 1888, Lt. Col. Peter C. Haines wrote, "I am of the opinion that the Eastern Branch of the Potomac River in the state of Maryland is not worthy of improvement by the National government."[13] The corps preferred to build parks rather than dredge a silted river.

In 1916 the corps attempted to "rejuvenate" the Anacostia by turning its upper reaches from malaria-ridden swamps and mud flats into an aquatic park of floating gardens, walled riverbanks, and facilities for canoeing and other sports. The corps planned to build a waterfront park that extended upriver from Geisboro Point to the District line on both sides of the river. Engineers envisioned an immense man-made lake to be carved out of part of the river, some nine feet deep with walkways and fountains gracing the shorelines. In most respects this plan was visionary rather than practical given how parsimonious Congress was with its appropriations for the river. Yet, at this early date we can see in outline what became Kingman Lake and the Kenilworth Aquatic Gardens.

Aside from the Corps of Engineers, the only strong support for the aquatic park came from rowing clubs and promoters of motorboat races, who wanted to have better facilities on the Anacostia.[14] It was not until 1923 that the engineers were able to break ground for the first section of "the Aquatic Mecca," a river park area near what is now the Sousa Bridge on the river's east bank. There was little park land in Anacostia, and city commissioners responded to the criticisms of the East Side Business Association that too much attention was being paid to developing parks and public amenities in the Rock Creek area of northwest Washington.[15] With limited funds, though, the Corps of Engineers could do only a modest amount of work on the Anacostia. Most appropriations from Congress centered on building a walled embankment on both sides of the river that would straighten the watercourse and protect against floods.

In 1914 the Washington Commission for the Fine Arts issued a report calling for the construction of an Anacostia Water Park to "balance" developments taking place to the northwest. The project was to open a fifteen-foot channel from the Anacostia Bridge upriver to Massachusetts Avenue and dredge a nine-foot channel to the District line.[16] Those living along the river were incensed by a rider in the 1924 appropriations bill stating that property owners would be assessed to underwrite the cost of reclaiming the flats and swamp land. Further complicating proposals for a river park were businessmen like Hugh Watson of Anacostia, who clamored to have the river developed as an industrial base with ample piers and wharves for factories. Most important in Watson's view was the need to dredge the Anacostia to a depth of twenty-five feet at low tide so steamers could come upriver to load and unload. Watson believed, and he spoke for many in the business community, that it would be a "capital idea" if citizens abandoned their plans for a waterfront park and instead petitioned Congress "to offer the land to corporations that are anxious to locate there."[17]

The Corps of Engineers only spent about $128,000 a year to reclaim the flats and swamps along the upper Anacostia out of a total multi-year appropriation of $1,706,000. Most of this large budget was devoted to keeping the channel open to the navy yard and facilitating navigation at the mouth of the river. Significantly, by 1924 the corps reexamined the plan of dredging a channel to Bladensburg for recreational boats.[18]

In 1914, in his *Annual Report of the Chief Engineers*, Maj. Charles W. Kutz wrote that reclamation of the Anacostia River for commercial purposes was unnecessary. "Until there is a commercial need for this reclaimed area, it should be developed as a public park."[19] That was in keeping with the earlier view of the Anacostia expressed by Lt. Col. Peter Haines in 1888. By 1926 the landscape outline for a five-mile aquatic park was already evident. The army earmarked 160 acres of marsh for the dumping of dredge spoil as the engineers carved out what would become Kingman Island. Plans the corps issued that year show four picnic areas on two man-made islands reachable by rowboat and skiff. The larger island was named for Maj. Dan Kingman, who was Chief of Engineers when the project was first conceived.

Unfortunately, support for engineering the twenty-mile-long river early in the twentieth century was not consistent but sputtered between periods of enthusiasm for improvement and years of cold indifference. Planning the river's improvement also faced a singular obstacle: the enormous amount of sedimentation caused by widespread deforestation and erosion of coastal plains upriver.

World War I delayed efforts on the upper Anacostia. By 1919 the work on Anacostia River Park was only 29 percent completed. As the park system along the river stalled, river-borne commerce was also becoming but a shadow of its nineteenth-century self. On the Potomac it declined from over $10.5 million in 1917 to $8.9 million two years later.[20]

In a project that gave new direction to discussion about parkland along the Anacostia, the Corps of Engineers took some seven hundred acres of landfill from the Washington channel of the Potomac and used it to create an island park and marina called Potomac Park. Earlier ideas concerning the Anacostia had centered on the concept of a bucolic safety valve from urban stresses reminiscent of the landscape philosophy of Andrew Jackson Downing. In 1924 the corps' park philosophy grew more urban-focused with plans for playground areas to get children off the streets and walking areas for adults interspersed with ball fields, tennis courts, and golf courses. This vision was in keeping with the Progressive Movement's emphasis on the vigorous life. The Anacostia system would imitate that of Potomac Park, but, given the racial diversity of Anacostia's population, no money would be spent to create a swimming beach on the reclaimed river like the sloping, sandy beach at the Potomac Park Tidal Basin.

In the spring of 1925, Congress entertained plans to construct a National Arboretum along the Anacostia to permit expansion of the Capitol Botanical Gardens. The project was estimated at $300,000 and was championed by conservationists and District leaders, who argued that an arboretum would be valuable to nurseries throughout the country as a source of desirable trees and as a bird sanctuary and game preserve. In this instance, the Corps of Engineers received strong endorsement for the creation of a bird sanctuary. In a letter to the corps dated November 9, 1923, the Audubon Society wrote that it was "deeply interested in the plans and development of the Anacostia Park between Benning Bridge and the District line ... the establishment of a National

Botanical Garden and at the same time preserving some of the natural features of the Anacostia marshes which will insure the preservation of migratory birds." How the army engineers were to build Kingman Island and preserve the marsh at the same time was a question neither the Audubon Society or the corps cared to explore.[21] The vicinity of the proposed arboretum was "unsightly and virtually neglected," and it was hoped that a National Arboretum would complete the ring of parks that Congress and the corps planned "ultimately to enclose Washington in living green."[22] President Calvin Coolidge, not surprisingly, thought the Arboretum cost too much money and threatened to veto the legislation. Plans therefore remained in limbo until the Garden Clubs of America, the Smithsonian Institution, and other agencies successfully argued their case for the park. Finally, in 1927, work began on the construction of a large National Arboretum on 446 acres situated between Mount Hamilton, Hickey Hill, and the Anacostia River Park. Upon its completion, the Arboretum launched a research program in ornamental horticulture, but the facility would not open to the public until 1959.

One part of the Anacostia wetlands was saved inadvertently because of one man's love of water flowers. In 1880, Walter Shaw, a Civil War veteran from Maine employed as a U.S. Treasury clerk, purchased thirty-seven acres of marshland from his father-in-law, who had deemed the flats to be worthless. For Walter Shaw, though, these wetlands were an excellent place to realize his dream of an aquatic garden. He and his daughter, Helen, built ponds in the marshes and grew water lilies for sale. Soon their garden hobby was doing so well they began to sell water plants. The Shaw Aquatic Gardens soon became one of the nation's largest exporters of water plants, and Walter Shaw became a prominent spokesman for the Anacostia marshlands. The Shaw Aquatic Gardens ultimately were acquired in the 1930s by the U.S. Department of the Interior and renamed "the Kenilworth Aquatic Gardens." Of the various plans to create "an Aquatic Mecca" on the upper Anacostia, only the

National Arboretum and the Kenilworth Gardens successfully evolved
by World War II.

The sense of urgency in acquiring parkland in the Anacostia watershed in the 1920s derived from the capital's desire to protect valuable
natural resources from urban development, and the need to control and
guide the new highway grid being constructed to facilitate automobile traffic in and out of Washington. Anacostia Park and Rock Creek
Park were targeted to receive highways that would provide "gateway
entrances" to the city. In 1920 the Federal Court of Washington issued
an order condemning 5,862 acres of land along the Anacostia River
held by the Washington Loan and Trust Company and seventeen owners for park and highway use.[23] This settled litigation that had been in
federal court since 1912. In addition to the private property issue on the
waterfront was the larger question raised in the 1880s: What was the
purpose of a river? Could it or should it have other than economic uses?
Community leaders like Mrs. Frank B. Noyes, president of the local
branch of the Garden Clubs of America and a member of the powerful
Washington Star publishing family, urged that the Anacostia be transformed from an urban sewer and industrial site into an urban park. She
was supported by the Audubon Society and most of the hunting and
sporting clubs in the District.

A Community of Homeowners

Behind the drive for more parks along the Anacostia was a real
estate boom fueled by the prosperity the capital experienced after
World War I. By 1920, Anacostia was a richly textured network of
stores, residences, and churches. The main street, Nichols Avenue, was
the area's most important business thoroughfare. This suburban area
was divided into two sections—white Anacostia and black Hillsdale.
Originally a freedmen's camp, Hillsdale was the residence of many of
the black workers at the navy yard and the federal post offices in the
District. For a city that experienced a race riot over the supposed black

manhandling of white women at the end of World War I, race relations in Anacostia were quietly amicable.* White and black children played together in the community and both races patronized the same stores and shops.

The capital's growth and prosperity created a demand for services in new neighborhoods. Suburban Anacostia's growth outpaced its infrastructure. Here was a classic argument for new water mains, a new reservoir on the top of Good Hope Hill, and additional sewer lines. J. S. Garland, the District Superintendent of the Water Department, declared that "the situation in Anacostia is fast approaching the point where a radical change is necessary to provide a permanent and adequate water system for all the territory east of the Anacostia river."[24] In 1926 several hundred houses were built in Anacostia, and Dr. George C. Havenner, president of the Anacostia Citizens Association, predicted that twice that number would be constructed in the coming year. "We have a community of homeowners," Havenner said. "In the southeast section of the city south of the Anacostia River we have a population of about 15,000 who are mostly mechanics and government workers."[25]

Anacostia was a healthy community, physically and financially. It had freed itself of the scourges of malaria, typhoid, and pulmonary disease. The stores were well-stocked and heavily patronized. The local Bank of Anacostia had deposits totaling almost a million dollars. The best thing about the community, argued Dr. Havenner, was that 50 percent of the homes were free of debt. The area was free of major crime and lacked only a sports stadium for public entertainment. Havenner believed that a sports stadium located on sixty-three acres close to the river near Benning Road would help Washington achieve international status in the world of sport. Thus unwittingly did the idea of a sports

* Soldiers and sailors back from the Great War rioted in the District over a suspected sexual assault on a white woman by a black male. In four days, 150 men, women and children were beaten and clubbed, and nine people died before the police and marines restored order.

stadium as a venue for mass entertainment enter into the equation for Anacostia's social and economic development.[26]

Throughout the 1920s, George Havenner tirelessly promoted the economic and social development of Anacostia and its embryonic river park system. The magnitude and importance of Anacostia Park, he argued, were "little understood." It had the potential to be "one of the most beautiful waterside parks in America," extending along the south shore of the Anacostia in a northeasterly direction six miles toward the Maryland state line and encompassing 820 acres. But, Havenner cautioned, reclaiming this area with sea walls and pumping material from the channel onto the river banks was only part of the process. "It necessitates the building of many new sewers and the extension of others to carry storm water to the river channel." In the 1920s, Havenner foresaw what would become the paramount problem of the Anacostia in modern times—too much storm water and insufficient sewerage.[27]

The irony of Anacostia was that although it was the District's first residential suburb, dating to before the Civil War, it never had the support of the District or Congress to develop in ways comparable to northwest Washington. Money and class created enclaves of power in DuPont Circle, Connecticut Avenue, and Meridian Hill Park. Residents of the Envoy, the plush apartment building on Meridian Hill, drank coffee on their balconies and looked westward to the Mall and the Washington Monument in the distance. Black residents of Anacostia came by trolley to Meridian Hill Park, not to take in the view of Washington Monument but to work as waiters in the Envoy's ornate public dining room.

Washington's post–World War I racial segregation followed the pattern in most southern cities, but what made the system especially odious was the official blessing it received in the capital's highest circles. President Woodrow Wilson and his wife personally intervened in capital life to prevent blacks from advancing in the civil service and gave tacit approval to the kind of informal racial controls that relegated blacks to "Negro restaurants" and the back seats of city trolley cars. Racial segregation also spilled over into nature. The new swimming beach on the Potomac that opened in the recently created tidal basin was reserved for whites only. Blacks, if they cared to partake of the waters, could swim in the Anacostia.

Although whites and blacks swam in different rivers, both races were swimming in polluted water. During late summer heat waves the District sanitary engineer warned that anyone who bathed in the Potomac or the Anacostia faced "a positive danger." The rivers were "teeming with the germs of typhoid fever, cholera, and other diseases." The whole of Potomac Park, with its beauty spots and golf course, tennis courts, and baseball grounds, was losing its attraction because of "the disgusting smells" and the "atmosphere of tainted sewage." Congress abolished the Tidal Basin bathing beaches in 1924 because of raw sewage in the river. Scientists who sampled local waters found Rock Creek and the Anacostia to be more polluted than the Potomac itself.[28]

Suburbia Overtakes the Watershed

In the 1890s, as commuter railways began to stretch out into the landscape beyond the District line, they brought major environmental change to the upper Anacostia watershed. An expanding government sent growing numbers of clerks looking for cheaper housing beyond the District. Railroads anxious to expand their passenger business followed them, or in some cases preceded them, into Prince George's and Montgomery Counties. Although the upper classes preferred to remain in the city, others of lesser means opted to leave out of fear of the District's black population or concern that urban life was in conflict with traditional American morality.

One of these early suburbs was Takoma Park, a town platted in 1883 by real estate investor and conservative churchman B. F. Gilbert. Capitalizing on the fact that the land was several hundred feet higher than the lowlands of downtown Washington, Gilbert promoted his town as a place where residents could enjoy comfortable, semi-rural living, breathe fresh air, and escape the city crowds.[29] The B&O's Metropolitan Line enhanced this development with its commuter passenger operations, as did the Brightwood Trolley Line, which extended tracks into Montgomery County in 1892. By 1922, Takoma listed more than four thousand adults living on the Maryland side of Takoma Park and 1,874 in the District. In Prince George's County growth was confined to the corridors of transportation provided by the B&O. By World War I, trolley lines extended to Berwyn Heights and Laurel, Maryland.

Takoma Park and the other suburbs in the watershed were much more primitive than their modern counterparts. Most lacked running water and bathrooms. Suburban expansion brought along the privy toilet and cesspools, and the use of streams to carry away sewage. After World War I, Maryland created the Washington Suburban Sanitary Commission to coordinate water and sewage disposal. Initial studies indicated that the most cost-efficient means of waste disposal was to direct effluent into the upper Anacostia. Later, Prince George's and Montgomery Counties placed sewer pipes parallel to the Anacostia's tributaries and connected them to sewage treatment plants, but that process would not be fully developed until the 1950s.[30]

The sewage problem in the suburbs repeated the same drama and angst that had afflicted the capital a generation or two earlier. Apparently little or nothing was learned until people had sewage in the streets and in their yards.[31]

The Army Corps of Engineers and the Upper Anacostia

The relative inactivity of the Army Corps of Engineers on the Anacostia had become a long-standing bone of contention in Washington. Limited as they were by a Congress that did not place as much urgency on reclaiming the Anacostia as it did on other rivers, the engineers dredged the flats with their limited budget and mostly confined themselves to clearing a navigable channel to the navy yard. That annoyed the business community, which wanted the corps to make the Potomac and Anacostia productive arteries of trade. Whether or not Congress was forced to take action is uncertain, but things began to change by 1913. An appropriation of $400,000 made it possible for the engineers to do more than make park space out of dredge spoil, and the corps geared up to "engineer" the Anacostia to protect communities from spring and summer flooding and bridges from flood damage. In 1913 and 1914, the engineers laid 33,158 cubic yards of riprap along the river's banks and constructed a sea wall 1,465 feet in length between the Anacostia and Pennsylvania Avenue Bridges. As summer progressed they extended the sea wall farther upriver, so that by June 1914 it was 10,185 feet long with another 2,934 linear feet scheduled.[32] The engineers also removed old wharf pilings, small wrecks and logs, and the ruins of a railroad trestle that had been destroyed by floods in the 1890s.

The U.S. power dredge *Dalecarlia* working on the Anacostia in the summer of 1914 excavated 21,806 cubic yards of silt and other materials from the riverbed. In twenty days it cleared 582 linear feet of channel that was about a hundred feet wide and twelve feet deep.[33] During this same period the engineers drained marshes and low-lying areas on the grounds belonging to St. Elizabeth's Hospital for the Insane.

One more problem confronted the corps: congressional appropriations to reclaim the Anacostia were made "with a view to the interests of commerce and navigation." Given the river's massive annual silting, it was not certain that the engineers could keep channels open without incurring massive dredging costs. Their best alternative, the corps insisted, was to engineer the Anacostia as a massive public park in much the same way it had dredged the Washington channel to create Potomac Park. This could be achieved by reclaiming mudflats and wetlands on the eastern bank, from Geisboro Point to the Anacostia Bridge, a twenty-mile-long stretch of river the engineers thought could never again be an artery of "commerce."

By 1921 the old familiar problems had returned to haunt the corps.

Tidal action appeared to be in league with nature, constantly rebuilding the marshes and mudflats as soon as the engineers had scoured them out. Silting rendered plans to make a dammed lake at Massachusetts Avenue impractical. Instead, in 1916 the engineers constructed "a lateral basin along the west bank of the river to a depth of six feet" and used the spoil to build Kingman Island.[34]

The corps also had a new priority—dredging the Anacostia to create an airport called Bolling Field out of the land between Geisboro Point and the Anacostia Bridge. Airplanes had come into their own in the War Department, which deemed a large military airfield a necessity for the nation's capital. These projects were done when riprap cost $1.74 a cubic yard and building stone for sea walls cost $2.25 per cubic yard—high prices for the time.

In February 1926, a pessimistic Maj. James O'Connor, the Chief Engineer for Anacostia Reclamation, reported that it would take at least six years to reclaim the upper river from its shallow and flooding waters, its mud banks and silted channel, provided the funds were forthcoming from Congress. Given his annual appropriation of about $360,000, O'Connor believed the job would cost at least $2 million, plus any additional costs to build intercept sewers to keep effluent out of the river. Most army engineers thought the fate of the Anacostia was linked to the navy yard and that attempts to improve the river upstream were not practicable.[35]

So it was that the Anacostia continued to be a shallow and frequently flooded river with little capacity to absorb runoff from heavy storms. From 1865, when it first started to reclaim the Anacostia, to 1936, the Corps of Engineers had dredged eleven million cubic yards of material from the river, but in 1945 a new report on soil erosion revealed that between 1891 and 1937 "the bed of the river was raised three feet and its width reduced from 210 feet to 75 feet."[36] In the 1930s, after many of the marshes had been destroyed by dredging and diking, the corps once more entertained the idea of remaking the Anacostia into a stone-walled barge channel for coal and lumber transport to Bladensburg, but that plan, long a part of the litany of Anacostia River development, failed during the Depression.

Left was a watershed that no longer reverberated with the sounds of birds. The river whose marshes, wetlands, and forest cover had so thrilled John Burroughs and Paul Bartsch had been subdued by the engineers and the reclamation people, and was now silent. To see the Anacostia in the 1930s was to see a river completely subjugated by rip-rap, sea walls, dredge spoil, and sewage outfalls. Pierre L'Enfant's noble vision of a river that would showcase the emerging American republic had reached its nadir. The Anacostia was now a storm water culvert, and a sewer.

CHAPTER SEVEN

Engineering the River,
1870–1909

*"With the Anacostia dredged beyond Bladensburg and thus opened to freighters
with their cargoes of factory and farm products and carrying to Norfolk the
goods now shipped there from the New England states, a new era of
prosperity will dawn for Washington."*
— William F. Gude, Anacostia Chamber of Commerce, 1909

In the 1870s issues of public health, cleanliness, and river navigation converged on the Anacostia Flats. The flats—large mud banks
along the river—were the creation of silt, garbage, and sewage.
When the Army Corps of Engineers first surveyed them they discovered that a man trying to walk across the flats to the river could easily
sink up to his waist in mud. During summer's torrential rains and heat
they became swampy mosquito-ridden bogs. Vagabonds and the homeless camped near the flats in dry weather, since neither the police nor
civic and business leaders cared to venture there.

Dredging the Anacostia

From 1870 to 1900 the corps maintained, through dredging, a navigation channel from Long Bridge to the navy yard for military use. It
also believed in "the importance of a radical improvement of this river
to the health and prosperity of the city."[1] It was during this period that
the Anacostia riverfront in the expanding capital became increasingly
industrialized.

By 1876 silting had forced the piers and docks along the Anacostia above the navy yard into disuse. Even at the navy yard, water depths were constantly shifting. A narrow channel, from five to seventeen feet deep, allowed smaller ships to pass at high tide. Most larger vessels had to dock off Greenleaf Point and Buzzard Point where water in the ship channel was between twenty and thirty-two feet deep.[2] To get to the navy yard, ships had to move carefully along the river's western side, through a narrow channel only twenty feet wide and marked by buoys.[3] To alleviate this situation the Army Corps of Engineers in cooperation with the District commissioners began drafting a plan to dredge the Anacostia and reclaim the river flats. But by 1880 dredging of both the Anacostia and the Potomac met increasing resistance from commercial fishermen, who did not want dredge spoil contaminating their fishing grounds. Sludge scows had to chug twenty-three miles south of the city to deposit their spoil on the riverbanks.

From 1880 to the turn of the century, the corps labored at dredging out the Anacostia tidal flats for development of parkland and businesses, and trying to create a channel in the Potomac from Arsenal Point to Georgetown that seemed to shoal up as soon as the engineers completed their task. At the bargain rate of 13.9 cents per cubic foot for dredging, the corps nonetheless calculated that a permanent dredging program involving the Potomac at Washington and a channel to the navy yard on the Anacostia would cost about $2.5 million.[4] While the corps devoted its manpower and congressional funds to rescuing Georgetown from its environmental fate, it only focused on the Anacostia when the mudflats became a menace to health.

When army engineers first studied the problem of navigation on the Anacostia, they recommended a $6 million program to dredge the channels of both the Potomac and the Anacostia, but no action was taken at the time, according to Corps of Engineers historian Martin Gordon.[5] In 1875 the engineers studied a proposal from the management of the Chesapeake and Ohio Canal for dredging a fifteen-foot channel to Bladensburg, followed by construction of a 17.5-mile canal to the Patuxent River and on to the Severn River. The idea was to let coal barges make their way to Baltimore more cheaply over a shorter distance. The Anacostia was navigable for the 1.75 miles from its mouth to the navy yard, but, as corps engineers pointed out, at Bladensburg it was heavily silted and at twenty cents a cubic foot for dredging the cost might be prohibitive. The engineers did not flatly turn down this proposal for another canal system. The Anacostia's riverbed was formed of hard sand, which would allow for the cutting of a ship channel, they reported.[6] From an engineering standpoint the project was possible, and over the years business groups tried to revive it.

This canal, it should be observed, was not a new idea. When the District's board of trade researched the proposal it found that as early as 1838 an engineer named Isaac Trimble had surveyed the terrain for a proposed canal that would reach ten miles above Bladensburg, cross a ridge 155 feet above high tide, and continue twenty-one miles to the Patapsco River.[7] But skeptics at the Corps of Engineers pointed out that the last waterborne commerce of any consequence to reach Bladensburg had taken place in 1835, when a load of 199 hogsheads of tobacco and a cargo of pine plank had labored up the shallow channel.

Yet the Potomac and the Anacostia still figured largely in the minds of regional businessmen when the subject turned to coal. In 1878 about 25,000 tons of hard coal was shipped down the C&O Canal, along with six million board feet of pine lumber. Given the escalating cost of rail transport, Washington shippers hoped to follow a water route, even one as implausible as the one through Bladensburg.[8]

Beginning in 1878 and continuing well into the twentieth century, the Washington city government in concert with the Army Corps of Engineers engaged in an extended dialogue with Congress about reclaiming the Anacostia Flats. In November 1881, Dr. Noble Young, the city's physician at the D.C. House of Detention near the river, wrote a lengthy report contending that the flats were the source of the malaria epidemic that had sorely afflicted prisoners in the penitentiary. A drought, Young argued, exposed the flats "to the action of a hot sun as well as rendering the surrounding marshes a moist slimy vegetable surface, laid down by all authorities as most productive of the poisons causing these diseases."[9] Concern for the sanitary conditions at Fort McNair and Washington Barracks prompted Congress in 1887 to focus on the health of its soldiers. At the time the James Creek Canal, which flowed into the Anacostia, was a malarial bog. After a quick study army engineers estimated that the canal, which ran from the foot of Capitol Hill through Southwest Washington, carried an estimated ten million gallons of sewage daily.[10]

Meanwhile, the city planned to dredge the flats and create a public park out of marsh, mud, and bog. First, it appealed to Congress for funds to reclaim the flats because the project was beyond the city's financial limits. Then the federal government and the District had to settle the problem of who actually owned the Anacostia Flats. Ultimately an eminent domain fight arose between the claimants of these tidal flats and the District of Columbia over who was the "riparian owner" of the land. As early as 1872 the District had mulled the problem of riparian ownership in order to secure river frontage for the city.[11] District commissioners took the position that ownership of the river banks rested with the federal government. The Anacostia River frontage, they argued, had been part of the land cession of 1790, which had been part of the 6,100 acres ceded by Virginia and Maryland for the new national capital. While owners of old docks and shoreline on the east side of the river grumbled that the flats were extensions of their legal property, the District let the courts decide the issue.

In the midst of this public debate, Lt. Col. Peter C. Haines of the Corps of Engineers drafted a plan of river improvement that entailed massive dredging of the Anacostia Flats and deepening the channel. Sections of the river, the colonel noted, had become uninhabitable owing to "the solid matter of the sewers." The channel from the Potomac to the navy yard was at constant risk of being silted up by spring and autumn freshets and had to be re-dredged to a depth of between sixteen and twenty feet. Dredging would eliminate the mud bogs in front of the sewer outfall at the old canal at James Creek and assist in dispersing effluvia downstream.[12]

Interest in reclaiming the Anacostia Flats came at a time of increasing commercial activity along the river. In the 1880s once vacant wharves were being rented by garbage, sand and gravel, and coal companies to provide industrial materials to an expanding city. Brickyards were running day and night. Riverfront real estate rose in value while riparian rights litigation simmered in the courts.

Over the course of several decades, Congress appropriated money to reclaim the flats and improve the navigation channel to the navy yard, and by 1898 the Corps of Engineers envisioned a project costing some $6 million that would dredge a ship channel all the way to Benning Road and the District line. Dredge fill would be deposited on the flats, raising them to a height of fourteen feet above low tide. Coming as it did on the heels of an ambitious District-wide plan to improve the city sewer system, the corps' plan engendered considerable optimism that the Anacostia would once more become a commercial waterway all the way to Bladensburg.[13] Suddenly there was big money to be made in the marshes on the Anacostia.

Great as was the promise of reclaiming the flats, little was done to improve the river north of the navy yard. As late as 1907, Congress had not appropriated any money for work above the Pennsylvania Avenue Bridge. Riverfront property owners as well as residents' associations from Lincoln Park and Anacostia bewailed congressional inertia.

The East Washington Citizens Association, a commercial group, was the most vocal. At a time when inland waterways were reviving in popularity, the association lobbied Congress for a twenty-foot channel to Bladensburg and to reconsider the construction of a ship canal from Bladensburg to Baltimore via the Severn River. While congressional critics dismissed the plan as just so much civic boosterism, the East Washington Citizens Association kept alive the issue of reclaiming a river that had once been an important part of the city's economic life. The prime movers in this agitation were George S. King, a well-connected real estate broker, and William F. Gude of the Anacostia Chamber of Commerce. The Anacostia, Gude argued, had to be more than a breeding ground of malaria. Communities east of the river were growing in ways that few could have envisioned thirty years ago. Now the river was at a critical juncture. It would either be a marshland for hunters and fishermen or a commercial waterway. Gude wanted the latter. "With the Anacostia River dredged beyond Bladensburg and thus opened to freighters with their cargoes of factory and farm products and carrying to Norfolk the goods now shipped there from the New England states, a new era of prosperity will dawn for Washington," Gude insisted, "and I can see in the future a waterfront edged with massive stone and concrete piers, at which will lie steamers from South America, the West Indies, and the Canal Zone."[14]

For others, the Anacostia's sanitary problems were the primary issue. In the winter of 1882 a special committee of the U.S. Senate investigated charges that the riverfronts and "flats" of both rivers affected the health of the city. Dr. Joseph Toner, the foremost health authority, downplayed the issue, claiming it was doubtful that the "flats" could cause enough malaria to cause an epidemic. Instead, Toner suspected, real estate speculators had circulated a malaria scare to encourage the reclamation and development of lands they owned.[15]

But communities on both sides of the river increasingly found the stench of the flats unbearable. Dr. Walter Reed reported that Fort McNair and Washington Barracks continued to experience high incidences of malaria. The sanitarian and medical researcher blamed the dredge spoil from the flats for malaria's increase.[16] Never had the situation on the river become so rank, complained Maurice Otterback of the Anacostia Citizens Association. "Fully a dozen sewers empty into the river and what in previous years was a clear channel that washed this filth away, is now so crooked that instead of being carried downstream, it is left on the already noisome flats."[17]

The Army Corps of Engineers began work on the lower Anacostia in 1902 and used hydraulic dredges to carve a channel twenty feet deep and three hundred yards wide. The project would not be completed until the 1920s. In the meantime, merchants and realtors in Anacostia looked enviously downriver towards the navy yard and wondered if reclamation upriver would ever come.

The only development that cleared the air with regard to the Anacostia Flats came in 1911, when a federal court finally ruled that the federal government had riparian ownership of the Anacostia riverfront. The decision ended nearly three decades of litigation. Public and private rights on the Anacostia had become so complex that Congress appointed Hugh T. Taggart, a respected Washington attorney, to research the issue and make a final determination on riparian rights. In 1911, Taggart and his staff submitted a report that concluded the federal government and not private interests had exclusive ownership of the Anacostia's riparian rights. Their report was upheld in federal court and ultimately solved this troublesome issue in city politics that dated to well before the Civil War, when the heirs of planter Notley Young claimed ownership of the Anacostia riverbanks and the mudflats they contained. Resolved too were contentions that claimants of the mudflats were entitled to $2,000 per acre for their land.[18] By filling in the flats on the south side of the Anacostia, army engineers hoped to create parkland at Poplar Point and provide a stable shoreline that would prevent the erosion of soil on the stream bank on which the B&O's tracks were constructed.[19]

Reclamation and Parks

In 1900, the year of the District Centennial, supply ships became grounded in the mud in front of the navy yard and had to be pulled off by tugboats. Reclamation of the Anacostia Flats finally began in earnest after 1909, when Congress specifically appropriated money for the purpose, partly in response to the public outcry over a boy who had drowned in five feet of swamp muck in the Anacostia Flats.[20] Business leaders also pointed out that real estate values in southeast Washington would improve considerably with the reclamation of the flats. Henry H. McKee of the National Capital Bank argued that "the reclaimed land would be valuable for business purposes and give ample sites for parks that are sorely needed in the southeastern portion of the city. The filthy condition of the flats at low tide makes it imperative that this nuisance be abated as soon as possible."[21] Ultimately Congress appropriated $220,000 for reclamation, but the work with hydraulic dredges in the area north of the navy yard proceeded slowly. By 1912 corps engineers questioned the viability of commerce and navigation on the Anacostia and proposed that the spoil be deposited on the riverbanks to create an "Anacostia Water Park" of lakes, parks, and fields. At the heart of this plan was a proposal to build "an immense earth dam" with locks and sluice gates across the river on a line with the extension of Massachusetts Avenue and "the enclosure of the river with masonry walls."[22] This was the beginning of what came to be called Anacostia Park, which Congress created in 1918 with appropriate legislation. In effect, for engineering purposes the river was now divided into two sections: the lower Anacostia below Benning Bridge for commerce and navigation, and the upper Anacostia for parks and recreation.[23]

Industrial Riverfront

By 1903 an industrial matrix corseted the Anacostia. An examination of the Baist real estate maps of the District between 1900 and 1909 shows growing commercial use along the river's western bank. An examination of insurance maps of the District between 1880 and 1927 shows what was happening to both sides of the Anacostia. Increasingly the riverfront was being defined by the industrial processes established there. The Washington Gaslight Company put in large coal piers north of the navy yard, while other companies like Smoot Sand and Gravel, a sewage disposal plant, and the Columbia Granite and Dredging Company wharves, together with the railroads, cut off the river from the community it had once served. On the east side of the river, sheep and cattle yards and the large slaughtering operations of the Washington Abattoir on Benning and Anacostia Roads gave unique refulgence to the Anacostia air.[24]

Starting from the southeastern sections of the city, one sees, in addition to the arsenal and an expanding navy yard, a grid of steam brick works, lumber yards, coal yards, ice houses, scrap yards, saw mills, and the sprawling Washington Gaslight Company between 12th and 13th Streets, SE, and the river. The strings of this tightening corset were the tracks of the B&O Railroad, which cut off the north shore's access to the river. Construction of a large sewage disposal plant that emptied its effluvia into the James Creek Canal completed the transformation of the lower Anacostia from a commercial river into an industrial one.[25] The ugliness of this process was compounded by the fact that railroads had appropriated most of the Capitol Hill side of the mall for track and a rail terminus. Similar developments were taking place in river cities like Pittsburgh and Louisville. Between 1870 and 1903 most riverfront cities would see access to their shorelines blocked by industrialization.

The expansion and development of Washington's infrastructure after 1870 created the first major real estate bubble in the city since the speculative frenzy that accompanied the founding of the capital. As long as the areas around the Anacostia and Potomac rivers remained health hazards, writes historian Howard Gillette, "elevated sites in the hills surrounding Washington beckoned potential settlement."[26]

As the number of federal workers in Washington increased from 7,800 in 1880 to 23,000 ten years later, Capitol Hill experienced a housing boom. Civil servants could buy a nice row house on Capitol Hill with their annual salary of $1,600 and still have enough left over to employ a maid at $8 a month plus room and board. Between 1870 and 1895, real estate speculator Charles Gessford built marketable row houses that had bay windows, stained glass, and slate roofs. The boom at the navy yard attracted Jewish merchants who opened stores in the southwest portion of the city and established the Southwest Hebrew Congregation four blocks from the main gate. Out of this congregation would come the famous jazz singer Al Jolson.[27]

African American Anacostia

Blacks contributed to the flurry of community building. Barry Farm on the banks of the Anacostia was a Freedmen's Bureau experiment in building a community of independent African American households. Beginning in the spring of 1867 the bureau developed a plan to sell land to the freedmen. Using $52,000 from the Refugees and Freedmen's Fund, General Oliver O. Howard, the head of the Freedmen's Bureau, purchased 375 acres on the east side of the Anacostia just north of St. Elizabeth's Hospital and divided the parcel into small lots to sell to the freedmen. The average cost of a one-acre plot was about $225 with mortgage payments of ten dollars a month, the equivalent of what African Americans paid for tenement apartments in the District. With lumber taken from razed military barracks, regional forts, and a train load of planks from Maine, construction of small two-room houses began. The proceeds of land and lumber sales went to operate the new freedmen's school, Howard University. Barry Farm "was one of the first, if not the first, government ventures into the field of public housing."[28] A free African American community of five hundred families sprang up on land that had once been part of the Barry plantation. The community rapidly became known as Barry Farm despite its unincorporated status.

Until the Civil War, the major taxable income and wealth of land east of the Anacostia derived from land and slaves. Now a sizeable portion of this same land was being acquired and developed by African

Americans.[29] New developments at Uniontown and Barry Farm gave
blacks an opportunity to move out of the river slums. Those who settled
east of the river had a less restricted life than those who remained in
the older sections of the capital. With the Freedmen's Bureau's support, freed blacks for the first time became property owners on the
banks of the Anacostia River. During this Gilded Age, they rallied
around the family of Frederick Douglass, the town's most influential
black man, and Solomon Brown, a civil rights leader who served in
the territorial government in the 1870s. Lacking a press of their own,
blacks worked through churches and civic organizations to improve
public education for black children east of the river and to install a
system of public transport that would connect the town with Capitol
Hill. In 1898 the Anacostia and Potomac Street Car Company, a line
of ten miles, installed tracks from the navy yard across what is now the
11th Street Bridge, past St. Elizabeth's Asylum, out into the rural parts
of the District to the new community of Congressional Heights. This
gave Anacostia residents an important transport link and opportunities for employment in the city, and Anacostia grew significantly. What
had begun as the all-white suburban community of Uniontown was
now a growing community of some ethnic and racial diversity. From
his stately mansion on a hill overlooking Anacostia and the Capitol,
Frederick Douglass served as an effective voice for the city's poor and
disfranchised. He was active in local literary efforts for black youth and
an influential bridge between white and black Anacostia.

By 1920, Anacostia had changed from a region of plantations and
truck farms to a small community of seven thousand people. In general
terms it consisted of three sections: Anacostia, Barry Farm, and Hillsdale, which, like Barry Farm, was primarily settled by blacks. Though
much of the area was decidedly rural, with open fields for raising tomatoes and other truck crops, all three communities experienced growth
and a modicum of prosperity in spite of the distressing lack of sewers
and water service. Indeed, for most blacks living conditions were primi-

tive. Some maintained their families by grazing their own milk cows at Fort Stanton Park. But blacks and whites alike aspired to an increase in public services and better financing for home building and community development.

Several streams of migration flowed into what came to be called "Anacostia Town" in the final decades of the nineteenth century. Irish and Italian immigrants settled east of the river, driven out of the central city by rising rents and a dearth of available housing. Developers dismantled many of the old and poorer areas of northwest Washington to make way for hotels, government buildings, and larger homes for the upper middle class.

From the outset, though, communities east of the river suffered from two disadvantages. First, the topography was hilly; little flat land was available for commercial and residential development. Infrastructure did not follow population shifts across the Anacostia, and communities like Barry Farm and Uniontown had to contend with a meager and unpredictable public water supply. Many homes had to rely on wells that often contained brown water. St. Elizabeth's Insane Asylum had to pump its water uphill from the turgid Anacostia itself. As late as 1900 visitors who crossed the river into "Anacostia Town" found open sewers and overflowing outdoor privies that contributed to a high incidence of infant mortality. Life expectancy for black males east of the river was almost thirty years less than that for white males.[30] Water and sewer issues fueled contention between the citizens of Anacostia and the District government well into the 1920s.

The second problem for communities east of the river was that by the 1870s the upper Anacostia had silted in so much that it was useless as an artery of commerce. After the Civil War, the Anacostia region became a place where the sick, the poor, and the working class, black and white, lived side by side but nevertheless uneasily with federal government workers.

Until the Civil War, Washington had been a relatively small river town. Its commercial vision focused on waterborne commerce, and the city fathers believed that its future was oriented towards its wharves, shipyards, and commodity warehouses. War, railroads, trolley lines, and new earth-moving machinery brought vast changes to the city's landscape. The steam railway and electric trolley, for example, made possible the development of urban corridors north and east of the Anacostia by the 1880s. As the size and complexity of Washington increased, the city's wealthier elements continued to move westward and northward from the urban core into soon-to-be prestigious areas like Kalorama, DuPont Circle, and Massachusetts Avenue. To the upper classes, the Anacostia presented a far less attractive environment.

The capital has retained but two of its important pre–Civil War aspects: It remained a city populated for the most part by people who had been born south of the Mason-Dixon line, and it remained, like its southern counterparts, a city with a substantial black population. By 1880 the city's 43,398, blacks represented 43 percent of its residents.

In the northwest, real estate investors developed the 240-acre Kalorama estate of the famous poet Joel Barlow, spearheading the settlement of that section by the wealthier classes. The purchase of the Joseph Bradley Farm on the northwest side also brought investors great profit. Called Chevy Chase by its developers, land that had previously sold for eight cents a square foot now brought six times that amount. By 1885 there were more than a hundred real estate firms in the District, testimony to the keen interest in developing the city in the heady afterglow of the Civil War. Owing to the expansion of the federal government, the District's population swelled to 230,392 by the turn of the twentieth century.

Development of the Northwest and the Anacostia revealed conscious decisions by political and business figures on the matter of how the District was to evolve in the late nineteenth century. The Anacostia, for example received the gas works, the factories, the rail yards, the almshouse, the prison, the arsenal and the garbage disposal sites. The

Northwest received mansions, excellent city services, sewer, water, and infrastructure—and the social cachet of an elite residential address. This was but the beginning of a process affecting the Anacostia watershed that would be anything but random.

What stifled the community most was its inability to capitalize on the Anacostia River for commercial purposes. A navigable channel up-river to Bladensburg would have given local businessmen cheaper access to barges of lumber and coal. Better docking facilities, argued bankers like Adolphus Gude, would have encouraged local boat builders and produce merchants to locate their operations in Anacostia. Georgetown tied its economic fate to the Potomac and through political influence and guile maintained a dredged channel of commerce on their river. Residents of Anacostia looked out on theirs and saw an economically worthless tributary clogged with silt and raw sewage.[31]

Storm Waters

On May 31, 1889, a torrential rain fell on Washington, flooding streets near both rivers and creating ponds and lakes out of what had been dry well-situated land. The storm came up the Atlantic, picking up gale force as it roared northward. Water levels rose above the city's docks and wharves, and by eight o'clock that night the Anacostia had risen to a height greater than it had reached in the floods of 1877. Within a single day, four and a half inches of rain fell on the city. Boat houses overcome by the swirling water lost their moorings and floated toward the navy yard. Lumber merchants feared that the floods would carry off their inventory, and citizens were alarmed by raw sewage and dead animals floating in the river.

All along the Anacostia calmer heads worried that the floodwaters and accompanying silt would add more muck to the flats and obstruct what little navigation remained. Streetcars on the east side suspended their schedules owing to the large number of overblown trees and pol-luted floodwater on the tracks. Sewers, choked up by the rising waters, flooded basements with effluent.[32] Sewage spilled onto the streets and gave thoroughfares a nauseating stench.

Summer freshets like this one accentuated the growing public call for channeling and diking the Anacostia to prevent future calamities. The District responded by placing renewed pressure on the Army Corps of Engineers to build flood walls and dikes. Members of the East Side Business Association also pressured the District to add new sewers to their community and to fix deficient ones. Increasingly, Washington's civic leaders believed that to prevent floods and sewage problems the Anacostia had to be "engineered."

Every time a major rain fell, community leaders like W. C. Dodge wrote angry letters to the newspapers demanding the reclamation of the Anacostia. In a fit of exasperation after several years had passed with little or no progress on reclaiming the Anacostia Flats, Dodge wrote: "Even if the Congress cared little or nothing for the health or lives of its citizens, it certainly should for its own officials and employees. If Congress as a body could be induced to go out there and see the actual condition, especially in the summer time, I apprehend there would be no hesitancy in providing relief."[33]

Though it is difficult to ascertain whether Congress was listening to the District's flood- and sewage-plagued citizens, it clearly was concerned about itself and appropriated money to build a major sewer that would take care of Capitol Hill. Work neared completion on "the Big Sewer" in the fall of 1898. What would come to be known as the third largest sewer in the world was a major engineering effort that would become the backbone of the city's sewer system. It ran beneath the Capitol grounds to 1st Street and followed the path of the old Washington Canal and supplemented the old Tiber Creek main that ran under the Botanical Gardens. At its outlet on New Jersey Avenue, the sewer was fourteen feet six inches high and fourteen feet wide. Constructed of brick, tile, and concrete with walking ledges, it was reminiscent of the Paris sewers. In the late nineteenth century the problems of nature were to be solved by feats of engineering, even if it required tunneling forty-six feet under the Capitol buildings to assure a satisfactory flow. On Capitol Hill, building the big sewer in 1898 was the closest thing to a major mining and drilling operation the city had. Power shovels dug underground at the rate of twenty feet a day, and trolleys run by cables brought tons of earth to the surface.[34] The new sewer dumped surface runoff and sewage into the Anacostia.

In a new age of industrialization, real estate development, and expanding government, entrepreneurs would impose their vision of shared space on the city, and it would be a vision that very quickly retreated from its historic riverine base. Since then, despite planning and zoning, entrepreneurs have continued to be the dominant creators of a landscape that reformers, conservationists, and homeowners could change only modestly.

CHAPTER EIGHT

The Iron Heel of Power:
Class, Race, and Social Ecology
on the Anacostia

"They constructed in Anacostia at first Bantustans, then simply Siberian outposts larger and more distant from jobs, a faux landscape of hideous monuments mocking the other side of the river."
— Brett Williams, *A River Runs Through Us*

Although the Great Depression of the 1930s with its massive unemployment and dislocation did not strike Washington as severely as it hit other cities in America, hard times played out in the District as a theater of social and economic protest. The Anacostia Flats became a battleground when World War I veterans struggled to gain fair treatment from the government. Henceforth Anacostia would figure larger in the public dialogue about human rights and social ecology in the region. The iron heel of power used to trample the bonus marchers in the 1930s would be used again in the 1950s and 1960s when Washington officials determined to move African Americans out of the center of the city. Urban developers focused their attention on what they called "blighted" neighborhoods in the southwest quadrant. This time the authorities did not need soldiers with bayonets to remove the people. They had a better weapon: the legal power of eminent domain to destroy a community. The subsequent destruction of a large black neighborhood in the southwest set the stage for future disruptions in Anacostia's racially diverse communities.

The Bonus March

In 1932 veterans came from all over the country to camp and protest on federal land known as the flats of the Anacostia River. Eventually some twenty thousand strong, they were men who had fought in World War I who came now to prod Congress for an early payment of the war service bonus that had been legislated in 1926. In the face of economic conditions that were quickly becoming desperate, Congressman Wright Patman had introduced a bill to advance the bonus payment immediately rather than waiting until the mandated payment year, 1945. Patman's bill passed the House in June but was voted down in the Senate. By that time, white and black ex-servicemen from all over the country had already taken to trains, trucks, and automobiles to march on the Capitol. Many arrived with their wives and children, having traveled all the way from the West Coast. The sights and sounds of these people echoed what reporters had seen of fugitives from the Dust Bowl migrating westward—dilapidated automobiles piled high with personal belongings and thin middle-aged men and women camping in cardboard shacks.

The fallout from the stock market crash and the general unemployment crisis had left large numbers of people destitute and panicked about their future. These men were no longer youngsters. They were, wrote John Dos Passos of the swelling Anacostia encampment, "getting on into middle life, with sunken eyes, hollow cheeks, off breadlines, and pale looking with knotted hands of men who worked hard with them, and then for a long time had not worked." They were a cross-section of American life, salesmen and steelworkers and immigrants who fifteen years before had barely mastered sufficient English to serve in Uncle Sam's Army. "The arrival of the bonus army," said Dos Passos, "seems to be the first event to give the inhabitants of Washington any inkling that something is happening in the world outside of their drowsy sun parlor."[1]

The veterans had returned home victorious to an affluent, expanding economy. Jobs had been plentiful then, and they were content to see a bonus for military service voted them even if its payday was far in the future. Then the Depression swept away dreams and left stomachs empty. Many of the veterans were now destitute. If they had to wait until 1945, they argued, theirs would be a "tombstone bonus."

Sympathetic friends like retired Gen. Smedley Butler of the Marine Corps saw in the arrival of what came to be called "the Bonus Army" a profound class issue at work in the country. Addressing a crowd of five thousand veterans on the Anacostia Flats, General Butler told the men to stick up for their rights and crusade for the bonus. Butler, a two-time winner of the Medal of Honor, told the cheering throng: "Remember by God, you . . . didn't win the war for a select class of a few financiers and highbinders."[2]

Elsewhere around the country, starving Americans had to seek charity relief at a time when farmers were dumping food in ditches because they could not sell it. The veterans did not want charity, only their promised "bonus" of a dollar a day for every day of home service and $1.25 for every day at the front, and they could wait no longer. "We were heroes in 1917," they grumbled. "Now the elite treats us like bums." In a bitter rendition of the stirring 1917 song "Over There," the veterans sang: "All you here — here and there / Pay the Bonus pay the bonus everywhere, / for the Yanks are starving, / the Yanks are starving, / the Yanks are starving everywhere."[3]

It was historically fitting that thousands of American veterans camped on the grounds of the Anacostia Flats to renegotiate a social contract of citizen-soldiers in a time of crisis. The flats had served as an encampment for U.S. Colored Troops during the Civil War and were where the first settlement camps for freedmen had been located, at Barry Farm. Now this mosquito-ridden haven for the poor and dispossessed became the staging ground for a political assault on the capital by men determined to make their representatives listen to them. The veterans promised that they would immediately feed and clothe their families with the $500 bonus and thereby help end the Depression.

The Bonus Army on the flats of the Anacostia took on a life of its own that was stronger than individual members and frightening to the police. At night by the light of bonfires the men listened to speeches from orators of all political persuasions. Conservatives, mostly local businessmen, gave them candy bars and appealed to them to go home. Members of the D.C. Board of Trade thought the Bonus Army was creating a revolutionary situation reminiscent of the Russian upheaval in 1917. The more radical among the veterans talked about the American democratic birthright and the need for change in an economically damaged country.

Twenty-one camps had set up around Washington, but the largest was on the Anacostia Flats across the river from the Capitol.[4] The headquarters and center of the encampment was on the old recruiting and parade ground on a District-owned field adjacent to Bolling Air Field. Called Camp Marks in honor of a friendly local policeman, it promptly became one of the largest shantytowns in America. Unlike Washington proper, the camp was racially integrated, and black veterans were given a respectful hearing at the organizational meetings for demonstrations in the capital. The ragged state of the Bonus Army came as a shock to the local gentility. A number of conscientious social matrons reached deep into their purses and sent truckloads of sandwiches and cigarettes to the distressed men.

Between the anxieties of Congress and the determination of the veterans stood Pelham D. Glassford, Superintendent of the Metropolitan Police. During the war, Glassford had been one of the army's youngest brigadier generals and had made a distinguished record in the American Expeditionary Force. When Glassford saw the veterans coming to the flats, he put out the welcome mat. Many were soldiers from his old units. A member of the Veterans of Foreign Wars as well as a policeman, Glassford sought to play a mediating role between the District government and the veterans and provided a pair of rolling kitchens to serve up hot food for the hungry men. Not to be outdone, Secretary of War Patrick Hurley sent over two thousand bed sacks and two tons of straw to make beds. Glassford set up a commissary at 473 G Street, NW, and persuaded bakers, coffee distributors, meat suppliers, and others to donate food. The veterans themselves organized their own police force about three hundred strong to prevent agitators and criminals from moving into the camp. The men saw themselves as patriots, veterans, and citizens who had come to Washington in search of well-deserved help.

Elsewhere though, tensions were running high. Communist-led marches in cities like Pittsburgh raised passions, and a bitter Detroit auto strike at the River Rouge Ford plant left four dead and more than fifty wounded. When jobless workers led by a former cannery union organizer named Walter W. Walters arrived in Washington, it seemed that the city was on the verge of being swamped by bands of dangerous radicals. Twelve Bonus Marchers kept vigil around Capitol Hill while the Bonus Payment Bill was being debated in Congress in June, a specter that unnerved many visitors to the House and Senate.

By July conditions in the camp were appalling. The place gave off the fetid odor of spoiled food and excrement. Rats swarmed over piles of rotting vegetables. Some of the men built "mansions" out of packing crates and a few lucky souls were able to sleep in pup tents, but most huddled under tarpaper lean-tos. District police counted 8,300 men in the Anacostia Flats camp, all living in squalor. Ominously, as conditions worsened, agitators and radicals emerged as leaders, replacing the older, more cautious veterans.

Across the river at the War Department, Army Chief of Staff General Douglas MacArthur became convinced that the Bonus March was a communist conspiracy, even though members of his own staff told him their informants could only identify three communists out of the thousands camped there.* On July 20, the bonus marchers made two attempts to demonstrate at the White House and had violent confrontations with the police. The atmosphere was already tense. Military leaders told Congress that providing surplus cots and blankets to the veterans violated "the basic principles of the War Department and the Army hoped there would be no future discussion of the matter."[5] As more bonus marchers flooded into the District, spies reported seeing men "of known communist leanings," and Army intelligence informed MacArthur that twenty-six leaders of the bonus marchers were men who were either communists or affiliated with communist organizations.

Fear of communism colored the army's perception of the veterans on Anacostia Flats, a fact reflected in MacArthur's decision to bring tanks, a T-4 armored car from Aberdeen Proving Ground, and a 75mm. self-propelled gun from Fort Myer in case trouble erupted. His concerns, though, derived more from class arrogance than solid information. MacArthur ordered his troops to be armed with bayonets and tear gas grenades. On the theory that armed men on horseback were useful in dispelling mobs, a troop of sabre-wielding horse cavalry was also brought to Pennsylvania Avenue.

The trouble General Macarthur anticipated and Pelham Glassford feared erupted on July 28, when the District government ordered Glassford and his police to evict veterans who were squatting in abandoned buildings near the flats. Some veterans, angered by the police intrusion, hurled bricks. A riot erupted. One policeman panicked and fired his revolver into the crowd, hitting Walter Huska, a demonstrator, who fell dead in the rubble. More police began firing blindly. A shower of bricks

---

* General MacArthur came from a military tradition. His father had served gallantly in the Civil War and later was active as a general in the pacification of the western plains. A graduate of West Point and socially well-connected, Douglas MacArthur distinguished himself in World War I and married an heiress to a banking fortune. An aristocrat in temperament and social outlook, he had neither time nor patience for the unemployed masses of the Great Depression.

answered them. Glassford told the police to holster their weapons and retreat.

In his command post on Pennsylvania Avenue, MacArthur met with his aides and readied the army's plan for dealing with the "communists." A brigade of six hundred specially trained troops donned steel helmets and formed into a four-column phalanx. Up ahead, Maj. George S. Patton spurred his horse and moved his cavalry into position. Behind the cavalry and the riot infantry lurched five old Renault tanks of World War I vintage to intimidate the veterans with their smoke and roar.

At 4:30 that afternoon, MacArthur gave the word and the troops moved up Pennsylvania Avenue and across the 11th Street Bridge at the navy yard toward the flats. Angry at being attacked by men whom they regarded as fellow soldiers, the bonus marchers retaliated with bricks, bottles and any missile they could seize. Some yelled profanities and wielded clubs and iron bars. Patton and his cavalry charged and struck the men down with the flats of their sabers. The tactics were textbook military, charges followed by tear gas grenades to disperse the ragtag assembly. The troops set the shacks ablaze, and the former inhabitants of Anacostia Flats retreated across the river to find shelter in the city. A confident General MacArthur, in freshly pressed riding breeches, rode a large, strong horse, riding crop under his arm and medals a-jangle, to inspect what was left of the camp.

Although President Herbert Hoover had initially ordered MacArthur to refrain from attacking the veterans, in the critical moment he lost his nerve and placed the safety of the city in an arrogant general's hands. While MacArthur polished his story of acting on "the president's orders" for the press, Hoover watched the red glow of the fires at Anacostia Flats from his office window in the White House.

By the end of the day the toll on Anacostia Flats was four dead, fifty-four injured and 135 arrested. A baby died of tear gas inhalation. More than a thousand suffered from tear gas and one man had his ear severed by a cavalry saber. Conservatives in the government insisted that the Army had correctly and properly squelched a "serious riot." Flush with victory, MacArthur claimed he had dispersed a mob "animated by the essence of revolution." The next day President Hoover reported to the nation: "A challenge to the authority of the United States government has been met swiftly and firmly." If he had any regrets, he kept them to himself.[6]

Across the nation others saw it differently. They saw an army on Anacostia Flats turn against its own, using guns, bayonets and gas against an unarmed gathering of peaceful, patriotic citizens. Senator Hugo Black of Alabama summed up the tragedy when he said, "As one citizen, I want to make my public protest against this militaristic way of handling a condition which has been brought about by widespread unemployment and hunger."[7] Tired and defeated, the Bonus Army left the capital and drifted across the nation, hopefully to more hospitable places. Few protest events in the 1930s lasted as long as the Bonus March or ended so violently.* During the conflict, the U.S. Army obtained a "lasting lesson in the use of soldiers during American disorders." Sending regular troops against unarmed civilians was a public relations disaster, noted historian John Killigrew. The debacle would haunt the federal government for years and provide the Anacostia with a fresh chapter of its history, written in blood and suffering.[8] Alas, it would not be the last time the Anacostia would receive an exodus of misery.[9]

When the Bonus Marchers Went Home

The presence of several thousand bonus marchers exacerbated Anacostia's sanitary problems for a time, but were only a small part of a

---

* In 1936, Wright Patman resubmitted his bonus-now legislation, and Senator Harry S. Truman of Missouri led the bill to victory in the Senate. In June 1936 veterans began to pay their food and rent bills with war service checks that averaged $580. According to one recent study, "nearly $2 billion was distributed to 3 million World War I veterans."

larger pattern. The long-standing issues of sanitation, water quality and the overall condition of the river only got worse during the 1930s and 1940s and illustrated how precarious the water and sewage infrastructure was in a metropolis undergoing record growth.

From 1930 until well into World War II the Anacostia community suffered from the presence of slaughterhouse sewage. The abattoir problem came to a head when the Adolph Gobel meatpacking company from Chicago proposed to construct a three-building slaughterhouse complex at Benning Road and Minnesota Avenue, NE. At first the District government capitulated after the Gobel Company's expensive legal talent overwhelmed its small legal staff. The slaughterhouse was scheduled to kill five thousand cattle and hogs a week, but the idea of an abattoir situated within a thousand feet of an area designated as a housing estate subsidized by the federal Public Works Administration enraged Secretary of the Interior Harold Ickes. It was "disgraceful," he thundered, and vowed to use his power and influence to stop the slaughterhouse from being built. "I can't understand why they should want to come into the District when there is plenty of space outside of it," he said. Ickes also warned the city government that even if a new sewage disposal plant were constructed in the Anacostia, it would be insufficient to prevent pollution of both the Anacostia and the Potomac. Having the abattoir in Anacostia was the equivalent 140,000 extra citizens in the community dumping their sewage into the river.[10]

The city finally won its fight against the abattoir by invoking a statute to protect fish passed in 1898 which stipulated that "No person shall allow any tar, oil, ammonia, or any waste product to flow . . . into the Potomac or its tributaries within the District of Columbia." Secretary Ickes posited the then-novel idea that if nuisance industries decided to locate within the capital they should be taxed to finance any new sewage plants necessitated by their operations.[11]

Nonetheless, by the 1940s the nearly eight hundred miles of pipes, sewers, and drains that composed the water system of the capital were hard-pressed to serve the capital's 10 percent annual rate of growth. Housing tracts in the Benning Road area sprang up, financed mostly with government money, to serve as an outlet for home-starved middle-class white families. Few sensed at the time the irony of building a community in an area increasingly known for its sewage and water pollution.[12] The Second World War brought with it a housing shortage, which Washington answered with yet another campaign to build more dwellings. Evidence of the widespread pollution contaminating Anacostia's water supply was thrust once more into the public eye. Polluted water was regularly detected at the Naval Air Station and Bolling Field and in 1943 led to the District commissioners' appointment of a special investigating committee. Although Deputy Health Officer Daniel L. Seckinger reassured the public that there was no cause for alarm, the city installed a chlorination machine at the municipal reservoir to combat "a positive bacillus coli, a sewage-borne bacillus."[13] The Anacostia community received its water from the reservoir through two thirty-inch water mains, one of which crossed under the Anacostia River and the other over the Pennsylvania Avenue Bridge. Faulty pumps at the Anacostia Pumping Station and St. Elizabeth's Hospital often created lower pressure and admitted contamination, hardly a new problem given the region's history.

After the Depression and World War II, growth came to the Anacostia only in fits and starts, mostly in response to urban renewal elsewhere in the city. Well into the 1940s much of the community was still rural. One social indicator provided a perspective on the changes taking place. In 1949 the most serious crime reported was "cattle rustling."

The "Sanitary City"

In 1926, Congress created the National Capital Park and Planning Commission to prepare a comprehensive master plan for the development of the capital. Ulysses S. Grant III, a military officer and adviser to President Herbert Hoover, served as executive officer from its inception until 1933, a period during which he was also appointed Director of Public Buildings and Parks.* Specifically, the NCPPC was interested in the expansion of the McMillan plan, a wholesale urban development plan for more parks, buildings, and monuments that would make the city aesthetically pleasing.[14] Commissioner Grant and his business allies believed that renewal of large sections of the city, much of which dated back to the mid-nineteenth century, would strengthen the central business and cultural matrix of the capital. His plan embraced federal buildings, transportation, sewerage, zoning, and residential subdivisions as well as parks and national monuments.

As early as the 1920s the capital confronted the problem of how to provide new office space for federal employees as the national government continued to expand. It was during this fateful period that the National Capital Park and Planning Commission began to mark certain areas of the central city as "blighted" and in need of physical, social, and economic change. First to be designated for renewal was an area south of Pennsylvania and New York Avenues and west of Maryland Avenue that came to be called the Federal Triangle, an area that now houses the National Archives and the offices of the Justice, Commerce, and Treasury Departments and the Federal Trade Commission. In 1926 there were few challenges to the concept of urban renewal, and President Calvin Coolidge appointed Secretary of the Treasury Andrew Mellon to work with Ulysses Grant III to spearhead this urban transformation.

* The grandson of the famous Civil War general and president of the United States, Ulysses S. Grant III was a graduate of West Point who served with distinction in the Cuban Pacification, the Vera Cruz Expedition in Mexico, and World War I. Grant married the daughter of Elihu Root, a wealthy lawyer and secretary of state under President Theodore Roosevelt. Grant entered public life in Washington after World War I and earned his general's star as an army engineer, public administrator, and smooth-operating "fixer" at the National Capital Park and Planning Commission during the period 1926–49. He flourished in the same Washington social circles as General MacArthur and shared a similar class outlook. Until his retirement in 1946–47, he was the most influential bureaucrat in Washington on matters of city and park planning.

Significantly, the Federal Triangle expressed more than civic idealism or a salute to the planning of Pierre L'Enfant. This seventy-acre slice of land was transformed from a variegated residential and business community into a series of mausoleum-like buildings.* It constituted the first major appropriation by the government of open space and neighborhood since the days of the McMillan Commission. A somewhat perverse application of the "City Beautiful" ideal in Washington emphasized basing urban design on some of the original concepts and philosophy of the first District architect, Pierre L'Enfant. City Beautiful advocates liked the "monumental look" of big parks, wide boulevards, public monuments, and few residential areas to detract from the vistas. It resulted in an area of monumental buildings and plazas that in design and execution contradicted the very idea of revitalized communities and flourishing neighborhoods. The monumentalism of the Federal Triangle would be used as a standard for other projects of urban renewal as the National Capital Park and Planning Commission and its business allies expanded their influence with Congress.

When Ulysses S. Grant III came to the National Capital Park and Planning Commission in 1926, he saw his first task as ridding the capital of what he called "blight." Identifying alleys and shacks in low-income areas with large black populations as "unsanitary bastions of crime," Grant sought to develop a "sanitary housing policy" that would attack slum areas by tearing them down. With the appointment of John Ihlder as the housing consultant at the NCPPC, Commissioner Grant had a loyal and capable ally. In a 1932 memo to Grant, Ihlder argued that "old slum areas may not contain suitable sites for housing and may be better directed to other uses."[15] Ihlder also observed that the concentration of blacks at the city core was encroaching on white neighborhoods. One way to change the character of a class of

---

* It was in this area that Andrew Mellon chose to house his art collection, which he gave to the federal government to solve an income tax issue. Out of his tax problem emerged the National Gallery of Art.

slum dwellers, Grant and Ihlder agreed, was by "complete neighborhood change."

In 1934, Congress passed the Capper-Norton Alley Dwelling
Bill. According to historian Howard Gillette, this legislation, while
ostensibly designed to rid the District of alley slum dwellings, gave
the National Capital Park and Planning Commission "broad powers of
condemnation to make over at will whole blocks of the nation's capital."[16] Under Capper-Norton, John Ihlder became head of the Alley
Development Authority—the city's first housing authority. He soon
created a sharp controversy when he sought to move protesting blacks
out of the Foggy Bottom neighborhood at St. Mary's Court. Later,
in 1942, with a major wartime housing shortage in Washington, the
Alley Development Authority's attempt to condemn black houses as
slums led to a quarrel with the black-led Lincoln Civic Association.
According to the civic association, the housing authority "disregarded
human habitation by removing dwellings, scattering and not rehous-
ing former tenants and shattering the faith and confidence of Colored
Citizens."[17] Such agendas caught the attention of the *Washington Star*,
which noted that the District parks and housing bureaucracies sought
to "eliminate the city's largest slum area that is within sight of the
capital and assure all the attendant benefits which accompany such an
elimination." Although slum clearance was suspended during World
War II—dwellings of almost any type were hard to come by during
the housing shortage—John Ihlder, now head of the National Capital
Housing Authority, wrote that forty thousand dwellings should be torn
down, many of them in the southwest quadrant.[18]

Toward the end of World War II, Ulysses S. Grant, as chairman
of the National Capital Park and Planning Commission, asked for
complete control over urban development in the District and got it in
the form of a new bureaucracy, the Redevelopment Land Agency. A
product of the District of Columbia Redevelopment Act of 1945, the
agency's mission was to tear down and "renew" large areas of the city.

The RLA reported directly to Commissioner Grant's office and became the slum clearance wing of the National Capital Park and Planning Commission.

The D.C. Redevelopment Act of 1945 required the NCPPC to approve the boundaries and plans for urban renewal projects.[19] Little thought was given to where people from these razed neighborhoods might be re-housed. When the war ended the NCPPC focused its attention on razing the slum neighborhoods in Southwest Washington. Many African Americans sensed that somehow a disaster was about to befall them and regarded all talk about urban renewal as "anti-Negro." As early as 1949, blacks criticized white development advocates who had "decided that the pauperized underdogs of color are too close to the seat of government and need to be relocated."[20]

Ulysses S. Grant III ran the commission with the authority of his major general's rank in the U.S. Army, but some people thought his tactics more Prussian in style.[21] Grant was empowered with authority to literally rebuild the city center, construct new highways, and embark on an ambitious program of building federal monuments. In 1947 he urged the removal of "the colored population dispossessed by playgrounds, public buildings, parks, and schools" away from Southwest Washington, Foggy Bottom, and Georgetown to rural, small town Anacostia, specifically to a remote section "in the rear of Anacostia." Once the relocation had been completed, Grant would have the government build simple "Negro housing complexes" screened from white communities by green forested areas." Thus in a perversion of New Deal planning, Grant envisioned a black belt screened by a greenbelt. Or in the words of one historian, David Levering Lewis, Ulysses S. Grant III envisioned "Potomac Bantustans" for the Anacostia.[22] Significantly, this approach seemed to complement the federal government's quest to develop highways and roads in the District to accommodate the growing use of automobiles. Slums and cars, Grant argued, were the impetus to transform traditional land use at the city's core.

When Grant's plan came up for funding in 1950, congressional leaders found it unpalatable. The Rosenwald Fund and other liberal foundations were reporting on the excesses of racial repression in southern cities, and neither President Harry Truman nor the Congress seemed anxious to be identified with Grant's relocation program. (By this time Grant had retired from the agency.) The NCPPC was renamed in 1952 as the National Capital Planning Commission, to reflect better the agency's mission of slum clearance and development in Washington.[23] The D.C. Redevelopment Act led to the creation of an urban renewal bureaucracy with the sole purpose of making the downtown a haven for shopping, an office complex for federal workers, and a middle-class residential neighborhood for the influx of new federal workers, most of whom were white. This new bureaucracy was housed under the leadership of the National Capital Planning Commission, the District Committees of the House and Senate, the National Park Service, the Army Corps of Engineers, and four appointed city planners, only one of whom had to be from the District.[24]

But just before his retirement, according to District Engineering Commissioner Gordon R. Young, Grant removed much of city planning authority from the District government and placed it under federal control. Large areas of taxable property became tax-free parks. One of Grant's final plans was what he termed the "East Mall," a "monumental development of East Capitol Street for a distance of two miles eastward from the Capitol to the Anacostia River."* As one of Grant's supporters put it, this was a part of the central area of the national capital "as L'Enfant had intended in 1791." Once the plan was carried out, wrote H. Paul Kaemmerer, "our National Capital would have one of the greatest compositions in city planning ever designed for a national capital."[25]

---

* If put into effect, all of the housing along East Capitol Street to the current Armory would have been condemned under eminent domain and demolished, to be replaced by monuments and federal offices much in the tradition of Federal Triangle and Albert Speer. That such a development did not occur is a matter of luck.

Southwest Washington was the first quadrant of the city to feel the pressures of urban renewal and social change. Historically, Southwest's social environment remained relatively unchanged until the Civil War, when forty thousand black refugees in search of food and housing descended on the capital and took up residence in shacks and alleys. The Union Army also created major sanitary problems that made the middle class want to avoid this section. Railroad yards cut it off from other parts of the city. Increasingly, nineteenth-century residents began to refer to the Southwest as "the island," a region set apart by rail yards, swampy terrain, race, poverty, and general neglect. Throughout the Depression of the 1930s, Southwest D.C. remained a poor but stable, and largely segregated, community of blacks, whites, and recently arrived Jews and Italians. Apartments were cheap, and residents had easy access to places of employment. Many walked to work. But as the city became more densely crowded during World War II, the effects of earlier planning and zoning decisions began to make themselves felt in the Southwest.

In 1960 Southwest was a blue-collar community of workers who lived in low-rise town houses. The neighborhood had a flourishing commercial heart with block after block of stores and small businesses on 4th Street, SW. The community attracted Jewish merchants, immigrant craftsmen, and black and white day laborers who could afford cheap rents. Southwest also had its dilapidated houses into which crowded large numbers of black recently arrived from the South in search of work.

Though little remarked at the time, two key developments portended what soon was to come. First, during World War II, the War Department uprooted a small black village in Arlington that predated the Civil War to make way for the Pentagon, a mega-office complex of thirty thousand workers and military officers. Residents were resettled in Anacostia in what marked the first use of that area as a place for resettling unwanted black populations that stood in the way of government construction and urban renewal or both. Blacks, though, were not welcome in white sections of Anacostia. In June 1949 a white-led riot broke out when blacks attempted to use the recently desegregated Anacostia Park swimming pool. Rather than deal with the problem, the Department of the Interior closed the facility and urged the metropolitan police department to learn proper techniques for quelling racial disturbances.[26]

Congressional committees controlled Washington politically, and most committee members were newcomers. Some were segregationists, like House District Committee chairman Theodore Bilbo, an outspoken white supremacist from Mississippi. Dubbed the "Mayor of Washington," Bilbo vented his spleen against District blacks by saying that twenty thousand should be driven from Washington's alleys and repatriated to Africa. He also advocated putting blacks in what he called "a self-liquidating" stadium."[27] After Bilbo's death in 1947, John Mc-Millan, a segregationist from South Carolina, ran the House District Committee, where bills for home rule routinely died in the 1950s. McMillan allied himself with William Press, director of the Washington Board of Trade, who routinely leapfrogged District officials to present the needs and desires of the white business community to the segregationist ruler of the District.

The second development was more directly related to the question of what kind of neighborhoods would exist in Washington after World War II. Because of the capital's housing shortage and a general dearth of construction materials during wartime, Charles Goodwillie, a federal housing official, prepared a report for the National Capital Park and Planning Commission entitled *The Rehabilitation of Southwest Washington as a War Housing Measure.* Its main theme was that rehabilitation of old buildings in Southwest would be cheaper than tearing them down and building from scratch. Rehabilitation, Goodwillie believed, would help not only the residents of that section; it would also enable the government to establish middle-class residences in an area notorious for its alley slum dwellings. Goodwillie saw in Southwest Washington a verdant neighborhood with wide and well-shaded streets and large interior blocks available for green commons and play spaces. He added that since the Southwest had been geographically cut off from the rest of the city by the old City Canal and railroad tracks, it had evolved as a neighborhood that was at once picturesque, racially integrated, and peaceful.[28]

To a great extent the postwar reshaping of Washington was the work of local architects and business leaders who wielded considerable influence in matters relating to slum clearance, housing, and parkland development. Both groups were generally opposed to the concept of public housing for the poor because they envisioned an affluent, white metropolitan core.* That model appealed to city officials and federal politicians as well, for they believed Washington's future lay in the expansion of the tax base through the construction of office and high-end apartment buildings.

The 1945 legislation gave the Redevelopment Land Agency and the National Capital Park and Planning Commission power to decree what areas of the city would be rehabilitated. It also gave those agencies authority to seize all residences that stood in the way under the law of eminent domain. As chairman of the RLA, Mark Lansburgh, the department store magnate, wanted to make the center city a place that would continue to draw middle-class shoppers. So, too, did his ally, the powerful architectural firm of Justement, Elam, and Darby, which proposed to make the Southwest one of the city's top flight middle-

---

* This was part of a national trend. Throughout urban America from 1949 to 1971, urban renewal razed five times as many low-income housing units as it created and evicted more than one million people from their homes. There was some truth to the comment by historian David L. Lewis that with "reactionary members of the Board of Trade" and "military misanthropes in mufti who were simultaneously proposing fixed menial occupations for the black population," Washington in the 1950s was "becoming a model for the nation for racial and residential repression." (*District of Columbia: A Bicentennial History*, [New York: W. W. Norton, 1976]), 78.

and upper-middle income residential sections."[29] Louis Justement, who had achieved national acclaim with his 1946 book *New Cities for Old,* was one of the most influential architects in the country. According to him, "cities were built for the sake of making money" and should be a profitable environment for the entrepreneur. American cities were old, decayed and "inefficient" relics, "built hastily and carelessly, even for horse-and-buggy days." He advocated complete demolition and re-building as a chance "to banish the ugliness which is almost as revolting as the squalor of our urban surroundings."[30] Washington's business community accepted Justement's vision of modern row houses, apartment buildings, and stores as gospel.

For John Searles, the new Director of RLA, the issue was one of making "sanitary housing." It was not difficult to ascertain from Searles's demeanor that black people were unsanitary. From 1945 onward the RLA had periodically taken congressmen on tours of Southwest, usually showing them the worst poverty-ridden alleys, the overflowing outdoor privies, and the houses that seemed more deteriorating shacks than neighborhood residences. (Neither Congress nor the RLA considered, discussed, or analyzed what the terms "blight" or "slum" actually meant.) Goodwillie notwithstanding, Southwest Washington came to be seen as blighted and in need of total redevelopment. That meant the wholesale bulldozing of the quadrant and the removal of its population to other sections of the city until redevelopment was completed.

Developers and their architectural allies happily supported an urban renewal project, two-thirds of whose cost would be financed by the federal government. The Federal Housing Act of 1949 permitted tremendous "write-downs" in the cost of land. Developers paid only 20 percent of the price; the federal government financed the rest with bond issues.

All that stood in the way were the people who lived there. What, for example, would happen to the displaced poor and working classes? A pamphlet John Searles prepared for the RLA assured them they could return to Southwest after redevelopment was completed "if they wish to and can pay the rents and prices of the new dwellings."[31] While the RLA, whose early meetings were closed to the public, was busily planning to destroy Southwest Washington, no one was giving much thought to how the Southwest and Anacostia would fit into the federal-state regional complex of metropolitan development. The only clear indicator of the RLA's plan was that thousands of dislocated people from the Southwest would be transferred to Anacostia for resettlement and warehoused in large-scale public housing projects.

In its enthusiasm for razing Southwest Washington, the RLA refused to consider other alternatives that would have been socially and environmentally ameliorative. In 1951, Albert Peets, a city architect, submitted a plan to the RLA that would clear blight but retain the historic quality of old neighborhoods. RLA rejected it. At no time did the agency consider including the citizens of the Southwest in the planning decisions that were about to affect them. Under the Searles-Justement-Lansburgh regime, the purpose of the RLA was "to make Washington a better place to live." This was code for what African American critics of the RLA came to refer to as "Negro removal" from Southwest Washington. Although urban renewal was considered a process for ridding an environment of substandard and inadequate housing, writes historian Elaine Todd, "it was not specifically designed to provide public housing."[32] Often the slum clearance proposals considered by the RLA, developers, and federal officials were carried out with undue haste. The *Washington Post* reported that one multi-million-dollar proposal was approved behind closed doors with no citizen audience. "Elapsed time: 10 minutes."[33]

The Redevelopment Land Agency interpreted its mission to be acquiring "blighted areas," clearing land, and selling it or leasing it for private development. Dividing the Southwest into Areas A, B. and C, the agency relied upon Albert M. Cole, federal housing administrator, and Mark Lansburgh to convince Congress that the demolition would "help people obtain better homes, better neighborhoods, and better communities." Lansburgh, as chairman of the Redevelopment Land Agency, wanted to create affluent neighborhoods that would bring high-end shoppers back to his stores and staunch the flow of consumer dollars out to the suburbs.

As Lansburgh and like-minded merchants sought to retrieve a migrating customer base, the city government attempted to expand its diminishing tax base. One of the strongest backers of the RLA was the Greater Washington Board of Trade, which worried about the District's eroding business dominance in the metropolitan area. Although the Board of Trade gave lip service to reducing pollution in the Anacostia River, it was consumed by the idea that urban renewal, not a pristine river, was necessary for commercial survival and so the city could continue to lure some four million visitors a year and attract over three hundred regional and national conventions.[34]

The federal agenda was not to preserve community in the Southwest. "Any redevelopment of the area based on the replacement of housing by housing," wrote land planner Pierre H. Ghent, "is not only illogical but so hopelessly uneconomic that it could never be fully accomplished." As Ghent saw it, the important thing was to mark the Southwest for "the necessary expansion of Washington's physical facilities to serve the hundreds of thousands of visitors who come to the capital." In short, the Southwest was to be a federal center of monuments and office buildings, not a residential area. Another planner and architect, Harland Bartholomew, argued that it was self-evident that the entire Southwest had to be cleared, but he hoped some residential housing would be constructed. Historian Elaine Todd remarks in her study of the RLA that the real reason for the demolition of the Southwest was that it was "embarrassingly close to national monuments and powerful people wanted it changed."[35] It was also the smallest of the city's four quadrants, and its population was incapable of putting up much of a political fight.

Public agencies in Washington in the 1950s mandated solutions that were worse than existing problems and often imposed great costs on those who were supposed to benefit. Politicians, city officials, and members of the congressional District committees were loyal to the idea of preserving a downtown business core, but they had no loyalty to the people living in the neighborhoods that would be affected by their renewal programs.

What planners saw as blight and slum was in many cases nothing more than the common disorder that could and still can be found in many urban neighborhoods. Everyday life in Southwest Washington had a rhythm and tempo that was quite healthy. For example, much of the housing stock was old but fundamentally sound, creating a neighborhood that was affordable and stable. Vincent A Holmes, property buyer for the RLA, commented in 1960 that many of the houses they seized through eminent domain for "just compensation" were "pretty good — three story houses with English basements." After the Southwest was razed the U.S. Comptroller General found considerable evidence that inspections had been falsified. Houses and buildings were classified as "slum" or "blighted" without an inspector having visited them.[36] Redevelopment planners saw only what they wanted to see.

The RLA ultimately expanded its authority to cover more than 750 acres. While distressed and angry home and business owners set about challenging eminent domain in the federal courts, crews of the General Wrecking Company rumbled into Southwest and began tearing the neighborhood down.

Property owners contended that many of the properties condemned and seized for demolition were neither slum nor blighted and that seizure was unnecessary to fulfill the purposes of the program. A former resident of Southwest recalled that "where residents found community," civic and charity leaders saw "deterioration."[37] Their legal arguments ranged widely, from the 1945 RLA statute's unconstitutionality to alleged "arbitrary and capricious" actions by the RLA and other agencies. District and federal officials countered that the government was entitled to the properties with fair compensation going to the contesting owners.

John Searles and the RLA feared that litigation threatened to upset the whole plan of urban renewal in the Southwest. "If owner after owner were permitted to resist these development programs on the ground that the particular program was being used against the public interest," he argued, "integrated plans for redevelopment would suffer greatly." The RLA had to seize all the property "to wipe out sniper attacks" on the program by outraged owners. Searles also worried that as long as the eminent domain cases were in the courts, banks, and other agencies would be afraid to lend the RLA money for development.[38] Particularly irksome to the Redevelopment Land Authority were the suits filed by Max Morris, a department store owner, Mrs. Goldie Schneider, proprietor of a hardware store at 716 4th Street, SW, and Max R. Sherman, owner of the department store at 712 4th Street. Schneider's son Joseph was a skilled lawyer who exposed many of the pretensions of the RLA and argued that they contravened the Fifth Amendment rights of citizens in the District of Columbia. Schneider pursued the issue and forced the federal government to convene a three-man tribunal of federal judges. In their review of the case, the judges declared that although the RLA's use of eminent domain was constitutional, the agency could not rely upon its own judgment in deciding which properties were slum or blighted or "what a well-balanced neighborhood would be." The RLA, panicked by the prospect of a bewildering array of citizens' suits over eminent domain, and endless scholarly and lay debate over what constituted blight or slum in the Southwest, appealed to the U.S. Supreme Court for a definitive ruling.

Optimistic that the Southwest could be spared, lawyers for property owners like Joseph Schneider, Meyer Sawyer and Joseph Toomey fought to save homes and businesses. On October 19, 1954, while the bulldozers continued razing the Southwest, the case was sent to the Supreme Court for argument. The case was argued for the estate of Max Morris, whose family members expected justice and wanted to continue operating their department store.

Justice William O. Douglas delivered the unanimous view of the court in *Berman v. Parker.* The decision revealed a host of assumptions about the judicial establishment's view of slums and blue-collar urban communities in the United States in the 1950s. First, the Court upheld an expansive view of eminent domain that continues to this day to allow cities and communities to seize property for public purposes. Working-class whites and blacks and immigrant shopkeepers have suffered greatly from a decision that transformed the meaning and intent of the Fifth Amendment.[39] Wrote Justice Douglas: "The role of the judiciary in determining whether that power (eminent domain) is being exercised for a public purpose is an extremely narrow one. . . . It is within the power of the legislature to determine that the community should be beautiful as well as healthy, spacious as well as clean, well-balanced as well as carefully patrolled." In *Berman v. Parker,* Douglas and the Court found that Washington had the right to decide what constituted a slum. This was part "of what traditionally has been known as the police power." If a government agency looked at a community and defined it as a slum, it was *ipso facto* a slum. Getting to the heart of the matter, Douglas declared that the "need of the area" took precedence over inhabitants and property owners. "If owner after owner were permitted to resist these redevelopment programs on the ground that his particular property was not being used against the public interest, integrated plans for redevelopment would suffer greatly."[40] Overruling the federal tribunal, the Supreme Court said it was not for the Court to determine what were "unsafe, unsightly or insanitary buildings" in a city. Southwest's property owners, it added, were entitled to receive just compensation for "takings" under the Fifth Amendment. The price of the "taking" was, in most cases, a low one.* In the words of urbanologist Sam Smith, the Southwest project was "reverse land reform, a further concentration of land wealth rather than its dispersal."[41]

The Urban League of Washington, D.C., began to point out in a number of public meetings that the Southwest was being razed merely to improve traffic patterns for commuters who wanted to speed home to the suburbs. Further, when the RLA announced that it planned to extend slum clearance across the Anacostia River to include Marshall Heights and Barry Farm, the District's black community grew increasingly restive. After a number of heated meetings with the Urban League and the Hillsdale Civic Association, RLA authorities canceled their plan to raze Hillsdale and Barry Farm. Mrs. Franklin G. Sartwell, president of the Southwest Citizens Association, asserted that it was time for the RLA to "stop destroying and begin building." During the initial urban renewal phase, more than five thousand people lost their homes, and Sartwell voiced citizen resentment about "the continuous upset in which the entire population has been thrust, deeper and deeper since the original redevelopment of this ancient and historic portion of our city was proposed."[42]

Although the RLA promised to build a new town of high-rise, air-conditioned apartments with elevators and extensive town homes, blacks feared the Southwest would become an enclave for families with higher incomes. When the RLA rolled out its final urban renewal plan for the Southwest in 1952, it initially involved 17,500 people, of whom blacks constituted 68 percent. While many whites were able to relocate with minimum difficulty, black residents needed assistance. As building

---

* Miss Mame J. Riley sued over the taking of her home at 823 Delaware Avenue, SW. She received a $7,000 condemnation award that left her still owing $1,900 on her mortgage. The award was $3,800 less than the purchase price of the house. Meanwhile the Washington *Afro-American* reported that new homes in Southwest would cost about $15,000 each—around double the compensation offered for the residences that were being demolished. Very few "colored" families, the paper noted, would have enough money to return to a redeveloped Southwest.

after building fell, it became increasingly difficult for low-income blacks to find accommodations in the $20–$70 a month range they were accustomed to paying. Additionally, many people liked living where they were and did not want to move, even if offered relocation assistance and financial incentives. The reluctance to move found among the middle-aged and elderly residents of Southwest soon reached the level of "immobilizing fear." James Banks, the sincere and hardworking black executive who served as housing director for the RLA's relocation assistance program, was not altogether successful in finding people alternative residences. Most blacks believed, and rightly, that Banks and the RLA intended to move them to the outer reaches of Anacostia, far away from friends, jobs, and families.[43] Despite Banks's well-publicized public information campaign to find dwellings for displaced blacks, most either had to move in with relatives or find another apartment on their own. In the meantime, the federal government razed 223 houses, twenty-three businesses, and four churches south of Independence Avenue between 6th and 9th Streets for the construction of federal buildings.

The irony in all this is that Southwest Washington was the same kind of community—with stable historic structures and a racially and economically mixed population—as Capitol Hill. But Capitol Hill, unlike Southwest, was identified by residents and historical preservationists, including Justice William O. Douglas, as the kind of community that should be lovingly protected, preserved, and restored.

In their rush to protect their shopping and tax base, businessmen and public officials like John Searles chose to follow a model of urban design that flowed off a planner's easel rather than one that responded to the everyday concerns of those who lived in the community. Jane Jacobs, who was already fighting to save Greenwich Village and other neighborhoods in New York City from the wrecker's ball, was well aware of the nightmare of urban renewal. In her seminal work, *The Life and Death of Great American Cities,* Jacobs noted that planners responded to what they thought was the "disorder" of the city by imposing new designs. They completely failed to comprehend—or respect—the far more complex order that healthy cities already embodied. Communities are not designed, they emerge out of the everyday life of people who live there.[44]

The Southwest eventually was rebuilt, and a community of townhouses designed by architects like Chloethiel Woodard Smith redefined its landscape in the 1960s and 1970s. Five apartment buildings with roughly four hundred units in each, and more than three hundred townhouses in a park setting, were built. Past residents of Southwest have often said that if the old neighborhood had been left alone, it would now be a restored historic area like Capitol Hill, and people would be fiercely competing to buy the houses. Instead Southwest is now a sanitized neighborhood of residential blocks and townhouses with little organic and architectural relationship to the monumental core of Washington. A solemn quiet prevails in the neighborhood. In yet another irony, the Southwest is now one of the primary targets for waterfront redevelopment by the District. Perhaps they will get it right this time. So residents fervently hope.

Southwest and Its Aftermath

In its June 23, 1963, issue, the *Washington Star* attacked the RLA and its allies for creating "the Frankenstein of Urban Renewal." This "monster," said the *Star*, "menaces the cherished property rights of every private property owner in this city." With a finger pointed at Anacostia the paper continued, "the slums of the Southwest have been transferred to other areas." Moreover, the notion that families displaced by renewal were finding adequate replacement housing was "a cruel joke."[45] There was no urban vision in the renewal—just "power hungry men in the RLA and NCPC." A later investigation by the *Star* revealed that "the RLA's record-keeping was so poor the agency didn't know how many properties it owned or who was living in them."[46]

Skeptics questioned the merits of federally subsidized urban renewal. After a relatively short run of popularity with city officials, writes historian Jon Teaford, urban renewal "evoked images of destruction and delay rather than renaissance and reconstruction."[47] Margaret Hadley, who resolutely attempted to defend her house from the wrecker's ball, surrendered in 1958. Her home was razed to make way for L'Enfant Plaza. After thirty-two years in the same house in Southwest, she became a neighborhood refugee. Charlotte Allen, a resident of Southwest described how the urban renewal project turned out: "I live on 4th Street SW, myself, where there is not now a single commercial establishment." The stores and residences had been replaced by impersonal concrete blocks containing gigantic residential or office buildings. Allen, in the post-renewal age of Southwest, finds herself living in "concrete wastelands that stretch from L'Enfant Plaza to the marina on the Potomac." "It's taking more than a half century," she reflected, "to restore the dense, rich urban life we lost when the Supreme Court gave a green light to government to intervene in cities' natural processes and rejuvenation."[48]

In 1952 more than twenty thousand people lived in the racially mixed community of Southwest. In addition to razing an entire neighborhood, the RLA demolished thirteen out of fifteen churches, and the synagogue long associated with the famous jazz singer Al Jolson and his family fell to the RLA wrecker's ball. When Southwest was finally rebuilt by 1970, only about fourteen thousand people resided in the renewal district, and many of those were not the original inhabitants. According to 1998 data, the median household income for the Southwest was $47,511—$4,500 greater than the median income for the District. The Southwest, in one respect, had fulfilled the planners' dream. It had become a predominantly middle-class community.

"The City Dump of Public Housing"

In the early 1960s the District Housing Authority reported a major shortage of housing that was reaching crisis proportions for the nearly five thousand people who were on the waiting list for homes. Increasingly, these displaced black families would be moved east of the Anacostia River to areas that had been rezoned, without community input, from single-family residential housing to large-scale apartment development. Almost overnight the city government threw up huge apartment buildings that covered acres of land and were built by builders who did not heed construction standards for public housing. The operative command was to cleanse the center city of blacks before home rule was implemented. According to Brett Williams, "they constructed in Anacostia "at first Bantustans, then simply Siberian-style outposts, larger and more distant from amenities and jobs, a faux landscape of hideous monuments mocking the other side of the river."[49]

Development occurred so sloppily and rapidly in Anacostia that it contributed to the wholesale undermining of a diverse community, which until that time had been remarkably stable. By 1970, Anacostia's white population had decreased from 82 percent to 6 percent, and a semi-rural community was on its way to becoming a violent, drug-ridden urban slum. Until the redevelopment exodus from Southwest Washington to Anacostia, the area had been home to several thousand whites, most of whom comprised the blue-collar work force of the federal government.

In its efforts to save the Southwest by bulldozing it, Washington urban redevelopment brought about the wholesale decline of the Anacostia community. Resident activists in Anacostia like Diane Dale remember "rezoning that designated [her community] Fairlawn for multifamily units, apartment buildings only." "They crammed people in," she said. "The buildings were cheap and shoddy, they never should have been there, developers took advantage of the market." Increasingly in the 1960s, whenever the District government looked for a place to build housing, it invariably decided on yet another three-hundred-unit project in Anacostia. Although thoughtful black observers like William Raspberry of the *Washington Post* recognized the city's crying need for low-income housing, they questioned why these developments always had to be placed east of the river. Anacostia, Raspberry observed, was rapidly becoming "the City Dump of public housing."[50] At the same time Anacostia's schools were bulging with children, and overcrowding became serious. Schools east of the river had 50 percent more students attending class than there were accommodations, whereas in the thirteen grade schools of the Northwest, enrollment was only about 5 percent above capacity.[51] In retrospect, Raspberry wrote, "the overriding sin of public housing . . . is that it concentrates persons of low income, low education, and low ambition into compounds where their problems feed on each other."[52] In the 1870s sewage from the District's prosperous sections was routed to the Anacostia. A century later the poor and their children were warehoused away from public view along the river. By 1967 almost half of Washington's forty-three public housing projects were located there. Eight developments sprang up just to accommodate residents forced out of the Southwest. For Raspberry and other thoughtful urbanologists, rent subsidies that enabled low-income families to live in neighborhoods that appealed to them was probably the best approach, for they diffused the poor into populations with diverse lifestyles.

Compounding the District's housing shortage in the 1960s was a major influx of low-income people from the rural South. Yet such events cannot explain the city's unwillingness to provide adequate public transportation to the area east of the river, or its failure to challenge racially exclusive residential covenants in white suburbs that turned Washington into a kind of racial pressure cooker. The National Capital Planning Commission seriously underestimated population growth in the 1950s and 1960s. That left but one option, it thought—profuse apartment construction in Anacostia. Other alternatives would offend white sensibilities. By 1970 apartment zoning accounted for over 75 percent of Anacostia, while elsewhere in the zoning laws dictated that 80 percent of housing was to be single-family dwellings. Intelligent zoning practices applied everywhere in the city but east of the river.

In August 1966 black impatience with the District's inability to satisfy the need for thousands of low income residences boiled over. In a demonstration reminiscent of the bonus marchers, hundreds of demonstrators camped on the Anacostia Flats at Bolling Field to demand that the Air Force cede its land for public housing. The demonstrations, though not as large as those of 1932, were the product of a common root cause, the protest of a minority demanding an equal place in society. They were fighting the iron heel that too long had been the way of controlling poor whites and blacks in the Anacostia. An American city, they shouted, could not exist "half prosperous and white and half depressed and Negro."[53]

In the 1950s administrators of the federal government and the District of Columbia declared the Southwest "a sore spot of crime, illegitimacy, refuse, and disordered lives." The same tragedy struck Anacostia. Until the tidal wave of urban renewal hit with its titanic replacement of blacks and the urban poor, the Southwest and Anacostia were both settled communities with an intricate layering of income levels, stable neighborhoods that had evolved over decades.

Once renewal began, Margaret Hadley remembers the scavengers who came at night in the Southwest to pry off fireplace mantels and strip off copper pipes. Now those scavengers swarmed through construction sites in Anacostia, stealing lumber, copper pipe, and building supplies and clambering over cyclone fences to make free long distance calls from the phones on the poles at the building sites. After the scavengers came the open drug markets and other criminal activities.

In a review essay on urban redevelopment in the United States in the 1950s and 1960s, Kathryn Oberdeck describes what she called the "grotesque paradox" of city planning. "Only near-diabolical planners could have arranged cities in which poor residents in the inner core are excluded from neighboring pockets of world-class downtown glamour, on one hand, and from protected enclaves on the urban edge, on the other."[54] Perhaps General Smedley Butler was right when he said in 1932 that America was now ruled by the "financiers and highbinders."

In its attempt at urban renewal, the Redevelopment Land Agency destroyed two communities, Southwest and Anacostia. Experts have alluded to the quasi-fascist orientation of urban renewal that marked America in the 1950s and 1960s. When it came to matters concerning the future of communities, those who inhabited them were the last to be asked. White supremacist congressmen and commercialist civic leaders were only too eager to sacrifice black neighborhoods in order to build a sanitized white enclave of affluent shoppers in Southwest. A stroll through its sterile streets today, and through the open drug markets of Southeast, shows the bitter fruit of the Redevelopment Land Agency. Meanwhile, men like John Searles "failed upward." After making a mess of things in Washington, Searles moved on to a better job in New York, leaving the local citizenry to reap the whirlwind.

CHAPTER NINE

Water Woes, 1945–1990

"During floods Washington looked like Venice."
— *Washington Star*

From the Second World War to the 1970s, the capital's problems with water increased exponentially. Many of these issues fell upon Anacostia and communities east of the river, which by the 1960s were undergoing demographic change. The watershed flooded constantly, causing damage and creating inconvenience for residents along the river and in the expanding suburbs of Prince George's County. The decision to use the Anacostia stream valley as the major automobile commuter corridor split the capital by bringing "white men's highways through black men's bedrooms." It also made the watershed an environment held hostage to a transportation grid.[1]

Water and Three Million People

If Washington did not have enough trouble with urban renewal, racial discontent, and the periodic inundation of the capital by a tsunami of tourists, the city could also add its recurring issues with water, which had been part of Washington life since before the Civil War. Early on, water never received the kind of critical attention that beautifying Washington through parks and public buildings did, and as time passed the city's needs for clean drinking water and wastewater treatment seemed modest beside the greater challenge of dealing with transportation in the postwar era. Compared to the powerful auto-

162

mobile and construction lobbies, clean water advocates were at best a marginal group.

In 1970, civil engineers working for the city reported that water quality in nearly all parts of the capital seemed to be "poor or worsening." Reservoirs and sewers were in critical condition, and the proposed expansion of a wastewater treatment plant suffered a cut in funds.[2] With nearly three million people living in the Washington metropolitan area, the demand for fresh water amounted to about 381 million gallons a day, a figure that was projected to increase to 600 million gallons a day by 1980. The Potomac and its tributaries provided nearly all the drinking water, with few reservoirs available to stockpile water during dry periods. Meanwhile, the Anacostia River suffered increased poisoning from industrial pollution and from storm water runoff that began in the burgeoning suburbs in Montgomery and Prince George's Counties.

Washington's water woes stemmed from the loss over time of important forests, fields, and marshlands in both the Anacostia and Potomac watersheds. This ongoing process increased erosion, sedimentation, and non-point source pollution (storm water runoff from farms, malls, parking lots, and housing developments) from the end of World War I on. Insuring safe drinking water for the District became ever more problematic. In 1929 a main source of drinking water had been the Anacostia River's Northwest Branch, but that became polluted with suburban sewage. To replace it, the District piped water into the city from the upper Potomac and from reservoirs on the Patuxent River.

As population continued to grow in the suburbs, the Washington Suburban Sanitary Commission bought up smaller water plants like those at Takoma Park and Mount Rainier and built a water filtration plant at Hyattsville. With a service area of ninety-five square miles and a population base of thirty thousand, the Washington Suburban Sanitary Commission cast its water-drinking future with the Brighton Dam on the Patuxent River and the new river filtration plant at Laurel in Prince George's County.[3] Significantly, the public water supply in the Washington area remained river dependent at a time when regional growth was placing heavy pressure on these waters, and sewer overflow and industrial waste were polluting the watershed.

During the 1930s, the Department of the Interior under the direction of Secretary Harold Ickes made a concerted effort to address pollution in both the Potomac and the Anacostia. As early as 1933 the District worked on a plan that would see construction of a relief sewer to curb the flow of raw sewage coming into Kingman Lake on the Anacostia.[4] At Ickes' insistence, the Public Works Administration sent engineers to test water in various parts of the rivers. Both were so heavily polluted they required major sewage and drain projects to make them less dangerous to the metropolitan community. In Anacostia, District Sanitation Engineer John B. Gordon reported, storm waters at Congress Heights regularly overflowed the sewer system and dumped effluvia onto the Air Force's Bolling Field.[5] In response, the PWA allocated $500,000 in public works money to keep untreated sewage out of streams in the Potomac and the Anacostia watershed, but Rock Creek, which flowed through affluent areas of Washington, was identified as presenting the greater threat. Resources were diverted to cleaning up that tributary.

River pollution reached such a critical state by 1938 that the District constructed a four-million-dollar sewage treatment plant at Blue Plains in an effort to prevent raw sewage from being dumped into the Anacostia and Potomac. The plant was initially designed to process raw sewage from a population of 650,000, but by 1943 the city's population had soared to 1.5 million, and more untreated sewage was entering the rivers than before Blue Plains was built.[6]

The Izaak Walton League of Washington, a conservation organization, lost patience with the molasses-slow efforts of the District and regional agencies to reduce pollution. After a child wading in a branch of the Anacostia River contracted typhoid fever, the league filed a temporary restraining order against the Washington Suburban Sanitary Commission but failed to obtain a permanent injunction against the agency because court calendars were congested with a two-year backlog.[7]

As legal delays stymied the anti-pollution cause, Maryland's suburbs continued to dump their sewage into the Anacostia watershed. Upon discovering that it would cost them nearly $1 million to build a sewage treatment plant at Bladensburg, nearby communities tried to dispose of their sewage cheaply with a proposal that sewage trunk lines in Prince George's County be connected to the District sewer system and the sewage transported from the suburbs to the Anacostia. The reply was blunt. "The character and capacity of the existing sewer from Benning Station to Poplar Point are not such as to prevent the discharge, at frequent intervals, of large quantities of raw sewage into the Anacostia River," District commissioners retorted. To place five million extra gallons of Maryland sewage a day in the city sewer line to Poplar Point "would completely vitiate the benefits of this program."[8]

In 1941 the District was able to successfully outline its problems with sewage to the newly formed Interstate Commission on the Potomac River Basin and to initiate plans for corrective measures through state and municipal legislation. The District, said Maj. Beverly Snow of the Army Corps of Engineers and a District commissioner, had just spent $5 million on sewer projects to end pollution in Rock Creek, and the Anacostia River now had to be rescued. Snow hoped that a four-state compact to end river pollution would see the beginning of cleaner water for Washington and its suburbs. Unfortunately, regional political figures like Senator Millard Tydings of Maryland pressed the District to cooperate with the suburban trunk line hookup in return for additional appropriations for wastewater management. As late as 1949 the standard suburban remedy was "for construction of pipelines to carry all sewage from Prince George's and Montgomery Counties to the District sewage plant at Blue Plains."[9]

Today many Prince George's County sewers and all major trunk sewers in Montgomery County are connected to the Blue Plains system. Forty-five percent of the Blue Plains capacity of 370 million gallons a day—170 million gallons of sewage daily—has been allocated by agreement to the Washington Suburban Sanitation Commission.[10]

Anacostia's sewers were vulnerable. Construction work in the city often damaged sewer lines, resulting in periods when raw sewage flowed into the river for as long as two weeks while the line was being repaired. That was standard practice in the 1940s. Residents in the Hillsdale section of Anacostia, who could not afford to bear the cost of installing pipes from the street to their houses, complained of the city's tardy response in piping potable water into their community. As late as 1950 some Hillsdale residents hiked to public water pumps with their jugs to carry fresh water home, a scene common in the Third World but exceptional in the capital of a world power. Sewer service came late to areas east of the river and only after a crisis of overflowing outdoor privies fouled the community. The Hillsdale Civic Association, an organization of black community activists who believed that contaminated water and outdoor privies should not exist in the nation's capital, sued the District to obtain adequate municipal services. Often it was an uphill battle.[11]

The Washington Suburban Sanitation Commission admittedly wanted to end pollution of the Anacostia watershed. It just didn't want to pay for it. This would be the start of decades-long contention between the capital and the suburban communities over the contamination of the river.

In 1952 the Interstate Commission on the Potomac Basin began to test the Potomac and Anacostia systematically to determine the quality and degree of pollution. Until this time, scientific reportage on the Anacostia had been sporadic, with brief episodes of concern followed by long periods of neglect in monitoring pollution. Harold Kemp, the District of Columbia Sanitary Engineer, warned that most of a five-mile stretch of the Anacostia from Hyattsville to the Potomac had become "an open sewer." The District's sewage plant, Kemp reported, was only capable of removing 35 percent of the pollution.[12]

After putting the Anacostia and Potomac Rivers in a "broader and more serious perspective," Edwin R. Cotton, director of the Interstate Commission on the Potomac Basin, warned that both rivers were "a great danger to the people of Washington." But Cotton noted that Congress was only willing to deal with one problem in the capital, the pollution of Rock Creek, for which it had appropriated $1.2 million. If the Anacostia and Potomac were to be addressed, he said, "the real solution — and the only solution — is for the District to be granted authority to borrow and finance its long-term capital improvements through bonds."[13] During the summer of 1952 city officials created a polio scare when they warned of "a remote, but nonetheless real" threat of poliomyelitis in the polluted waters of both rivers. Sanitary Engineer Kemp warned that the polio virus was "present" in the sewers and polluted streams.[14]

Well into the 1990s, Wards Seven and Eight continued to suffer from serious water pollution long after other wards had solved theirs. Ward Seven was 97 percent black and comprised most of the neighborhoods in the hills beyond Anacostia's Sousa Bridge. Ward Eight was 91 percent black and contained most of what was known as the old Anacostia community. Sewer maps of the city showed that most of the toxic storm water runoff, effluvia, and other matter that combined in the sewer overflow began in the affluent Northwest quadrant of the city and traveled through the sewer system to the poorer black sections of the Southeast. Compounding the problem was the often sluggish nature of the Anacostia River, which allowed discharges to remain at certain parts of the channel and shoreline for significant periods.

The District of Columbia's water pipeline system is an old one, with some 1,300 miles of pipes reaching into the communities of the Anacostia watershed. Although water authorities by 1970 had replaced many of the wooden and terra cotta pipes in use since before the Civil

War, water still circulated through many pipelines that were more than a hundred years old. The city's main water source was the Dalecarlia Water Treatment plant, which is located in Ward Three. According to a recent study, "by the time water has circulated through 1,300 miles of pipes in reaching Wards Six, Seven, and Eight, it has greater potential for accumulating numerous pollutants." In the past the federal government has threatened to sue the District because of high levels of fecal coliform and other bacteria in the water.[15]

During the period of explosive growth following the Second World War, the city and surrounding suburban counties ran sewer lines along the tributaries of the Anacostia. From an engineering standpoint, following a stream valley with a buried pipeline was easy and cheap. But over the years the increase in storm water overflows in the creeks and tributaries eroded the banks of streams like Pope's Branch Creek, Sligo Creek, and Northwest Branch, leaving the sewer pipes sometimes hanging in the air, where they cracked under gravitational pressure and leaked sewage directly into the streams. By 1990 citizens on nature walks often complained of the raw sewage smell in the woods and along stream paths. Joseph Glover, a retired government analyst living in Ward Seven along Pope's Branch Creek awoke one morning to find something he never anticipated. "My yard was full of effluvia," he remembers. "I called WASA, the city sewage authority and reported the problem and the man said his people would get to it when they had the time." Understandably upset by the fact that his well-tended yard had suddenly become a toilet and a toxic threat, Glover then called the health department, which promptly dealt with the broken sewer pipe. Apparently the health department was more concerned about the possibility of an outbreak of hepatitis or cholera, or general bacterial infections, than the sewer department.

Floods

Floods were also part of the Anacostia's history. Newspapers recorded destructive Potomac freshets in the nineteenth century. Before the telegraph, when the water began to rise men on horseback were dispatched from Harpers Ferry on a wild and furious ride to warn the capital of the coming flood. On July 6, 1842, for example, a flood demolished bridges and brought a continuous sheet of water sufficient to float boats at the base of Capitol Hill. The great flood of 1870 destroyed much of the Potomac and Anacostia waterfront and swept away houses and lumberyards in low-lying areas. Residents learned that floods were a regular part of capital life. In June 1889, "every cellar in the lower section of the city was full of muddy dirty water which climbed even to the next story. Ruined household furniture floated adrift." That flood resulted from a May rain of 11.7 inches. The depot of the Pennsylvania Railroad was "so full of water," said a *Washington Star* reporter, that he easily rowed his boat through the front door. Other floods in the 1880s caused a great deal of damage to houses and businesses in the District. During a flood, "Washington looked like Venice."[16]

On August 3, 1906, after several days of heavy rain, a torrent of floodwater surged down the Anacostia and overflowed its banks along the Riverdale Road to a depth of four feet. In Bladensburg and Hyattsville residents were forced to evacuate their homes. At midnight the Chesapeake Railroad bridge in Hyattsville verged on collapse. The floodwaters caused the structure to sway back and forth, and all train service between Baltimore and Washington was cancelled. Yards, gardens, and farms were submerged, and cascading water carried away livestock. Women swept into the flood were rescued by men who waded into the torrent as they frantically clung to ropes and trees. Both the Potomac and the Anacostia rose so high that District officials feared for the safety of the White House. Older residents of Bladensburg could not remember when they had seen such a heavy torrent of floodwater engulf them in so short a time.[17]

On April 29, 1923, Anacostia was inundated with twelve feet of water. The rushing torrents swept away automobiles and marooned passengers atop streetcars. According to the *Washington Star,* "the flood centered its force on the low-lying portions of Anacostia and that area lying between the old Benning race track and Capitol Heights in the east." At 50th Street and Grant Road the flood lifted a barbershop from its foundation and carried it two blocks downstream. Nine major sewers in Anacostia and Southwest Washington failed. Ten bridges in the Hyattsville-Riverdale area were washed away and hundreds of homes flooded.[18] For good reason did residents in the Anacostia watershed fear the torrents of spring.

In August 1933 a hurricane drove a storm surge up the Chesapeake Bay and the Potomac River and hit Washington with a flood tide 11.3 feet above normal. At high tide Alexandria and factories on the capital waterfront were under six feet of water. The devastating tide moved up the Anacostia River and swept a train off a bridge it was unwisely attempting to cross, leaving ten people dead. Washington recorded another eighteen fatalities in the District. Bolling Air force Base was hit by a surge of water five feet deep. There were no flood controls to keep the raging water out of the capital. Waist-deep water swirled over wharves and waterfronts and disrupted local navigation. Large boats and small craft broke from their moorings and floated helplessly in the torrent. Backwash from the flood inundated homes and businesses near the waterfront, and Lt. R. T. Harney of the Washington Harbor Police declared that at nearly twelve feet above median high tide "the river was the highest in history."[19]

Flooding in the Anacostia became more frequent as land was cleared for new suburban communities and the forest and brush cover essential for storm water retention began to be seriously diminished. In 1936, Washington again suffered from high water and storm damage. The rivers raged as April storms flooded Hyattsville, Bladensburg, and other parts of Prince George's County. The flood threatened to cover most of the low-lying parts of the capital. District and federal authorities hastily assembled a "flood control army of 1,500 men" to dike low points of the Anacostia and Potomac waterfronts with sandbags. A flood tide twenty-four feet high rolled up the Potomac from the Chesapeake, and angry water surged down Sligo Creek and the Northwestern Branch Creek in the Anacostia watershed. Many residents of Brentwood and Riverdale in Prince George's County had to be rescued by boat.

President Franklin D. Roosevelt authorized the Civilian Conservation Corps to load 217,000 sandbags to build emergency dikes against the rampaging currents. Six thousand people were rendered homeless, most of them residents of Prince George's County. After the flood, District and regional officials indulged in the usual round of blame and recrimination and complained that the region's almost complete absence of flood control left lives, homes, and businesses at the mercy of capricious rivers.

Suburban communities like Colmar Manor and Bladensburg at Peace Cross saw no end to the flooding they had to endure. A memorial area dedicated to the soldiers of World War I in Prince George's County, Peace Cross was flooded in April 1937 and again that December. The *Washington Herald* editorialized that "this condition will not be remedied until the upper channel of the Anacostia is dredged sufficiently to take care of the volume of water that now overflows a wide area of low-lying land. Maryland can't get cooperation from the federal government to begin dredging," the *Herald* complained.[20] Locals joked that when it rained at Peace Cross the best mode of transport was a canoe. In 1951 the Washington Suburban Sanitary Commission reported that the Peace Cross area of Bladensburg had been flooded twenty-nine times since the first records were kept.

Throughout the 1930s Bladensburg was equally vociferous in demanding some kind of flood control that would liberate residents from the four times a year flooding cycle. In November 1937, Congress appropriated funds to purchase flood plains along the Anacostia River, Sligo Creek, Indian Creek, and the Northwest Branch to create parkland and prevent deforestation and construction of low-cost housing developments in that area.[21] Development of a park system in the Anacostia watershed, argued Maj. Walter Luplow of the Army Corps of Engineers, would help to prevent flooding. Shortly afterward, the corps built flood control levees at the Anacostia Naval Air Station and Bolling Airfield. The levees at the naval air station were seventeen feet above the mean low water mark and were thirty feet thick at the top and seventy feet at the bottom. The solution to flooding on the Mississippi that had been first addressed by the army engineers under the federal Flood Control Act of 1933 now came to the Anacostia.

Suburban authorities pleaded with the Army Corps of Engineers to build a large levee to keep the area dry during storms.[22] Historically there was ample precedent for levee building in the Washington metropolitan area. As early as June 1875 the Army Corps of Engineers planned a dike to run along the eastern shore of the Potomac tidal flats near the Washington Monument. "The place within the dike was to be formed into an artificial lake which would have sluice gates and be periodically dredged to prevent the growth of aquatic plants." The dike was to be riprapped on both sides, and "the level of the top of this was to be such that a flood, like that of 1877, would not pass over it." This dike was to be 2,500 feet long and would enclose 173 acres of Potomac River flats. Out of this plan came the Tidal Basin, which was finally constructed in the 1880s by the Corps of Engineers at almost twice the price of the 1878 plan.[23] Flood control in both the Potomac and Anacostia did not begin to evolve until relatively recently. Congress authorized a levee for the Bladensburg area in 1949, but only in 1952 did construction of the Anacostia dike truly begin. Even then flood control amounted to a series of scattered quick-fix solutions in response to unique events.[24]

The National Capital Park and Planning Commission used creative landscaping to build flood control dikes in the 1930s that looked nothing like levees to protect the Lincoln Memorial from periodic inundation. That was no help to the people of Bladensburg, though. In 1942,

Washington was again caught flat-footed when a major storm with a swirling, surging tide of brown, murky water arrived that October. Many flood victims in the watershed had to be given emergency housing. Bladensburg flooded, and war-workers commuting to the District foundered in a sea of mud and debris. Bus routes between Washington and Baltimore were closed, and B&O officials worried that the flooding would overwhelm their trains stationed at Hyattsville and Riverdale. The swollen currents reached fifteen miles an hour and overwhelmed Haines Point. The Anacostia's torrents caused sewage back-ups on Half Street, SW, and Gallinger Hospital in Anacostia was flooded. In all, though, there was less damage than in previous floods. The reason, according to District Sanitary Engineer John B. Gordon, was that the city closed off its trunk and interceptor sewers and allowed storm water to flow down through the main drain without additional sewage burdens.[25]

The *Washington Daily News* had long asked city and state authorities when Bladensburg's Job-like sufferings from floodwaters would be put to rest. The *Post* added that floods like this had "wrought more interruption and damage to the war-effort in this part of the country than a group of saboteurs could have caused in a comparable period."[26]

Floods increasingly became a political issue. Citizens who regularly bore the brunt of the water damage saw their political leaders spending tax dollars on everything but well-orchestrated flood control measures. Communities in Sligo Creek and Berwyn Heights, Colmar Manor, and Bladensburg continued to suffer from periodic high water. The issue was compounded by the fact that flooding in the Potomac and Anacostia watersheds was exacerbated by storm-generated flood tides. When flooding in the watershed was in congruence with a high flood tide rolling up the Potomac, the stage was set for chaos and destruction.

After Hurricane Hazel dumped heavy rains on the Potomac in 1954, causing severe flooding and extensive damage, Maryland and the District finally appropriated major funds for flood abatement. But a dozen years later, in September 1966, Mayor William Gullett of College Park was begging the Army Corps of Engineers and the Washington Suburban Sanitary Commission for more dikes or levees to protect the local communities. Three years passed with nothing done, and Washington newspapers once more carried photographs of half-submerged cars at Peace Cross and at Sligo Creek near Takoma Park. As late as 1968 the *Washington Post* reported that flooding in the District had turned Resurrection City, the camp of the Poor People's Crusade, into a muddy morass.[27] Rain-soaked Washington commuters walking from their offices to higher ground with their shoes in hand were a common sight in spring and fall. Although irritated and inconvenienced, few made the environmental connection: Aggravating the floods were the acres of apartments, parking lots, and new houses—their homes—that had replaced the forest and natural cover that once absorbed the floodwaters.

People who lived in the vicinity of Peace Cross, Colmar Manor, Hyattsville, or Riverdale knew one salient fact. After a heavy rain the Anacostia could rise eighteen inches in an hour. Piney Branch Creek in Tacoma Park regularly flooded four times a year as this area saw an increase of subdivisions in places that were flood-prone. Storm sewers and concrete culverts eventually helped to alleviate flooding in Piney Branch, but they just moved the water down the pipe into some other community. Flood control and sewerage construction proved unable to keep pace with a rapidly expanding metropolis, owing to the lack of adequate appropriations from federal, state, and local agencies.

Until recently the environmental effects of flooding were rarely examined. Today scientists have found that flooding creates and nurtures far more diverse and complex habitats than exist when floodwaters are controlled thorough levees and channeling with concrete sluices. Plants can colonize new areas in stream fields when old vegetation is swept away and help to create a more complex mosaic of habitats than had existed before the flood. But in the 1950s policy planners gave little thought to maintaining flood plains, riparian buffers, and associated wetlands. Concrete was king, and the suburbs were growing exponentially in Maryland.

Additional metropolitan development into the 1970s increased the number of paved roads, parking lots, and shopping centers. This in turn increased the flow of storm water in the absence of suitable drainage. Urban development resulted in greater sediment yields and storm water overflows containing high levels of manufactured debris that eroded stream banks and contributed to the destabilization of the watershed.[28]

A change for the better came in 1972 with the completion of the Anacostia River Flood Control and Navigation Project. Levees to protect Bladensburg and surrounding communities were finally completed. When the Army Corps of Engineers finished the project, the watershed had 28,000 feet of levees, 14,400 feet of improved channels, many lined with concrete, and four sewage-pumping stations.[29] The fully contoured dike was so large that one could only see the tops of the houses behind it. The engineers dredged the river to a depth of eight feet in its channel to create better flow.

After this massive construction, the philosophy of the Corps of Engineers showed signs of growing with the times. Since the Civil War, the corps had been something of a blunt instrument on the Anacostia River, responding to congressional imperatives. Engineers from Col. Peter Haines onward had argued that engineering the river was a waste of taxpayers' money. In the late 1970s, the corps began to give "serious attention to the environmental implications of its activities" and examine new approaches to flood control that emphasized community education about land and flood plain usage. Now when it came to flood control, the corps searched for "non-structural solutions as alternatives to structural measures."[30]

The Washington Suburban Sanitary Commission became the operating agency for flood control along the upper Anacostia. New projects like the Bladensburg recreational marina south of Peace Cross were designed to give a new image to a much-troubled river. Progress was coming to the Anacostia at last, boasted the *Washington Star*. "Instead of eroded banks and broken down docks, National Capital Parks will seek to develop grassy stretches and modern marinas."[31]

The Automobile in the Watershed

At the center of the Anacostia's troubles lay demographic change. For example, at the time the National Arboretum was being planned in the 1920s the combined population of Montgomery and Prince George's Counties was a little over 100,000. By 1960 that number had ballooned to more than 700,000 residents, whose water and sewage use would continue to undermine the ecology of the Anacostia watershed. The Beltsville Agricultural Research Center, the growth of the University of Maryland and development of the Goddard Space Flight Center in 1958 all helped to create a corridor of growth until nearly half of Prince George's County (181,946) was living in some part of the Anacostia watershed. New transportation routes like the Baltimore-Washington Parkway (1954) and Kenilworth Avenue (1957) ran parallel to Route 1 and facilitated a major growth spurt in suburbanization.

The automobile was the biggest environmental issue in the Anacostia watershed in the 1950s and 1960s. Although many praised the way it allowed District workers the opportunity to live in suburbs increasingly distant from the capital's urban core, others saw the automobile as a device that would destroy Washington. The National Capital Planning Commission began to focus on ways to control suburban growth. In its comprehensive plan of 1952, the commission sought to reverse the outward-bound move to the suburbs by stimulating housing and retail efforts to revitalize the central city. Washington in 1960 was so eaten up by automobile traffic and parking, the commission argued, that without a region-wide system of mass transit automobile thoroughfares by 1980 would have to include expressways "with capacities from four to twenty-six lanes." The automobile, indeed, seemed poised to bring environmental disaster to the nation's capital, not just with traffic but also with the attendant chemical pollution that thousands of cars everyday give off through their exhaust systems.

Washington was soon the most automobile-oriented city in the country, having outdistanced even Los Angeles, according to one postwar study. "The city had one car registered for every three residents, the highest figure in the nation. . . . A hundred thousand automobile commuters severely strained Washington's slowly expanding highway system."[32] By 1976 automobile ownership in the Washington metro area had increased to one car for every two people. The penetration of Washington's inner core by roads like the Southwest Freeway and Route 395 exacerbated pollution for those who remained there. In the 1950s and 1960s builders in Washington bulldozed one fragile neighborhood after another for superhighways that critics said were "white men's highways through black men's bedrooms."

In retrospect one can trace the Anacostia's automotive woes to congressional authorization of the George Washington Memorial Parkway, which was constructed along the Potomac River in 1932. That established a precedent for building auto corridors through river valley systems much as railroads had done decades earlier. By the end of World War II, Washington's streetcar system began to falter in the congested traffic.

Despite initial reservations, the comprehensive plan of 1950 developed by the National Capital Park and Planning Commission gave special emphasis to highways. Specifically the NCPPC advocated the construction of ring expressways or "beltways" around Washington that would allow traffic to flow around the capital without disrupting city neighborhoods. Only one beltway was developed, and it was put into operation in 1964. Other freeway plans ran into determined community opposition in the 1960s, especially those scheduled to bisect affluent or historic white communities like Glover Park and Takoma Park. The latter community put up fierce grass roots resistance because the route recommended by the Maryland State Highway Commission would slice a freeway through some of their oldest and architecturally significant neighborhoods. This victory kept one expressway out of the Anacostia watershed, but it set no precedent. Controversy over highway and expressway construction in the 1960s demonstrated that wealthy highway protestors with connections in the federal government, and those with effective protest organizations, could force transportation policy away from the inflexible insistence on urban freeways—in their neighborhoods.[33] The Southwest Freeway, on the other hand, running along the old and now destroyed Southwest quadrant, was testimony to the fact that urban renewal may have been expressly initiated to make roads and parking lots for commuters rather than giving residents an alternative to slum housing. The Anacostia Freeway, constructed along the east side of the river through public lands, bisected a valuable green space and the surrounding African American community with a barrier of asphalt and concrete. These corridors were operational by 1972 and part of the regional transportation grid.

The ceaseless noise and fumes caused by streams of vehicle traffic along the Anacostia River created a plethora of toxins, ranging from mercury to carbon dioxide. Disposal of oil, transmission fluid, battery acids, and other auto excretions caused further environmental damage. In the poorer areas of Anacostia, the watershed became the dumping ground for junked cars and auto tires. Oil slicks from thousands of drained crankcases contaminated the shoreline and harmed wildlife.[34]

Because of the urban nature of the watershed and the long history of pollution in the region, the U.S. Geological Survey in a recent study speculated that the ground water of the lower Anacostia tidal watershed was "contaminated."[35] The agency did not discuss what kind of impact this contamination would have on white and black neighborhoods there.

CHAPTER TEN

The View from River Terrace

"Anacostia is a community of people of color who happen to live on the wrong side of the river. They get unequal protection. If Georgetown whites lived at River terrace they would be raising hell."
— George Gurley

I n the 1970s and early 1980s, environmental justice, the idea of protecting specific classes and racial groups from the depredations of polluters, did not find much support among mainstream ecologists and environmentalists. According to environmental researchers George Middendorf and Bruce Grant, ecologists especially seemed to shy away from environmental justice issues affecting black people in urban areas.[1] Many ecologists felt the idea was too unscientific to warrant their serious consideration. African Americans, on the other hand, saw the concept of environmental justice as a "new civil rights battleground." Most of the hazardous waste dumped in the American South, argued activists like Dr. Robert D. Bullard, ended up in the black communities.[2]

Air quality for blacks became another ongoing challenge. A 1999 Clean Air Task Force study, "Out of Breath," discovered that "excessive ozone pollution" contributed to 130,000 asthma attacks in Washington, D.C.[3] Blacks in the nation's capital lived along massive commuter highways with heavy air pollution. These freeways, black critics pointed out, had been bulldozed through black communities in the capital during the 1960s. Getting sick from the environment, whether from auto

179

pollution, trash dumps, or toxins in the Anacostia River, also placed a special burden on blacks who could not afford medical insurance.

The African American community was also caught up in the ongoing social science argument about the nature and scope of environmental justice. Did poor black communities really bear the brunt of pollution? In 1997, Vicki Been and Francis Gupta tested this question and found on the basis of their research "no significant evidence" that a greater percentage of African Americans in a tract of land increased the likelihood that the tract would be selected to "host" an environmentally harmful industry or facility. The research did suggest, though, that high levels of toxic pollution were usually to be found in blue-collar working-class areas and lower-middle-income communities.[4]

Although it is true that Anacostia became polluted while it was still a white working-class area, it is also true that in the 1970s and 1980s its toxic problems affected the local black population to a greater degree than the capital's white population. As Ryan Holifield has pointed out, scholars have spent an inordinate amount of time arguing over the precise definitions of *environmental justice*, and *environmental racism*. Environmental definitions are popular in urban scholarship, but they mislead, he argues. "Environmental justice and environmental racism have never been simple descriptive terms, and we must stop treating them as though they ever will be." A better approach, he concludes, would be to "address the diversity of issues that grassroots activists and federal agencies include with their interpretation of environmental justice."[5]

Certainly issues of race and class entered the public thinking in Washington, D.C. Many urban middle-class whites believed that east of the Anacostia River was a dark and forbidding place—a source of drugs and crime that helped to make the city the murder capital of the nation. Visitors to Anacostia well into the twenty-first century saw everywhere the signs of decline and hopelessness. Anacostia, wrote Linda Goldstein in *Legal Times*, was "A Tale of Two Cities."[6] Unlike posh Georgetown and Connecticut Avenue, Anacostia had gutted storefronts and unemployed men and women standing listlessly on street corners. The smell of urine and trash-strewn streets conveyed a sense of economic and psychological hopelessness. The riots of 1968 and the violence in the housing projects scared a lot of whites out of Anacostia, observed Dorn McGrath, a professor of urban planning at George Washington University, "and many businesses followed their customers who were afraid to come here anymore."[7] So stereotyped as a violent depressed area was Anacostia, reflected resident Carl Cole, that few outsiders could see the good parts—well-tended houses on leafy streets often overlooking a beautiful riverfront. "There was a park with rolling meadows, ball fields, a golf course and recreational facilities that in many respects was Anacostia's own private green space."[8]

In the 1970s and 1980s most of the environmental concern for the Anacostia River originated in Washington's black community. Blacks complained that coliform bacteria in the river was climbing to unhealthy levels in the 1970s and argued that sewage pollution was highest along the river banks where people were most likely to come into contact with the water. Community activists like Joseph Glover, Kevin Chavous, Frazer Walton, and George Gurley worried about toxins in the river. They knew why the Anacostia and its many problems were forgotten by white environmentalists—primarily, it flowed through low-income or poverty-stricken neighborhoods. African Americans were convinced that disparate enforcement of environmental policies contributed to Anacostia's environmental decline, residential segregation, and low property values. In short, said Gurley, "Georgetown on the Potomac boomed while Anacostia communities suffered."[9] To activists this was far from being just a race issue. They noted that there were plenty of places in the country where polluted waterways affected whites and other non-black racial groups, but in Washington it seemed that all the environmental problems flowed through the city's struggling black communities. In the latter part of the twentieth century, race and ecology were clearly linked in Anacostia.

Rivers often flow in strange courses through contemporary metro-politan life, and sewage and toxins have never let Washington health officials dismiss the Anacostia. Further, the District's dependence on the Potomac for its drinking water forced it to join interstate compacts to protect that river. Strangely, few people made the connection that the Anacostia ultimately flowed into the Potomac. While the Potomac was sometimes called "the river of presidents," journalists referred to the Anacostia as "the forgotten river."

But the Anacostia had one man who made the river a metaphor of the black struggle—Mayor Marion Barry. In Ward Eight, the hilly neighborhood that was Barry's center of power, a population 80 per-cent black eked out life in the 1980s on a median household income of $16,000 that was half that of whites and well below the national average of $19,758 for blacks.[10] After a meteoric rise to power as a civil rights leader with the Student Non-Violent Coordinating Committee (SNCC) and election to the city council, Barry captured the mayor's of-fice for four terms and dominated Washington's political scene for more than twenty-five years. As councilman and mayor, Barry saw the Ana-costia River as the great social divide in Washington. He argued that those living east of the river were cast off from the American Dream and condemned to violence, unemployment, poor housing, and a de-graded environment. Barry gave voters a short course in environmental and racial geography with his constant references to "Anacostia." While mayor, he sparked commercial and tourist interest in the waterfront by having the District sponsor an annual river fest on the Southwest wharf to get people from various strata of society to come down to the water and see the potential of the Washington riverfronts.[11]

In Washington, African American resistance to environmental threats was a grassroots phenomenon. Blacks in the 1970s had few na-tional advocacy groups to rely upon. With growing hostility, blacks in Anacostia viewed power plants and trash dumps and polluted waters as unfair, inequitable, and discriminatory.

Background: Down in the Dumps

In 1942, Washington ran out of places to dump its garbage and began to fill in a large marsh opposite the National Arboretum. This dump was one of three major disposal sites (one was below South Capitol Street and one was located on Oxon Cove outside the Anacostia watershed). For a while the city used refuse as landfill to cover holes in parks and public grounds, but by 1961 it was overwhelmed with trash. The city created a million tons a year of non-burnable garbage that created health problems in the Kenilworth Gardens area.[12] In addition to building an incinerator for burnable waste, municipal authorities also routinely burned trash in large "dump" piles on the ground.

The Kenilworth Dump had been a pollution issue for a long time. In 1963, Bruce E. Hogarth, head of the District health department's air pollution section, deplored open burning of trash at the dump as a "psychological insult" that held back other efforts to combat pollution.[13] Little mention was made of its presenting a biohazard to the people living nearby. Making matters worse were construction firms who also burned their refuse at the landfill site.[14]

During the winter of 1968 children from Grant Street routinely played among the dump fires, lighting sticks from the burning garbage. According to the *Washington Post*, on Thursday, February 15, Kelvin Tyrone Mock, age seven, was playing with two teenage boys in the dump not far from a trash fire. "Suddenly the wind shifted and the boys were surrounded by flames leaping 10 to 20 feet in the air. They ran, but Kelvin fell and his clothes caught fire." By the time firemen responded to his mother's anguished phone call, Kelvin Tyrone Mock had perished in the flames, and all the firemen could do was remove his charred body.[15] Officials of the Greater Washington Citizens for Clean Air expressed condolences over the boy's death and urged city authorities to end immediately the open-air burning at the dump. Meanwhile, outraged mothers in the neighborhood took the law into their own hands and blockaded the road to prevent trucks from adding their trash to the inferno that had consumed the life of a small child on the banks of the Anacostia.[16]

Soon afterward, the dump closed. Most of the city refuse was sent to the Oxon Cove Dump until 1972, when Washington began sending trash to the huge Lorton Prison complex in Fairfax County, Virginia. To celebrate the closure of the Kenilworth Dump, Mayor Walter Washington, Norman E. Jackson, head of the Department of Sanitary Engineering, and other dignitaries hosted the first picnic ever held at a Washington dump. As the bulldozers moved tons of earth to begin covering the smelly landfill, the mayor and his colleagues lunched on fried chicken, potato salad, and jelly rolls.[17] Unmentioned during this celebration was that for years, six days a week, heavy trucks had brought more than nine hundred tons of trash, from bottles to bedsprings, into the heart of the capital's African American community.

Today the old Kenilworth Dump is a grassy recreational area with football fields. In 1972 the city thought the newly christened "Kenilworth Park" would also be a place where area residents could have gardens, raise vegetables, and grow flowers.[18] But beneath the park's long grassy knoll were two large underground domes of methane gas produced by buried decomposing garbage.* Although some scientists speculated that the gas could be used to heat public buildings, as had been done at the Blue Plains waste facility since 1938, Kenilworth residents viewed the park less rosily, uneasy as they were about the prospect of "swamp gas" in their neighborhood.[19]

In April 1970 the District began dumping garbage at a federally owned landfill in Prince George's County. Even though the city received permission from the National Park Service and the Maryland

---

* As of 2005 the old Kenilworth Dump still had large underground pockets of methane. Nor were the suburbs free from garbage pollution. What were once dumps in Prince George's County are now recreation fields. The Colmar Manor Ball Fields, for example, near Bladensburg in Prince George's County, were large garbage dumps in the 1960s, and the waste from these covered-over landfills was still leaching into the Anacostia in the 1980s.

Health Department to use the site, Maryland Senator Joseph Tydings and other political figures incited suburban resistance to the practice. Tydings claimed that the District of Columbia demonstrated "an incredible insensitivity" by dumping trash on a site across the county line. Prince George's County commissioners sought to void the city's dump permit by arguing that the District had violated a 1967 county law prohibiting garbage trucks from crossing Prince George's border without the specific permission of the county commissioners.[20]

Illegal dumping along the Anacostia and its environs in the Northeast and Southeast sections also plagued the city. Leroy Brown, Chief of Maintenance for National Capital Parks–East, estimated that as late as the year 2000, the Park Service spent $350,000 annually removing illegally dumped debris from parkland in the eastern portion of the capital. Enough unauthorized trash came into an area adjacent to Kenilworth Park that residents dubbed it "Mystery Mountain." (How the trash came to be in a park supposedly closed to dumping was a "mystery.") Contractors illegally dumped construction dirt and debris into Kingman Lake and on a portion of the Langston Golf Club course. Much of the Langston Club itself is a landfill of dredged, polluted river spoil. The buried waste leached into the Anacostia from the tenth to the fourteenth holes. Hazardous waste and illegal dumping alarmed District of Columbia delegate to Congress Walter E. Fauntroy. In response to a growing chorus of national and local black complaint, Fauntroy in 1983 initiated the U.S. General Accounting Office (GAO) study of hazardous waste and landfill siting in the region.[21] For Robert Bullard and other black environmentalists, people in communities like Anacostia had to reclaim "the basic right of all Americans—the right to live and work in a healthy environment."[22]

Tied to the Fate of the River

Grass roots activists like George Gurley and Councilman Kevin Chavous in 1990 successfully organized opposition to a proposal by the

Potomac Electric Power Company to construct two combustion turbines across Benning Road from their power plant, which would have created significant air pollution for local residents. This incident was all part of what black environmentalists in Washington pointed to as land misuse and public apathy over the pollution of the Anacostia. Blacks identified the Washington Navy Yard, the Capitol Power Plant, and the Pepco Benning Road electric plant as major sources of air pollution in the city's black wards.[23]

Black people living along the Anacostia were acutely aware that their socioeconomic situation was tied to the fate of the river. A cleaner river, they believed, would lead to improvement of their community. Its stench made the river a constant source of community unhappiness. "Sometimes," said one Anacostia resident, "there's a smell all over Southeast, like dead bodies or something." Many participants expressed "feelings of sadness and frustration" about the river's condition, and most of those interviewed regarded the river as more of a barrier to civic improvement than an environmental asset.[24] In places like River Terrace and Barry Farm, people were long aware of the human health risks of consuming fish caught in the Anacostia.[25] Residents also complained that Anacostia Park, a facility presided over by the National Park Service and the major park area east of the river, offered few employment opportunities to people of color.[26]

Brett Williams, a professor at American University who studied the Anacostia, wrote in detail of the environmental dangers from all the detritus of the automobile culture facing people on the east side: "Exhaust fumes poison its neighbors, who suffer alarming rates of blood lead contamination and asthma. Used motor oil, tires, and metal parts; antifreeze containing lead, benzene, cadmium, chromium, copper, mercury, and zinc, sulfuric and lead acid batteries, oil and transmission filters" were all part of the Anacostia environment.[27] Today, adds Norris McDonald, a child suffering from asthma in the Anacostia can be exposed to "multiple sources of pollution"—fumes from power plants, vehicle exhaust from neighboring highways, and "living next to abandoned mass-burn incinerator ash."[28]

Residents in River Terrace, a black community of apartments and single family dwellings literally on the banks of the Anacostia, held meetings to dramatize their concern about the rates of asthma, chronic bronchitis, lung disease, and cancer in their community. Leaders like George Gurley believed these ailments were related to exposure to air pollutants from the local power plant and other nearby facilities. Gurley, a retired air force sergeant, first became interested in the health problems of River Terrace in 1985. "Back then," he recalled, "Pepco was burning coal and waste fuel and people were complaining of coughs and asthma from the smoke that was released at night from the plant. We fought against Pepco's building additional generators at Benning Road because we knew that Washington would only get about 10 percent of the electricity generated and 95 percent of the pollution. We had to fight the money and the power with bad publicity. We made them withdraw the turbine project."[29]

Public health authorities investigated these complaints and found that while exposure to the air did little to affect healthy River Terrace residents, air pollutants did aggravate pre-existing respiratory diseases like asthma, bronchitis, and emphysema.[30] But Gurley argues, "We have to think of the cumulative effect on our health from power plants and other pollution on our lives. You just can't come in and take a test and say everything's okay." A 2000 study showed that more than three thousand new cases of cancer were reported in the District of Columbia each year, which translates into "one of the nation's highest prevalence rates for cancer."[31]

George Gurley believes that no community or river should be the dumping ground for other people's waste. What Gurley sees on the Anacostia is that the issues of race, poverty, and environment are clearly out in the open. "We can't ignore what is happening to our river and to our community. We need to get the level of pollution in Washington ratcheted down so that we don't get sick. Anacostia is a community of people of color who happen to live on the wrong side of the river. They get unequal protection." Environmental contention festers at River Terrace. A massive trash transfer site is located a short distance from where people live. "It's been there for years. In the summer its fumes are awful. Why do we have to smell it? What is that transfer site doing to our health?" "If Georgetown whites lived at River Terrace," Gurley concludes, "they would be raising hell."[32]

The Washington East Foundation, a citizens' group led by Deborah Jones and other community leaders, conducted an "environmental justice land tour" of the area. It was one in a series of events "to educate residents on environmental issues" and "lead to effective advocacy by the community for clean air, safe drinking water, vibrant waterways, and clean beautiful streets, parks, trees, and greenspace."[33]

The leadership of the EPA, the Department of the Interior and the Department of Transportation, all of which have a major impact on the life of the capital, was very slow to become involved with the Anacostia. Civil Rights Commissioner Mary Frances Berry complained that government agencies "lacked commitment to ensuring that low income communities and communities of color are treated fairly during the decision-making process" on environmental issues.[34] For example, argues Carl Cole, an Anacostia resident and community leader, it was not until 1985 that the District and the State of Maryland issued state and local advisories on fishing in the Anacostia River because the fish were contaminated with chlordane and PCBs. "This was some thirteen years after the passage of the federal Clean Water Act."[35]

In 1994, President William Jefferson Clinton issued Executive Order 12898, "Federal Action to Address Environmental Justice in Minority Populations and Low Income Populations," to insure that these populations were not subjected to "a disproportionately high level of environmental risk." The order was basically about distributive justice, specifically the distribution of environmental quality among different communities. It said little or nothing about the important issue of procedural justice, which refers to the access of citizens to decision-making processes that affect their environments. Furthermore, the Environmental Protection Agency did not apply the order to its day-to-day operations. In a report issued ten years later, the EPA admitted that it did not fully implement this executive order and "it has not developed a clear vision or a comprehensive strategic plan, and has not established values, goals expectations, and performance measurements."[36]

In its study of race and pollution in Washington, the African American Environmental Association, a grass roots organization that emerged during the pollution controversy, compiled a lengthy case of environmental injustices in the capital in general and in the Anacostia in particular.[37] The study cited city wards six, seven, and eight, which contained large, majority-black populations suffering from "serious pollution." According to the study, "Home Rule authority has had limited to non-existent impact on pollution sites, particularly federally owned toxic sites." A combination of air and water pollution made the Anacostia River area a "toxic soup." Washington's residents, daytime workers, and visitors "are consuming this broth on a daily basis."[38]

Environmental scientists since the 1970s have used the term "impaired water" to refer to the quality of the Anacostia's water and wildlife. But the logic could be extended to the people who ate the fish, suffered the stench, and lived on the riverbank. Black people too, George Gurley asserted, were becoming "impaired."

Toxic Soup

By far some of the most dangerous substances found over time in the Anacostia River are polychlorinated biphenyls. PCBs are a mixture of up to 209 chlorinated chemicals. Until banned by federal regulation for having adverse public health effects, PCBs were used as coolants and lubricants in transformers, capacitors, and other electrical equipment because they do not burn easily and are good insulators. PCBs are also found in old fluorescent lighting fixtures and in hydraulic oils. PCBs entered the air, water, and soil during their manufacture and through use and disposal at waste sites where incinerators released them into the air. Until 1977, waste from electric transformers and hydraulic oils leaked into the Anacostia River at utility plant sites and at the Washington Navy Yard. PCBs bonded with the sediment of the river bottom and entered the food chain through bottom-feeding fish.

A report prepared by the engineering and consulting firm CH2MHill in 1979 concluded that "the dramatic changes to the physical habitat and water chemistry of the rivers and streams in the District of Columbia leave no doubt that the biological integrity of the aquatic resources has been compromised." CH2MHill found the benthic macro invertebrate* communities in District streams to be "severely degraded."[39] The report also found a significant decline in fish species compared to historic levels. The Atlantic sturgeon and short nose sturgeon, once a mainstay of Anacostia's fishermen, had completely disappeared from the river. The large mouth bass was the only game fish found in substantial numbers much of the year, and its populations had declined as well. On the other hand, channel catfish, an introduced species, increased in abundance in the 1970s but with elevated levels of PCBs and chlordane.[40] According to one study, more than 50 percent of brown bullhead catfish caught in the river had liver tumors, and 37 percent had skin tumors. Both are linked to toxic polynuclear aromatic hydrocarbons (PAH), which found their way into the Anacostia as residue from the incomplete burning of fossil fuels, dyes, and pesticides. The chemicals also inhibit reproduction.[41]

Later reports by the Environmental Protection Agency documented "clear evidence that PCBs cause cancer in animals" and are a "probable human carcinogen." Pregnant women who had eaten PCB-contaminated fish gave birth to babies with low birth weight and "problems of motor skills and a decrease in short term memory" that lasted for sev-

---

*Benthic macro invertebrates like mayflies, stoneflies, and caddis flies hatch in water and are a link in the food web of streams.

eral years. "Studies in humans provide supportive evidence for the potential carcinogeniety and non-carcinogenic effects of PCBs," the EPA concluded. "The different health effects of PCBs may be interrelated, as alterations in one system may have significant implications for the regulatory systems of the body."[42]

Chlordane is another toxin found in dangerous amounts in Anacostia River sediment. It was manufactured in the United States between 1948 and 1988 under the trade names of Octachlor and Velsicol, among others. Until 1983 chlordane was used as a pesticide on crops and on home lawns and gardens. In the District chlordane was widely used to control termites. Chlordane sticks strongly to soil particles, does not dissolve easily in water, and builds up in the tissues of fish and birds. It enters the human body in a way similar to PCBs, through the consumption of contaminated fish. Men who have skin contact with chlordane can develop liver jaundice, experience stomach cramps and diarrhea, and have nervous tremors in their arms, hands, and legs. Although the International Agency for Research on Cancer has determined that chlordane is not classified as a carcinogen in humans, it has found that when mice were fed low levels of chlordane in food, they developed liver cancer.[43]

Mercury, a toxic metal that can lead to neurological damage in children and present other dangers to childbearing women, is also found in the Anacostia. Mercury was not widely publicized as a river toxin until the 1980s. In 1991 fish and eel samples taken from the Anacostia revealed not only high levels of PCBs and chlordane, but mercury in quantities sufficient to exceed acceptable risk levels for the general population. Mercury was also discovered in high concentrations in bass filets, meriting a caution about eating predator fish from the top of the Anacostia's food chain. An EPA-funded study concluded that "concentrations of chemical residues in fish from the Anacostia and Potomac Rivers could pose a public health hazard for sport fishermen."[44]

Recently, Paige Doelling Brown, a doctoral student at George Mason University, performed an extensive sampling of the PCB-ridden bottom of the Anacostia River. She found that sediment concentrations of PCBs were high enough to call for the implementation of sediment reductions or bottom capping to reduce fish contamination.[45] Another researcher, Dr. Harriet Phelps, a scientist at the University of the District of Columbia, experimented with the placement of freshwater clams. At Hickey Run, a tributary of the Anacostia before it enters the National Arboretum, the clams only had a 6 percent chance of survival. Clams placed in the Northeastern Branch of the Anacostia had the highest concentrations of pesticides and chlordane. Other fish and invertebrates were similarly impaired. Phelps's research revealed that parts of the watershed were having great difficulty cleansing themselves by stream flows because toxins were present in the tributaries' sediment. The Bladensburg Waterfront Park at the upper end of the tidal Anacostia, Beaverdam Creek, and the areas near the Washington Gas Light Company and the navy yard also had significant levels of toxins. In her report, Dr. Phelps wrote, "significant PAH (polynuclear aromatic hydrocarbons) contamination (from coal smoke, soot, and auto exhaust) appeared widespread in the Anacostia estuary."[46] In short, in certain areas like the "hot spot" near the Washington Navy Yard, the Anacostia was too toxic for humans and fish.[47]

Anyone counting toxins in the Anacostia also has to add those that stemmed from nineteenth-century industries. When the Washington Gas Works was established before the Civil War, it used coal to make gas for home and industrial illumination. The company dumped the coal tar waste into pits where, over time, it leached into the river to produce coal tar slicks on the surface. At places the odor of petroleum tars, tuline, benzene, and other toxic substances was strong enough to cause nausea.

African Americans residing along the polluted riverbanks in the 1980s were, therefore, in many respects fishing for trouble.

Swimming in Sewage

For at least seventy years, bacteria and pathogens have limited commercial use of the river and reduced its potential for recreation. Since scientists first began testing for it in the 1940s, they have found exceptionally high levels of fecal coliform, most of it coming from animal and human waste entering the river in storm water runoff and through dysfunctional or broken sewer lines. Although only 14 percent of the effluent contains human pathogens, the human content is decidedly the more dangerous. If fecal coliform counts are high (over 200 coliforms/100ml of water sample), a person swimming or wading in the river has an excellent chance of getting sick from swallowing the water or by introducing pathogens through the ears or nose or cuts in the skin. Hepatitis A is usually transmitted through fecal matter, and though infection rates in the Anacostia have been low, a small number of people, especially those with liver disorders, can develop serious complications. Because the risk of hepatitis depends on the sanitary conditions of a specific area, parents whose homes are near the Anacostia have cautioned their children over the years to stay away from the river.

Cholera, which greatly afflicted District residents in the nineteenth century, has not been eradicated. It can easily return to the Anacostia if nutrient levels from organic pollution such as human feces are high.[48] In wet weather sewage bacteria climb to unhealthy levels that remain high for several days after the rain stops. In 1980, University of Maryland microbiologists found that professional scuba divers working on the river faced potential cholera-like infections from pathogens in the water.[49]

In recent years outbreaks of waterborne disease have been on the rise in the United States. According to Nancy Stoner, director of the Clean Water Project for the Natural Resources Defense Council, "waterborne diseases can threaten the lives of seniors, young children, cancer patients and others with impaired immune systems." Washington for years under-invested in its sewer infrastructure. Since most people believed that sewers underground were working satisfactorily, little was done until the 1970s, when the media began to discuss sewer leaks and toxic waste issues.[50]

The issue of sewage in the Anacostia is not a single problem but a combination of many. The river has never been able to flush out sewage and toxins the way some bodies of water can. Unlike the steep-sloped Potomac, two-thirds of the Anacostia is on flat land, and there is nothing to aid the flow save the tides washing in and out of the bay. The tides, though, are in no hurry, and while other rivers might accomplish it in a matter of days, flushing the Anacostia can take up to three weeks. When marshes, wetlands, and forests were abundant enough to act as natural water filters, the Anacostia could cleanse itself before reaching the Potomac. But after the Army Corps of Engineers' efforts at reshaping the river, and the immense growth of housing and commercial development in the watershed, the conditions that once made for clean water, spawning fish, and abundant bird life are no longer readily at hand.

By the end of the twentieth century, more than 80 percent of the Anacostia watershed was developed. Whereas formerly Washington had only the ills created by its own sewers and sewage overflows, in the last several decades it has had to deal with vast sewage and storm water overflows entering the watershed from the malls, highways, and residential communities of the surrounding Maryland suburbs. Making matters worse, Prince George's and Montgomery Counties are served by antiquated sewer systems that were built in the 1950s and 1960s and which, as mentioned earlier, parallel and cross the streambeds of the Anacostia's tributaries, leaking human waste into the watershed. The D.C. Water and Sewer Authority and the Anacostia Watershed Society's annual Water Quality Monitoring and Flagging Project have found that fecal coliform counts are higher upstream in the suburban tidal portion of the Anacostia than they are in the District. Storm water rushing off paved surfaces and broken sewage pipes flood the Anacostia with human waste long before it passes beneath the capital's bridges.[51]

Washington, in the late twentieth century, was not the only urban center whose rivers were awash in sewage. Similar conditions prevailed in Los Angeles, Milwaukee, Baltimore, Atlanta, and a host of other cities that over the years had seen growth overwhelm antiquated and dysfunctional public sewer systems. In terms of wastewater management, the problem, said John Hanlon, the Environmental Protection Agency's sewer expert, could be summed up in two words: "miserable infrastructure."[52] By 2004 the Environmental Protection Agency estimated that the volume of combined sewer overflows nationwide was around 850 billion gallons, and that did not account for the leaks in sewage lines in watershed tributaries.

Swimming in the Anacostia River in Washington has been off-limits for decades and the public is warned not to go near sewage outfalls or to eat bottom-feeding fish like catfish and carp taken from the river. When viewed from a national perspective, though, inadequate sewage management puts nearly 3.5 million Americans at risk for infection and serious illness every year. "Not only are urban rivers with sewage problems disgusting, and smelly," said Jim Connolly, executive director of the Anacostia Watershed Society, "they are a serious health problem because with raw sewage comes all kinds of bacteria and dangerous pathogens which can cause serious illness." Yet, as it approached the twenty-first century, the nation's capital lumbered into the future with a sewer system that had not been systematically updated since 1907. By the 1990s, the only appellation the Anacostia had was its listing as one of the top ten most endangered rivers in the United States.[53]

In the words of Brett Williams, "the river runs through us." In Washington, D.C., the capital of one of the most powerful nations on earth, a toxic river flowed languidly though the city, endangering the local African American population as well as the general community, and holding up the District of Columbia to opprobrium.

CHAPTER ELEVEN

Rescuing the Ruined River, 1980–2000

"The river needed healing and we had to get Nature back on course in the watershed."
— Robert Boone

By the end of the twentieth century, the story of the Anacostia River was being played on a much wider stage. Added to the interplay of race and urban development was a growing public interest in environmental responsibility and stewardship that gave environmental problems a new sense of urgency. With greater involvement by federal agencies like the Environmental Protection Agency and organizations like the Anacostia Watershed Society and Earth Justice, the river received a level of scrutiny and protection it never before had enjoyed.

Earth Day and After

On April 22, 1970, twenty-five million Americans joined around the country to demand a safer, cleaner, and healthier world. In Washington, it was a perfect spring day with sunshine, temperatures in the low sixties, blue skies, and light cottony clouds that served as a rich natural counterpoint to the capital monuments. Earth Day brought activists and worried citizens to the Mall to sing, meditate, and hear speeches from educators, scientists, and politicians whose concerns ranged from nuclear annihilation to the Vietnam War to dealing with pollution and toxic wastes.

Earth Day was also an intensely political occasion. Its rationale was to alert people to the activities of high-pollution industries and to agitate for the passage of federal laws to focus on the real-life issues—neighborhoods dissected by freeways, air fouled by auto exhaust, rivers filled with sewage and toxins, and factories without pollution controls. Earth Day and the resulting environmental agitation tapped a deep well of political progressivism. Jewish intellectuals referred to the spirit of the new movement as *Tikkun Olam*, "the repair of the world." In rapid succession Congress passed the Clean Air Act, the Clean Water Act, the Superfund legislation for toxic dumps, and the Endangered Species Act, and established the federal Environmental Protection Agency. Earth Day built upon earlier twentieth-century reform efforts that led to forest and soil conservation and the creation of our national park system. Most remarkable, Senator Gaylord Nelson later reflected, was that Earth Day had sprung up spontaneously from the grass roots.[1]

In 1965, local environmentalism had received a major boost when President Lyndon B. Johnson labeled the sewage- and toxin-ridden Potomac "a national disgrace" and ordered a massive clean-up of the waterway. Through the efforts of environmentalists acting in concert with the Potomac Basin Commission and the significant advocacy of well-connected figures in politics and Washington society, the Potomac began to recover from its poisonous ordeal. Real estate promoters snapped up waterfront property in Georgetown to build condominium-office-restaurant complexes. That was all to the good. Middle-class entrepreneurs and the wealthy did not want businesses or residences overlooking a sewage conduit. Yet from the outset environmentalism was a tangled skein of affluent individualism, anti-capitalist rhetoric, and spiritual devotion to preserving and protecting God's creation. While concerned with the good of the community, environmentalism contained a strong streak of middle-class "not in my back yard" complacency. Historian Roderick Nash remarked that the movement was "a full stomach phenomenon."[2] Clean water had become fashionable.

Environmentalism was also fueled in the 1960s and 1970s by organizations like the Audubon Society, the Sierra Club, and the Rockefeller Foundation, whose leadership and ample trust funds sponsored programs and organizations in accord with their own environmental interests. In the District of Columbia groups like the Izaak Walton League, Ducks Unlimited, American Forests, and the Pew Charitable Trust (a creation of the Sun Oil Company fortune) carried the environmental standard. Affluent Georgetown leaders Roger and Vicki Sant took an interest in Washington's urban environment and in rescuing the Anacostia through their foundation, the Summit Fund.

The Clean Water Act

The Clean Water Act of 1972 grew out of public concern about the condition of rivers and streams in America. During the 1960s scientists reported record fish kills in American rivers and lakes and fish contaminated with as much as nine times the limit for harmful pesticides like DDT and PCBs. Ecologists warned Americans in the 1960s that they could lose fifty to one hundred species of birds by the turn of the century because of toxic chemicals in waterways.[3] By the time the Clean Water Act passed into law, one-third of U.S. waters were in the EPA's words "characteristically polluted," that is in violation of federal water criteria. Significantly, Congress defined "clean water" in terms of ecosystem integrity, and the legislation required Americans to restore watersheds and other aquatic ecosystems before they became a significant public health risk. The Clean Water Act was predicated on the belief that citizens should be able to swim and fish in our lakes and rivers, and that no foreign materials should enter our waterways in "toxic amounts."[4]

In their recap of the Clean Water Act twenty years later, historian Robert Adler and his colleagues noted that it was an activist measure. The heart of the law was embodied in Section 301, which stated that no one has the right to use the nation's waters as a dumping ground for pollution. The law focused on a permit system for all point sources of pollution. Sewage discharges, especially, were required to have all water go through secondary treatment. Industrial discharges had "to meet minimum control levels defined by the EPA on the basis of what the 'best technology' could achieve."[5] The Clean Water Act of 1972 appeared to be tailor-made for the rescue of a benighted river like the Anacostia but for one detail. With all the energy employed in cleaning up the Potomac, the hubbub of fashionable environmentalism in Washington, and the euphoria over the Clean Water Act, the Anacostia was overlooked.

Putting the Problem into Focus

That was something of an oddity, because from Earth Day 1970 until the late 1980s the Anacostia was much in the news. In 1971 the D.C. Council prohibited water contact sports—swimming, fishing, and boating—in the Potomac, Rock Creek, and the Anacostia. Throughout the 1980s the city worried about increased sewage and toxic contamination resulting from urbanization of the watershed. The press routinely reported spills of oil and hazardous substances. By 1987 urban planners gloomily reported that 98 percent of the Anacostia's tidal wetlands and 75 percent of the river's freshwater wetlands had been destroyed. Information on the monumental environmental loss was readily at hand.[6]

Despite all this concern, saving the Anacostia River came rather late to the environmental reform agenda, which raises a difficult question. Why did it take so long for environmentalists and government agencies to rescue a river that by all accounts was in great jeopardy? A few tentative answers come to mind. For one thing, Washington never had an organized political community with effective representation on Capitol Hill. For another, Washington was often regarded as nothing more than an arena of protest over war, race, and social issues, precluding many congressmen from taking a larger, more sympathetic view of its problems. Unlike other cities where environmentalism took root,

Washington was also a transient community whose sense of place was never clear to the populations that moved in and out of the capital with the tides of presidential elections. Lastly, much of the city was black, poor and largely invisible to the wealthy or to political groups, lobbying organizations, and lawyer-led special interests. The Anacostia's rescue therefore had to await a local effort that was slow in coming. When that effort finally did emerge after 1987 in concert with the African American community, it was self-organized at the grass roots, dedicated, and articulate.

In the winter of 1987–88, Curtis Peterson, a wealthy Maryland contractor and developer, approached Robert Boone, a stream coordinator for the Interstate Commission on the Potomac River Basin, to discuss the possibility of forming an environmental organization to clean up the Anacostia. The environment, Peterson said, had been very good to him and his business over the years, and now, as he approached retirement, he became an environmentalist. Whether prompted by guilt, cynicism or eleventh hour moral fervor, Peterson decided to give back to that which had sustained him. Boone was tired of the Potomac Commission's bureaucracy and eager to form an organization that would speak critically about local environment issues and address the Herculean task of rescuing the polluted Anacostia. Calling itself the Anacostia Watershed Society, the fledging organization consisted of Boone's reformist energy and $60,000 in "seed money" from Curtis Peterson. For a long time the AWS was a one-desk operation in Peterson's office, and Robert Boone often reflected wryly that he was sitting in a developer's office while engaged in a program to save the watershed from developers.

Building a cadre of engaged citizens took time and effort. In the meantime, Boone's one-man army took aim at polluters who were most likely to be embarrassed by media exposure. Using pictures and scientific documentation, Boone exposed D.C. Metro for its violation of Maryland state sediment controls at the construction site of the Prince

George's Plaza Metro. He then went after the D.C. Metro Bus Maintenance Yard near the National Arboretum on Bladensburg Road, a facility whose underground oil tanks had, over time, leached thousands of
gallons of oil into the Anacostia. Boone told the public that unless the
leaching was stopped, oil on the water would make the river nothing
but a highway of "dead rainbows." Boone also publicized the fact that
the National Zoo was storing vast amounts of manure from its pens on
the banks of the Anacostia at the National Arboretum—manure that
added still more coliform bacteria to the river.

Working in concert with Hope Babcock at the Institute for Public
Representation at Georgetown University Law School, Boone combined bad publicity with the threat of lawsuits over violation of the
Federal Clean Water Act and other state and local statutes. Eventually the District spent $6 million to clean up the oil waste in the bus
yard, and the Arboretum planted an "Asia Valley" of bushes, shrubs, and
flowers in place of what was once an unsightly manure pile. Boone's
campaign captured the attention of the Morris and Gwendolyn Cafritz
Foundation, which gave him the financial support to begin recruiting
citizens and staff to the new environmental society.

Robert Boone paddled his kayak up the Anacostia after a career
that ranged from studying Eastern philosophy in India, to Woodstock
rock, to vegetarianism and teaching psychology at a New York university. Quick-witted and a stormy petrel when it came to polluters,
Boone dramatized the river's problems from 1989 to 1996. A south-
erner by birth with a deep love of his region, Boone also reached out to
black churches, giving the AWS a strong connection with Anacostia's
African American community.[7] Saving the river, Boone argued, transcended the color line. He vowed that the Anacostia Watershed Society
was not going to be some "wine and cheese" organization for pampered
city dwellers and suburbanites.

His early days on the Anacostia were rough, Boone recalled. "I had
to take three lawyers out to a business run by some pretty tough char-

acters who were dumping into Beverdam Creek all the waste from their automobile recycling operation." The company, Joseph Smith and Sons, Inc., was located in what Boone described as a pretty dysfunctional neighborhood, and the men who ran it left their junk everywhere, even depositing fuel tanks on the lawns of residents. They drained antifreeze, brake fluid, and oil onto the ground where it flowed into the stream when it rained and threw tires and auto parts into the river. Theirs was one of the worst industrial sites in the watershed, and to halt their pollution of the Anacostia's tributary, the AWS sued them. "These recycle guys broke a lot of laws and they got cited," Boone said.

Litigation, the AWS discovered, did not always bring about all the desired environmental results. Polluters like Joseph Smith were tough, politically well-connected, and wily, and there were times when Boone went out to the site in fear for his personal safety. It took four years to force a change in their practices. In the end the company built a storm water runoff pond and planted trees and other green buffers between their operations and the water. It also submitted to increased public inspection.

As Boone patrolled the bureaucratic halls in the District and suburbs touting his "Anacostia mission," officials did not quite know what to make of him. Sometimes he sounded like a 1960s tree-hugging hippie, at others like a southern preacher, and at still others like a seasoned ecologist. But regardless of his public image, Robert Boone stayed on message: Unless changes took place in our rivers, they would become lost habitat that could lead to extinction for the creatures that live in, or depend on, aquatic ecosystems. And man, he reminded everyone, was as endangered as any other species.

Besides confronting polluters, Boone and volunteers at the Anacostia Watershed Society organized efforts at restoration. "The river needed healing," he explained. "We had to get nature back on course in the watershed by getting back to basic stream ecology. This meant planting trees and vegetation on the banks and looking for areas . . . where we could restore some of the marshes that had once been so characteristic of the river. Trees and vegetation keep the water cool. The warmer the water gets, the less oxygen it carries. We vowed that we were going to plant buffers. We were going to reclaim wetlands and help to bring the Anacostia back."

That was a tall order in the late 1980s and 1990s. Despite the fact that Washington was home to more environmental groups than any other city in the United States, most of them were concerned about the environment in some other place. "They were on planes, living in their heads and too broadly focused to think of something as regionally specific as the Anacostia," Boone said. "These groups did not even get excited about the fact 1.2 billion gallons of raw sewage flowed into the river each year from sewage overflow systems and that none of the District's waters at that time were in compliance with the federal Clean Water Act!" During a heavy rain, members of Congress and Justices of the Supreme Court flushed their toilets into the Anacostia without giving it a second thought.[8]

While some in the local political community dismissed Robert Boone as "a crank," others were impressed by his dedication and single-minded effort to rescue the Anacostia. Bringing together citizens from all walks of life, the AWS pursued what many thought to be a radical agenda—to make it possible to once more safely swim and fish in the river, the minimum standard for a waterway under the Clean Water Act.

With publicity and a few victories the AWS membership soon swelled to 1,200, and it employed four full-time staff. Larry Silverman, an environmental lawyer, and Jim Connolly, a former teacher with organizational skills and a solid grasp of public policy, completed a leadership trio for rescuing the Anacostia. Through Silverman, the Anacostia Watershed Society came in contact with Earth Justice officials, attorneys, and environmental activists who were beginning to see the Anacostia as not just another polluted river. It was an important part of the nation's capital with a history that spoke to centuries of inequality and environmental degradation. Jim Connolly advocated programs to get school children and adults "out on the river" and see firsthand its beauty and recreational possibilities as well as its pollution.

Within a decade of its inception the AWS had filed lawsuits against polluters, helped more than twenty thousand volunteers plant some ten thousand trees, stenciled 820 storm drains with the words "Don't Dump—Anacostia River Drainage," involved 6,300 inner-city youths in canoeing and conservation work, and removed from the river almost three hundred tons of debris and an additional seven thousand tires. That record was by Washington standards astonishing.[9] The early work of the Anacostia Watershed Society helped to coalesce forces for environmental and social change that heretofore had been isolated or politically invisible.

The Anacostia and the Clean Water Act

By 1987 the federal Clean Water Act had been in force for nearly fifteen years. When first enacted, the country was facing water pollution of crisis proportions. Environmentalists saw the EPA failing in its mission to protect American waters at a time when 40 percent of the nation's rivers, lakes, and streams were polluted. In Cleveland the Cuyahoga River, which had been so loaded with toxic waste in 1969 that it had actually caught fire, was still a major threat. The District of Columbia regularly issued health advisories about the Anacostia, urging people to avoid contact with the water and to severely limit consumption of fish caught in it.

Congress found that the Environmental Protection Agency routinely delayed enforcing the law under the guise that polluting industries "needed flexibility." The agency was reluctant to get involved in protracted court cases with corporate and other polluters whose ample legal talent could frustrate the EPA bureaucracy indefinitely.

Despite some progress, many of the promises of the Clean Water

Act were unfulfilled, and in 1987 Congress reexamined the legislation. It did little to solve the problem of budgetary constraints on federal aid for wastewater treatment, but it did enact a number of amendments, most of which had to do with setting requirements for states to develop total daily maximum loads (TMDLs) in order to restore pollution-impaired waters. TDMLs refer to the amount of pollutants a body of water can receive without violating water quality standards. By defining pollution in an empirical framework, clean water legislation set the stage for legal battles between environmentalists and would-be polluters over how much pollution was tolerable.

When it came to implementing the Clean Water Act for the Anacostia River, the devil was in the details. Much of the pollution came from non-point sources through storm water runoff, and both Maryland and the District were hindered by a lack of financial and technological resources to deal with it. Furthermore, just as the enforcement of the Clean Water Act was beginning to register some successes in controlling toxins entering the river, the federal government in 1995 cut back on funding wastewater treatment. Not until 1999 did the Environmental Protection Agency propose regulations to clarify and strengthen rules that governed the Clean Water Act. This meant, observed Jim Connolly, that "for nearly twenty years the Anacostia watershed was pretty much on its own. Sure we had lots of meetings with EPA and other agencies but not much came out of them."[10]

Dishonorable Discharge

Robert Boone and his allies soon grew weary of waiting for salvation at the hands of government agencies and marshaled their resources for a fight in the courts. The first major adversary was the Washington Navy Yard, a major industrial polluter. Prior to the formation of the Anacostia Watershed Society there was "no voice speaking for the river," Boone recalls. "Maryland refused to have anything to do with the Anacostia, and treated it as a District problem, even though 82 percent of the Anacostia watershed was in the state boundary."[11] The District of Columbia was undergoing its own political and social stresses as a majority-black city struggling to achieve racial justice and political freedom while forced to depend upon Congress for much of its revenue. Black neighborhood groups had long protested against the Pepco Power Plant and the navy yard, but they had no ready advocate at city hall.

In the summer of 1995, Greenpeace, the activist environmental group, took sediment readings at the sewer outfalls of the navy yard and were hardly surprised to find in them large amounts of mercury, PCBs, and chlordane. A number of federal agencies, most notably the U.S. Department of the Interior, had long been aware of the problem but had done nothing with the information in their possession. Damon Whitehead, a law student, became interested in the Greenpeace findings. Through his mentor, Hope Babcock, a Georgetown University law professor, Whitehead filed a number of freedom of information requests to ascertain the extent of the navy yard's pollution. Greenpeace and the Anacostia Watershed Society positioned one of its own boats at a navy yard sewer. They placed a large sign in front of the pipe that read, "Dishonorable Discharge."

After much discussion, the AWS decided to file a suit against the Navy for violating the Clean Water Act. Earth Justice and two African American community groups, the Barry Farms Residents Association and the Kingman Park Civic Association, joined it. "The pollution caused by federal activities is on federal property, so it is only fair that the federal government step in and take responsibility for cleanup," argued Howard Fox of the Earth Justice legal defense fund.

The suit came just as the Navy received congressional approval and $200 million to convert the yard's old factories into office space and erect a new building and a five-level parking garage. Now those plans encountered foul weather. When in response to the suit the Navy undertook an extensive environmental study, it discovered a number of contaminated waste sites dating back to the yard's days as an armaments facility and containing PCBs, mercury, lead, mineral spirits, paint, batteries, spilled fuel, adhesives, and acids among other things.[12] The evidence simply confirmed the fact that for over a century the navy yard had considered the Anacostia as nothing more than a convenient repository for waste. Naturally the Navy was embarrassed to be revealed as a toxic polluter sued by a small and noisome band of environmental activists, but the problem was the river. "The pollution may start out at those sites, but it doesn't stay there," said Robert Boone of the AWS. "It has been leaking out through storm drains into the Anacostia where it has caused a conspicuous 'spike' of toxic pollutants adjacent to these sites."

In the midst of all this, the Naval District of Washington, which ran the yard, received a new commander, Rear Admiral Christopher E. Weaver. An environmental makeover, Weaver quickly realized, was essential before any modernization could take place. In meetings with Anacostia Watershed Society representatives, Weaver stated that the Navy would hereafter strive to be a source of solutions. The yard, Weaver told the media, offered the Navy the chance to be "a fulcrum—a point against which a lever is placed to get purchase—for change along Washington's waterfront and within the Navy itself."[13]

The Environmental Protection Agency took control of the suit against the sixty-six-acre installation and designated it a Superfund Site for toxins. According to Elizabeth Freese, environmental director for the Naval District of Washington, these were "historic issues that developed at a time when environmental regulations did not exist. EPA has acknowledged that and is working very clearly with us in that view." The Sierra Club and other organizations opposed designating the yard a Superfund Site because it would make room for a large number of "bureaucratic delays" in the cleanup. According to attorney Damon Whitehead: "From 1983 to 1997, the Navy hasn't done anything. Why give them eight to ten years to sit on their duffs and do nothing?"[14]

Navy and EPA officials immediately set to work to get the navy yard out of the unwelcome spotlight. Along "Admiral's Row," a group of twenty-one residences assigned to flag-rank officers, crews removed lead paint and landscaped the grounds. Admiral Weaver himself directed the effort, and the installation hummed with environmental improvement. Unused underground oil storage tanks were removed. Toxic soil was excavated to remove mercury. Weaver placed a high priority on renovating the yard's antiquated storm sewers, which fed toxin-laden storm water directly into the Anacostia. Almost six miles of sewer lines were examined by video camera and their contaminated sediment removed. The yard even experimented with rain gardens and other low impact storm water controls. The Navy offered job-training opportunities in environmental control to local youth and conducted bimonthly open house sessions with the Washington environmental community to convey news about the cleanup.

The Washington Navy Yard, once a major polluter, became a model for other agencies seeking to prevent toxins from entering the nation's waterways. Brent Blackwelder of Friends of the Earth, an organization active on behalf of the District's environment, saw this as a major development. "Powerful agencies like the Navy," he said, "need to lead the way in cleaning up their toxic pollution, so that the Anacostia can become the pride of the nation's capital instead of its dumping ground." Dorothea Farrell of the Barry Farm Residents Association said that "as the people who live closest to these facilities, with children and other residents currently at risk from the pollution there, we are pleased that the Navy and the GSA are beginning to see the need to be good neighbors."[15] Through determined litigation, EPA coordination, and the actions of a civic-minded and innovative admiral, the Washington Navy Yard was able by 2004 to wipe its "dishonorable discharge" off the books. Once adversaries, the Navy, the Anacostia Watershed Society, and Friends of the Earth created a strong partnership to save "the forgotten river." Issues first raised by African Americans in Anacostia were gaining acceptance and urgency in the wider community.

Earth Conservation Corps and the River

In 1992, Robert Nixon joined the crusade to help save the Anacostia and ended up saving the kids who lived nearby. A producer of environmental documentaries who made the motion picture about Dian Fossey entitled *Gorillas in the Mist*, Nixon was appalled by a film clip showing the garbage in the Anacostia River. He flew to Washington, won a $50,000 corporate grant, and immediately began to recruit and employ youths from public housing projects to pull old tires out of the river. "Here was a white guy racing around taking these young African American kids down to the creek to pull out old tires," recalls community activist, Brenda Richardson. "Nixon won over the kids by getting them excited about the project, offering them jobs, and simply staying put despite the mayhem around them. It was like he had a shroud of protection — like a disciple leading them to the waters." Nixon took over a nascent, financially troubled non-profit organization called Earth Conservation Corps. He and his volunteers shoveled tons of garbage, replanted the banks, and built a small riverwalk trail. He and his crew also successfully introduced bald eagles to a place where they had not nested since the 1940s.

In working with area children, Nixon learned that more than the river and its wildlife were at risk. These young men and women lived in neighborhoods where half of the city's two hundred murders were committed every year. Against this forbidding backdrop, Nixon used Earth Conservation Corps to get them off the mean streets. Working on the river gave them a chance to see hope and improvement in their lives. Nixon was straightforward. "Just because these kids come from serious poverty doesn't mean the river doesn't speak to them. Our model is very simple and very powerful: Let's pull on waders and go down to the stream." Nixon saw it as a way of revitalizing the local economy. In

Anacostia alone at any given time there were about 2,200 unemployed men and women between the ages of seventeen and twenty-five who could benefit by paid employment in his organization.

Since its inception Earth Conservation Corps has had a long waiting list of applicants. Nixon realizes that his environmental work can achieve much more than conservation. He has worked with crack addicts and those who were homeless and abused. One corpsman, Rodney Stotts, recalled that before he met Bob Nixon and the Earth Conservation corps he was selling drugs on the streets of Anacostia. The organization, Stotts admitted, "prevented me from ending up dead." Unfortunately not all of the Earth Conservation Corps workers went on to a better life. Since 1992 nine have fallen victim to street violence. One was raped and killed, another beaten to death with lead pipes. When Bob Nixon came to the river in 1992 he did not realize that young African Americans as well as eagles were an endangered species on the Anacostia.[16]

Up in the Anacostia Watershed

As environmentalists and ecologists took to the river in canoes and kayaks, they saw a river of discomforting contrasts.[17] Many tributaries showed no influence of human activity, while others reeked of sewage. Some streams were encased in concrete channels or enclosed in pipes. So heavily urbanized was the watershed that it surprised them to find that, despite heavy pressures from metropolitan development, the stream valleys and flood plains had been preserved by flood control legislation. In cooperation with the National Capital Planning Commission and various other state and county agencies, Maryland had been working since 1927 to set aside approximately 4,600 acres of stream valleys as park lands and open spaces in the Anacostia watershed.

Nevertheless, many of the natural channels were not very scenic. Stream banks were heavily eroded by storm water that hurtled in from parking lots, housing developments, and shopping malls. Portions of some were imprisoned in concrete trapezoids with uniformly wide channels, no meanders, and no vegetation. Farther downstream were grass-covered levees but no trees—engineers did not want to compromise the levees' structural integrity.

Sligo Creek was at once the most interesting and the most depressing of the tributaries. Where its lower reaches were not heavily channeled in concrete it had fallen victim to erosion, but its upper reaches had great recreational value. The Maryland Park and Planning Commission had designated this area as primary park land for ball fields, hikers, and nature lovers. Along Sligo Creek visitors found stark contrasts in the 1980s: attractive bird life and children on bikes; tires and shopping carts in the stream; and sewage surging out of manholes. The Northwest Branch flowed through some of the most densely wooded areas of the watershed, and parts of this well-shaded stream supported a wide variety of aquatic life. The upper reaches of Paint Branch Creek in eastern Montgomery County had excellent stream bank vegetation and silt-free habitat.[18] Maryland's Department of Natural Resources had introduced trout into the stream in 1937, and in 1984 this was the only self-sustaining trout population in the watershed.

At the same time, one of the most dismal streams in the watershed was Northeast Branch. Surrounded by several factory zones, the Beltsville Agricultural Research Center, the University of Maryland, and huge low-density residential communities, it was choked with algae and sediment.

Urbanization changed how water flowed in the watershed, what was present in the water, and how quickly or slowly water found its way to the river. The watershed had to accommodate greater flows in the aftermath of storms. Runoff sped across paved surfaces toward the river, with little time or opportunity to infiltrate ground water tables. That meant reduced flows during dry periods and lower ground water levels. Storm water "flashes" in the 1980s had the additional effect of scouring channels out of the streambeds, thereby greatly reducing animal habitat.

Sediment from the storm water and the eroded stream banks kept light
from underwater plants and clogged the gills of fish. Residents standing on the banks after a storm reported a host of unwelcome intruders
in the streams: bottles, cans, motor oil, grass trimmings, and a flood tide
of Styrofoam packing materials broken into myriad white pieces.

Managing storm water became a central issue for environmentalists in the 1980s, but the task was expensive, and District and state
agencies were reluctant to embark on expensive storm water retention
and debris catchment technologies. In 1988 the House Committee on
Public Works and Transportation commissioned the Army Corps of
Engineers to study the water resource problems of the watershed. By
this time the corps had been involved in one activity or another in the
Anacostia for 115 years, mostly with dredging work, navigational operations, and flood control. Between 1902 and 1940, it had channeled
the river and built sea walls on the portion of the Anacostia inside the
District. It had dumped spoil from the river channel on the banks and
filled in over a thousand acres of productive wetlands. In the 1950s it
had embarked on the last phase of engineered river stabilization and
flood control with construction of a levee at Bladensburg. By 1984 the
corps had destroyed some 2,600 acres of aquatic wetlands, 99,000 linear
feet of aquatic habitat, and 700 acres of bottom hardwood trees in the
forest buffer. Despite these losses, and one of the largest metropolitan
urbanization processes in the country, the watershed somehow endured.
The engineers reported back to Congress in 1990 that the watershed's
worst problems derived from "urbanization and past Corps of Engineer
activities." Such an admission does not come easily to a military organization, let alone one that had spent more than a century transforming
the American environment.[19]

By 1990 nearly 70 percent of the Anacostia watershed had been
developed. Residential subdivisions were the largest component of this
phenomenon. With more houses came still more roads, parking lots,
and other impervious surfaces, but no storm controls. The Anacostia

tributary system became ever more "flashy" after a rainfall. Add partially or entirely untreated sewage from the District's combined sewer overflow system and the unsurprising result was devastated aquatic life, diminished aesthetic quality, and reduced economic vitality and recreational potential. Combined sewers, a state-of-the-art technology in 1900, were designed to transport sanitary waste to the treatment plant, but in storms a century later the system quickly overloaded and dumped sewage directly into the river to prevent it from backing up in people's homes. The combined sewer had become a hopeless anachronism, and worse, a major health hazard.

Some notable public developments did take place that were generally salutary. In 1984 the State of Maryland and the District of Columbia addressed the fact that they had a troubled river system on their hands. Three years later the District, Maryland, and the governments of Prince George's and Montgomery Counties, joined in a six-point action plan to clean up the river. As in most such agreements, the signatories eyed one another warily and squabbled over how much money to put toward the river's restoration. Once the Army Corps of Engineers, the EPA, the National Park Service, and the National Capital Park and Planning Commission signed on though, restoring the Anacostia changed from a grand idea to a practical matter with measurable benchmarks of progress. Since the signing of the Anacostia Watershed Restoration Agreement, more than seven hundred restoration projects have been identified in the watershed, and $150 million, mostly federal dollars, has been expended. Most of the projects addressed runoff. Maryland and its counties worked with the Corps of Engineers and other agencies to stabilize stream banks and "retrofit" areas suffering from excessive storm water overflows.

Montgomery County worked to rehabilitate the Sligo Creek area and recreated wetlands. The county also established a special protection area on Upper Paint Branch Creek to protect environmentally sensitive brown trout residing there. Prince George's County over time developed a low impact development plan of swales and rain gardens to curb storm water runoffs in new developments. The basic issue facing the coalition in the 1990s, though, was that funds were tight and population was increasing throughout the watershed. Moreover, the problem of sewage made reconnecting citizens to the river a challenge.[20]

Saving the Streams, Saving the River

By 1990, Anacostia's watershed was home to nearly 805,000 human inhabitants, making it one of the most densely populated watersheds in the Chesapeake Bay basin. As we have seen earlier, its degradation has altered important forest and wetland habitats, altered natural drainage patterns and stream flow, and increased sedimentation. When environmentalists first began to consider improving conditions, they had to approach the problem of extremely dense metropolitan development. Impervious surfaces—roads, parking lots, and roof tops—had come to constitute 23 percent of the watershed. According to geologists, streams typically become degraded or impaired when impervious surfaces cover 10 percent of a watershed.

As in many such cases involving severe environmental issues, the first thing to occur was the creation of an Anacostia Watershed bureaucracy with advisory committees and workgroups. Thus the Anacostia in 1990 was well on its way to becoming one of the most closely studied rivers in the mid-Atlantic. Meanwhile, river advocates like Robert Boone demanded more action and greater funding.

While Boone, Jim Connolly, and an army of volunteers pulled tires and debris out of the river, a new kind of individual appeared on the Anacostia. Calling himself the "poop detective," Charles Hagedorn, a professor of microbiology at Virginia Polytechnic Institute, spent time in places well off the tourist map—in a tunnel under Benning Road, near sewer outfalls, and along river banks. With a methodology borrowed from forensics, Hagedorn sought to identify and quantify the kinds of fecal coliform coming into the river. He looked at the environment as a fecal source and was as much interested in geese as he was in humans because a goose produces as much fecal matter in twenty-four hours as a human being. In the Benning tunnel he found that wildlife was contributing its feces to the river, but, he said, this was wonderful, because "Wildlife has made a comeback." Back on the Anacostia, Hagedorn confirmed that the biggest single source of fecal contamination continued to be people, not wild animals living in the woods.[21] Hagedorn and scientists like him wanted to learn what conditions were bringing wildlife back to the Anacostia when it was merely in the first phase of its clean-up. The answers seemed more spiritual than empirical.

Landscaping to Save a Watershed

The Corps of Engineers decided in the late 1990s to change its approach and attempt to retrofit the Anacostia for low impact development. Over seven years the corps spent more than $17 million on the restoration of wetlands at Kenilworth Marsh, stream restoration, and storm water management. It no longer engineered the Anacostia but tried instead to find the best possible fit for its expertise and the kind of engineering that would save a good deal of what was left of the landscape. The corps tried to restore 2,600 acres of wetland lost since the end of World War II and to create clear streams by rebuilding stream beds and meander in accordance with nature, not trapezoidal concrete storm water sluices. The new approach, said corps spokeswoman Stacey Underwood, was "to start at the headwaters of the watershed and work our way down. This is why we are building economic partnerships with Montgomery and Prince George's to improve stream management." By 2000 the corps had enhanced wildlife habitat in the area of Kingman Island by creating more area for birds. In what was perhaps a revolutionary insight for the engineers, Stacey Blersch, the corps' environmental affairs specialist for the lower Anacostia, said, "We are trying to get the older hydrologic regime back as much as possible."[22]

In the 1980s and 1990s, landscape designers began to take a hard look at the Anacostia to see how they could reduce the destructive pulses of rain water that were overloading Washington's outdated sewer system. Low impact development (LID) represented a relatively new approach for reducing storm water from developed areas. In the past, storm water management was based on moving massive flows off the land as efficiently as possible, channeling them into drainage systems, sewers, and rivers. "This had a devastating impact on the region's biomass," said Tom Schuler, director of the Center for Watershed Protection in Ellicott City, Maryland. The task, he believed, was "to reduce the harm caused by mass drainage from so-called impervious surfaces." By keeping storm water on the land, natural hydrological processes associated with grasses, trees, and soils could filter out pollutants.

One technique, the humble rain garden—a dry pond or fixed area of grasses or other vegetation that absorbs water—could eventually play an important role in stemming runoff. Scientists estimate that rain gardens can trap 94 percent of the sediment, 70 percent of the nitrogen, and 43 percent of the phosphorus that is washed off the land by rain. Low impact development for the Anacostia means using nature to "volatilize" or break down some toxic compounds in water.

In the 1990s, Neil Weinstein, a landscape engineer, began to attract wide notice for his work in developing rain gardens. Weinstein, head of the Low Impact Development Center in Beltsville, Maryland, believed that vegetation had a tremendous ability to treat pollution and reduce runoff, and he made a successful career out of those beliefs. Weinstein was instrumental in planning a rain garden at a restaurant (IHOP) parking lot that became an environmental showpiece for the Anacostia. He and other proponents of LID projects demonstrated how a different type of landscape engineering could minimize runoff and offer cost effective approaches to hydrology that would allow businesses to meet regulatory and resource goals.

Larry Coffman, for many years the Associate Director of Environmental Resources in Prince George's County and a national expert on maintaining the ecological function of watersheds, was instrumental in helping developers plan innovative projects such as the eighty-acre Somerset development in Prince George's County. This community, on 10,000-square-foot lots, used LID techniques to reduce the burden of storm water management. By showing developers how to use swales, rain gardens, and other bioretention areas, Coffman helped them reduce the cost of a finished lot by four thousand dollars and create a more aesthetically pleasing landscape for buyers while helping the environment,

Throughout the Prince George's section of the Anacostia watershed, Coffman spearheaded the use of rain gardens, which have proven to be cost-effective for developers and enormously beneficial for the area's hydrology. Said Coffman: "If you can disconnect runoff and distribute your drainage, you can reduce storm water volumes by up to 50 percent and it doesn't cost anything. In the long run it is easier to deal with storm water at the source than at the end of the pipe."

Coffman admitted it was difficult to change conventional thinking about controlling storm water. "When we first talked about rain gardens, we were ridiculed," he said. "Now bioretention is the new mantra of watershed management." The task at present is to educate residents in the watershed and enlist property owners' participation in LID efforts. "If we are going to recover the Anacostia, we need to come up with better technologies that mimic natural processes to save these ecosystems."[23]

The Environmental Protection Agency and the Anacostia

Earlier, in the 1970s, the EPA had aggressively protected Americans from the harm of pesticides and toxins, particularly in American waterways. It demanded that municipalities use secondary treatment to curtail high bacterial levels in common sewage waste, even to the point of fining waste water plants for noncompliance. According to Jon

Capacasa, an EPA water director, the agency's task in the 1970s and 1980s "was to create a level playing field for environmental protection based on using technological approaches for secondary water treatment in sewage plants. We focused on leveraging financial assistance for construction of new sewage facilities. We were concerned with sewage plants whose major point of service was over 500,000 gallons per day and upwards. Blue Plains was the only plant in the Anacostia in this category."[24]

By the 1990s, the EPA found itself in the role of a broker between industry, environmental groups, and the environment itself. It was in this broker's role that the agency scored a notable success in helping to solve the pollution problems of the Washington Navy Yard. Another success was convening in 1999 the Anacostia Watershed Toxics Alliance (AWTA), "a coalition of over 25 different groups and institutions to address the complex environmental issues in the Anacostia watershed." By pooling more than $20 million with other agencies and groups, the EPA was able to generate important studies of toxins in the river that helped to secure scientific understanding of the problem and build consensus on strategies for a cleanup. The interim results of the AWTA were impressive. With EPA backing the alliance removed more than 7,500 gallons of coal tar, 20,000 gallons of petroleum, and twenty-five pounds of mercury from the watershed. It also abated over 27,000 tons of contaminated soil and greatly reduced the pollution of surface and ground water. The EPA hoped that AWTA would be a model for restoring other ruined rivers in the country like the Elizabeth River in Virginia.[25]

This was the kind of work for which the EPA was well-suited. The agency legitimized environmental issues as public policy and used its bureaucracy to apply resources and staff. It took environmentalism such as that at work in the Anacostia watershed and transformed it from niche "green" activism to something more mainstream and politically palatable.

That is not to say all went smoothly. Since 1987 the EPA has played an often controversial role in cleaning up the river, sometimes moving as slowly as the Anacostia itself. Like any new bureaucracy, it has kept one eye on its mission as defined by the federal statutes and the other on Congress, where many of the people's representatives appeared less than friendly to the idea of protecting the environment.

As the EPA confronted combined sewage overflows in American cities and the problem of deteriorating and broken sewer lines, it entered a thicket of local stakeholder controversy that often crossed municipal, county, and state lines. Controversy arose over the permit process. Was the permitting process actually a means to facilitate pollution, as some environmentalists claimed? Or was it, in the words of one spokesman, "a permit to control discharges into water sources in keeping with ambient monitoring of streams and waters?"[26]

As a regulatory agency, the EPA consisted mainly of lawyers, engineers, and economists who were more accustomed to the world of legislative enactments, hearings, findings, and memoranda of understanding than working with grassroots organizations. This bred misunderstanding and conflict, because the EPA perceived itself to be a legal-technical bureaucracy above the fray of politics and public pressure. In the Washington area, the EPA concentrated on cleaning up the Potomac and working in concert with the Interstate Commission of the Potomac Basin to remove toxins from the river.

Although Jon Capacasa maintained that the EPA "tried to connect the Anacostia River to initiatives that we were developing to improve water quality in Chesapeake Bay," it seemed to organizations like the Anacostia Watershed Society that the agency in the 1990s had stopped looking at watersheds.[27] As Robert Boone and Jim Connolly of the AWS viewed it, the EPA was lumbering along on a pollutant-by-pollutant approach as it bargained for pollution permits and marginal environmental benefits while losing sight of the fact that the watershed as a whole was in continued decline. According to Boone, some time in the 1990s "the EPA lost sight of the watershed picture. Every day officials of the Chesapeake Bay Program of the EPA drove from Capitol Hill to their jobs in Annapolis, crossing the Anacostia River twice. They did little to help the river at that time."[28]

Late in the decade the EPA changed its focus to small-scale projects in the Anacostia that were non-controversial and easily funded. It seemed less receptive to grassroots strategies that emphasized pollution prevention and environmentally sound land use. To many environmentalists it looked like the EPA had entered a different galaxy of effort and statutory enforcement. Organizations like Friends of the Earth, Earth Justice, the Audubon Society, and the Anacostia Watershed Society found that the EPA had become at best a reluctant advocate.

In 2001, Earth Justice sued the EPA over its lax pollution permitting process with regard to the Anacostia River. That same year, Maryland and local authorities decried the EPA sewage permit system and complained bitterly of the numerous storm water sewage overflows in Maryland. In December, Maryland's governor, Parris Glendenning, held a press conference to dramatize his annoyance with this "go slow" attitude. The Anacostia had failed every water clarity test the Chesapeake Bay Program had conducted that year.

An EPA official, commenting on the suits in a 2005 interview, replied: "We are a federal agency. Federal agencies get sued all the time. We have been in the forefront, launching our own suits to curb sewage pollution in the Anacostia watershed. In our litigation against the Washington Suburban Sanitary Commission some environmental groups like Friends of Sligo Creek and the Anacostia Watershed Society only joined us at the eleventh hour."[29]

Advocates at Earth Justice and other litigious organizations were unimpressed, and environmentalists in the Anacostia Watershed Society wondered if EPA was part of the solution or part of the problem. Without engaged neighborhood and environmental constituencies at its side, EPA lacked an informed, critical perspective in dealing with the influence of corporations on the design and enforcement of environmental laws. The agency saw things differently. "We were in the process of getting away from a national policy of 'one size fits all,'" Capacasa recalled later. "We had to develop partnerships with state groups in order to leverage money and research to solve complex problems."[30]

Environmentalists along the Anacostia remained skeptical. They believed that when it came to civic action, community and regional planning, and environmental justice, the Environmental Protection Agency's mandarins were decidedly out of touch. At the dawn of the twenty-first century, the EPA found itself in the role of defendant in Anacostia watershed lawsuits as often as it did that of plaintiff.[31] Increasingly the river's problems surfaced in national media, on CBS's "Sixty Minutes," in the *Washington Post* and the *New York Times,* and in a blizzard of reports, editorials, and commentary in the nation's environmental press.[32]

CHAPTER TWELVE

Waterfront Fever, 1996–2005

"The river is like a library. To learn from it you have to use it."
— Carl Cole

In the late twentieth century, rivers became focal points for city planners, developers, and political leaders who sought to revive America's center cities by reclaiming river waterfronts as commercial, residential, and recreational amenities. Washington joined a host of waterfront restoration cities like Providence, Pittsburgh, and Baltimore. The idea of a restored waterfront along the Anacostia River excited politicians and attracted investors, but, like most urban development plans, waterfront restoration prompted citizens to raise a number of civic, environmental, and racial concerns.

Boating Life

In the light of a summer dawn in 2005, sleek racing shells skimmed across the water against a backdrop of rich green trees on the far shore. The scene could have taken place on the Eastern Shore's Chester River, or near one of the many ports in the Chesapeake Bay country. Instead it was the Anacostia providing a more than eight-mile row through the heart of Washington, D.C.—past cave-like sewer outfalls and trash collectors, abandoned marinas, and the navy yard, and under four bridges that carry thousands of commuters in and out of the capital each day.[1] Jim Connolly and his crew pulled their oars with strong, smooth strokes as the primrose sun gathered strength. A few lone fishermen cast their

222

lines from the shore. In the sycamore trees cormorants paused in their feeding to watch.

Jim Connolly didn't think about the fact that the American Rivers Association once counted the Anacostia among the most dangerously polluted rivers in the nation. He concentrated on the cadence of the oars. In summer the river is warm and placid, a great time to be rowing. "It puts you in touch with the rhythms of nature," he said. "Out in a crew boat you just concentrate on rowing, on being on the river."[2]

The river and its environment have not always been so hospitable to rowers. Recently, though, there has been a rehabilitation of the shoreline below the Marine barracks in southeast Washington. Connolly and Carl Cole, another advocate for the river, helped to establish the Anacostia Rowing Center and obtained the use of an old warehouse owned by the Army Corps of Engineers for their racing shells. Both men have seen the reality of sports-minded men and women coming down to the river.

Connolly envisions a time when charitable foundations will provide rowing and recreational opportunities to children who know nothing of Anacostia save the meanness of its city streets. Currently the river is home to several canoe and kayak clubs. The community boathouse is host to regattas for high school rowers and Chinese dragon boat races put on by the National Capital Area Women's Paddling Association. Connolly admits that it is still a long haul to making this area into a regatta paradise. But it is a start.

Recreational boating in the Washington metropolitan area reveals the stark polarities of race and class on the rivers. Along the Anacostia there are no townhouses and restaurants like those that face out on the Potomac. The port of Alexandria, just a short row downstream from the Anacostia Rowing Center, shows off a manicured waterfront, well-kept parks, and fashionably dressed tourists. The Alexandria Rowing Club is toney and spacious. The discreet quarters of the Old Dominion Boat Club exude the aura of wealth it has enjoyed since its founding in 1880. A short distance away, the Anacostia Club sits behind a torn chain link fence. Picnic tables constructed from river debris offer a weak amenity. The few marinas show their age. The noise and whine of automobile traffic on the 11th Street Bridge makes peaceful contemplation at the river's edge all but impossible.

In the days of racial segregation it was only on the Anacostia that black mariners could find boat slips for their craft. The Seafarers Yacht Club points with pride to its founding in 1945. Lewis T. Green, a black teacher in Washington's segregated schools, in that year patiently sought rental rights for a marina on federal property on either the Potomac or the Anacostia, but the Department of the Interior did not rent land to blacks for marinas. Green asked Mary McLeod Bethune, a friend of Eleanor Roosevelt's, to intercede for him. The two women persuaded Secretary of the Interior Harold Ickes to establish waterfront rights on federal land for Green's newly organized boat club. That is how Seafarers became the first African American boating club on the East Coast.

Before there was Earth Justice or Friends of the Earth there were black yachtsmen who loved the Anacostia. Yes, they admitted, it was a tired old river, but there was also delight to be found in the sound of fish jumping on a summer's eve, and gentle breezes offered refuge from Washington's intense summer heat. Moreover, the river was theirs— beyond the purview of haughty whites whose expensive boats seldom ventured farther than Haines Point. These black men are the spiritual heirs of John Burroughs, the naturalist, who loved the river when it was not fashionable.

From the beginning the Seafarers Yacht Club was more than just a recreational boater's venue. The club was actively involved in community life. It offered emergency assistance to flood victims and delivered grocery baskets at Christmas to poor families. Over the years, reflected former Commodore Howard Gassaway, "we've been spearheading the way for a cleaned up river." The club has pulled 150 tons of trash and debris out of the water.

The Seafarers Yacht Club continues the African American tradition of boating on Washington's rivers. Blacks have worked and sailed on the Anacostia since the days of "Jack-Tar" seamen before the American Revolution. Norris McDonald, one of the younger members of the club, believes it is important to maintain that tradition. "That is the great achievement of Seafarers. During a time of severe segregation and oppression, African Americans took to the water. So we'll continue the tradition of hopefully training the youth coming up in the 21st century to continue boating."[3]

In the summer of 2000 the Seafarers Yacht Club took part in the Smithsonian Folk Life Festival by building a river skiff on the Mall. Blacks on the river have survived marginalization by whites, claimed boat-builder Bob Martin. "They have been trying to get rid of us and our club for years." The skiff symbolized the history and enduring maritime presence of blacks on the Anacostia.[4]

For African Americans like Carl Cole, the Anacostia is "the most fantastic part of Washington, bar none." Within easy reach of his house in Fairlawn, Cole can count "at least three yacht clubs, a rowing club, sixteen tennis courts, a swimming pool, a golf course, a park with scenic bicycling, excellent bird watching and abundant wild life, and a river with some of the best bass fishing anywhere."[5] For him the Anacostia is the very heart of the capital's history. Diplomats landed on its banks during the city's early years, and the area experienced the worst of the War of 1812. The river, he says, was ultimately ruined by industrial development. "This has nothing to do with race. Until recently many of Anacostia's neighborhoods were not populated by minorities but by whites." Cole believes that the best way to rescue the river is by getting people down to the water where they can see its beauty and its advantages. "Above all, we need to get people out on the water. Get them used to it. Get people out racing in dragon boats. That's how you make a difference." People tend to fear the river and "that fear leads them to search for demons and scapegoats," he adds. "The river is like a library. To learn from it, you have to use it."[6]

By 2004, Washington had awakened to the possibilities of Anacostia's waterfront.

Waterfront Fever

Ann Breen and Dick Rigby are waterfront experts. They have traveled the globe looking at how cities went about reclaiming their waterfronts and what successful development meant to their economic, cultural, and social vitality. The important cities of the world are located on waterfronts, they note, and now, after years of industrialism, pollution, and neglect, cities like Washington have begun to reengage their shorelines.

Breen and Rigby suggest that monuments, amenities, and vistas have "a significant effect on the civic psyche" and give "renewed pride to their residents." New waterfronts score well in this regard. Waterfront development at its best is part of "the resilience of cities" as they adapt to changed circumstances, new economic opportunities, changing neighborhoods, and popular interest in creating new recreational amenities. "It is a worldwide success story." Although waterfront development breeds astonishing successes like that of Sydney, Vancouver, and Barcelona, "there is no cookbook for waterfront success that you can follow."[7] The history of Washington's waterfront offers a recipe both sweet and sour.

The Evolution of a Waterfront

Pierre L'Enfant envisioned a busy waterfront for the nation's capital, a "water street" along the river's edge, and a network of wharves, inlets, and canals, a landscaped quay, and wide plazas for markets, businesses, and residences.[8] The most successfully realized part of this plan was the creation of the Washington Navy Yard, which gave a distinct industrial cast to waterfront development in the District. Setbacks were numerous. Destruction of the navy yard during the War of 1812 and Washington's military occupation by federal forces during the Civil War hampered development. Trade rivalries with Alexandria and silting in the Potomac diminished commerce. By 1880 Washington's waterfront was little more than a steamboat wharf and fish market.[9]

Yet, L'Enfant's dream of a dynamic waterfront never quite died. Throughout Washington's history, there were civic leaders, businessmen, and planners who tried to incorporate a sadly neglected waterfront into the capital's economic and architectural matrix. In 1928 the National Capital Park and Planning Commission supported creating two miles of piers and slips and rail headings along the area of 14th and P Streets, SW, to compliment the activities of the Army War College and the navy yard. The project came to roost at Buzzard Point, a geographic favorite of L'Enfant's. It would establish rail terminal facilities on the Anacostia River and "give the best shipping facilities for the national Capital for many future years." Washington would become a major shipping terminal for bulk cargoes like sand, gravel, and coal. But neither Congress nor the District would fund the $3 million waterfront makeover.[10]

Eight years later, in 1936, the U.S. Army Corps of Engineers offered to give Washington's Potomac waterfront a major facelift by dredging the channel at Haines Point to a depth of twenty-three feet so that battleships could moor at the island. The engineers also suggested tearing down a lot of the "dilapidated shacks" along the Anacostia waterfront and replacing them with new structures that could be used either for commerce or tourism. According to Maj. R. G. Guyer, army engineer for the District, this refurbished waterfront would make the city "a real seaport" and "offer more sightly facilities for existing commerce including yachting."[11] As it happened, most of the $325,000 in federal funds went to expanding the harbor in front of the navy yard and dredging the channel for coal boat traffic to the Washington Gas Light Company.

Even during the Depression, Washington was abuzz with ideas. In 1939 the city approved plans to build a stadium and sports center on the Anacostia flats. The reason, according to *Washington Post* sportswriter

Jack Munhall, was to create a sports venue larger than Griffith Stadium to accommodate the crowds attending the annual Army-Navy football game and big-time professional football. Included in the plan were an ice hockey rink, tennis courts, and a swimming pool. "The possibilities for increasing better amateur sports attractions would be unlimited with the birth of a sports center," Munhall wrote with evident enthusiasm.* "It's up to all Washington fans to get behind the movement to obtain the necessary appropriation, and then work together until the sports center does become a reality."[12] For the first time, Washington's waterfront was being defined by sports, but the reality was slow in coming.

In the spring of 1945 the Washington Board of Trade offered a program of waterfront development that would be covered by a new federal rivers and harbors bill that President Roosevelt had just signed. Among the Board of Trade's objectives were completion of a local sewage treatment plant, the dredging of mudflats at Haines Point, the construction of additional berths along the waterfront, and the improvement of yacht club facilities. The last item on the agenda was "the beautification of the Potomac and Anacostia River fronts."[13] The project dragged on for a year with hearings and arguments for and against the improvements. The port of Alexandria wanted to be included. Georgetown and Roslyn, Virginia, wanted docking facilities as well. The most that people

---

* After the 1960 season, the Senators baseball team moved out of Griffith Stadium and relocated to Minnesota. The District acquired an expansion team which it promptly named "Senators." After 1961 the stadium was able to house the crowds for baseball and the Washington Redskins football team that Munhall had hoped for, but the stadium's construction and layout satisfied neither the baseball club's owners nor the Redskins football club. The Senators stayed only until the end of the 1971 season, when they opted to locate in Arlington, Texas. During the last game on September 30, 1971, the Senators were leading the Yankees 7 to 5 in the final inning when a large crowd of youths spilled onto the field and vandalized the park, taking anything they could carry away as a souvenir of the Senators' last game. Because of the crowd on the field the Senators were forced to forfeit the game. Concerning football: after lengthy negotiations with the District and some acrimony, Redskins owner Jack Kent Cooke took his club to FedEx field in suburban Prince George's County in 1997.

could agree on was the preparation of a survey-report to be conducted by the Army Corps of Engineers.

New stimuli for developing Washington's waterfront appeared as the twentieth century passed its mid-point. The wholesale destruction of Southwest Washington through urban renewal made possible the construction of new middle-class neighborhoods in the 1960s that connected to the old waterfront and offered possibilities for tourism and recreation. What sociologists called "emerging communities of middle-class whites" began returning to the city ostensibly to take advantage of the many new cultural amenities like the Kennedy Center and the refurbished Smithsonian Museum complex. Property in historic, well-established neighborhoods like Capitol Hill, Georgetown, and Southwest Washington was attractive and inexpensive, close to federal workplaces, and possessed a fairly decent infrastructure. District businessmen and community leaders launched Heritage Tourism and Historic District initiatives to promote business at the city center. Through building codes and tax policies on residential property, the city quietly encouraged the rehabilitation of many "historic" urban neighborhoods. Some black activists and scholars, looking back at what had happened to the Southwest, thought historic districts and heritage tourism were "harbingers of displacement."[14] They worried that gentrification would bring about the same kind of "Negro Removal" that had made urban renewal infamous in the capital a generation earlier.

In 1961 the National Capital Planning Commission drafted plans for waterfront development that it hoped would be in place by the year 2000. The commission proposed adding several parks along the old Southwest waterfront and a continuation of parkland along the Anacostia south to the 11th Street Bridge. Working in concert with the navy yard, the commission drafted provisions for access to the water along a part of the Anacostia River currently closed to the public because of industrial development. In 1967 the commission enlarged the plan to include the entire river frontage of the District.

Neither the federal government nor the District had ever established zoning controls over the waterfront, which had become a mélange of piers, channel markers, semi-discarded industrial sites, and sewage outlets. The Maine Avenue fish market seemed disconnected from the river despite its popularity with Washington locals. Meanwhile the Board of Trade was advocating a restored Washington waterfront as central to Washington's continued tourism and economic development.

As the National Capital Planning Commission studied the Potomac and Anacostia Rivers, it became aware that the waterfront had to be redefined as an environmental entity rather than a commercial one. According to a 1972 report, "The pressures of urban growth have made the protection and conservation of the environment imperative." For the first time, planners heeded the idea of preserving the historic and environmental character of the Anacostia and Potomac Rivers and of their shorelines as well.

In 1972 the commission envisioned intensive urban development at selected sites on the Anacostia's edge, broken by parks and wetlands that would provide "handsome vistas and cooling breezes" to reorient the city to the rivers. The keystone of the project was a new recreational area. Boat landings, and, "as the rivers are cleaned sufficiently, swimming areas should be developed . . . especially in the clean lake areas of the Anacostia."[15] Central to the plan was the idea of a clean water swimming lagoon at Kingman Lake. Planners wanted promenades and embankment quays to provide "continuous access to the water." Some areas, the commission noted, would undergo "major alterations." This was particularly true with regard to the area around Buzzard Point and South Capitol Street. In contrast to what the commission called a "hard edge" redevelopment–office building approach to Buzzard Point/South Capitol Street, it wanted a new park that "would be a gentle sweep up from the river, across a terrace over the freeway to the intensely developed uptown center near Martin Luther King Jr. Avenue and Good Hope Road." Planners wanted thick screens of trees along the bridgeheads. Finally, they said, "a small docking basin could be established around Good Hope Road."[16]

Plans for the waterfront had come full circle. The 1972 proposal was much closer to L'Enfant's original plan than those of 1928 and 1945. Recreation, aesthetics, and a nod to the environment had replaced the older idea of a commercial waterfront for large vessels. Conceptually at least, most of the major problems were addressed in 1972. The NCPC urged that it was time to develop waterfront Washington. More than enough studies had shown that something had to be done with the miles of inaccessible, environmentally degraded, unsightly, and under-used waterfront.

The Legacy Plan

In 1996 the National Capital Planning Commission unveiled a plan to "offer Washington residents the same intimate connection to their rivers as Londoners and Parisians enjoy." This "Legacy Plan" called for a "continuous band of open space from Georgetown to the National Arboretum with a mix of festival, concert, and urban uses. Hoping to expand what it called "the Monumental Core" clear to the Anacostia River by creating monuments and public spaces along the river's edge, the NCPC was certain that "New and redeveloped commercial and residential neighborhoods will evolve. Complicated and unsightly stretches of freeway and railway will be removed."[17]

Architects and private planners were quick to point out problems. Some wondered how the federal government would fit into this grand scheme. Others, like experienced planner and architect Mark Seasons of the University of Waterloo, worried that plans for developing Washington were always majestic in vision but notably short on practical detail, with "no feel for the grim reality of life in much of Washington's urban core." With regard to the Anacostia waterfront, Seasons complained that "large scale projects are described but not their cost. Details about cooperation, roles and liabilities are missing."[18]

While planners argued, Washington's waterfront became desirable real estate. In the 1980s developers had sought land accessible to the capital's urban core. In 1988 the architectural and development firm Theodore F. Mariani and Associates became interested in eight acres at Buzzard Point as an office space and housing venture. When the firm presented plans to the District, which was considering the wholesale facelift of the five-hundred-acre peninsula south of the Capitol, one thing became clear—developers were already aware of the waterfront's potential.

When they learned the city was going to rezone the Anacostia shoreline from industrial to commercial and residential use and open a Metro subway stop at the navy yard, developers invested in land nearby, particularly Buzzard Point. Influential builders like the John Akridge Company and the Sigal/Zuckerman Company bought land "in the expectation," said one newspaper report, "that waterfront development will stimulate a wide transformation."[19] Businessmen with long-standing real estate holdings formed the Buzzard Point Planning Association to influence the course of development and to insure that infrastructure costs on roads and amenities were evenly distributed.[20] By 2000 the components needed for a massive transformation of the Anacostia waterfront began to come together.

The task was to broker a business and government alliance with real estate development into a new urban matrix for Washington's rivers in the twenty-first century. When he was elected mayor, Anthony Williams was a well-known financial administrator who had served well on the D.C. Control Board during the capital's time of fiscal crisis. Williams spoke the language of business but also believed that the environment and the city's working class had to be incorporated into any vision of the future. Williams and the city council put together a plan that came to be known as the March 2000 Anacostia Waterfront Initiative, a joint venture of community partners, the District Office of Planning, the National Capital Planning Commission, and the federal government.[21]

Anacostia Waterfront Initiative

Most people who studied economic trends in the city were aware that the Anacostia's banks constituted the last real area for major unimpeded economic development. Land was priced reasonably, and the city and federal government were willing partners and allies to a vision of "growing" this area. The District also had a talented and imaginative planning staff at the D.C. Office of Planning and the National Capital Planning Commission.

When Richard Rogers, a prominent architect who helped design the London waterfront, first ventured forth in a boat, he was startled by the stark contrast between the Potomac and Anacostia waterfronts. On the Potomac were cafes and a riverfront walk extending north toward the C&O Canal and connecting with a bikeway to Bethesda. As his boat turned into the Anacostia, he saw only trash, dilapidated structures, and a few industrial cranes scooping up sand at a cement plant. There was "no great public space where you can come down and enjoy the waterfront." No cafes, no restaurants. Here was a riverfront, in Rogers' view, that was being "dramatically underutilized."[22]

Mayor Williams and the city council in January 2004 vowed to change that and transform a blighted shoreline into residences, offices, shops, and restaurants to attract city residents, commuters from the suburbs, and tourists. The District hoped that new development would unleash a powerful stream of tax revenue that would in turn energize the whole city. Officials estimated that nine hundred acres of development along the Anacostia riverfront would generate $1.5 billion in taxes over twenty years. "Growth is going to happen," said Andrew Altman, head of the newly formed, quasi-public Anacostia Waterfront Corporation. "We want to make sure that it results in a great waterfront." The city buzzed with anticipation. Eight hundred public housing units in the neighborhood now known as the "Near Southeast" were slated to be torn down and replaced with 1,600 homes, some subsidized and others at market rates. The Federal Hope VI program, which supported replacing distressed public housing with mixed-use communities, financed the project. Displaced residents received housing vouchers, Altman assured the press and the public.[23]

As the Anacostia stood on the brink of change, the most exciting centerpiece of the Waterfront Initiative was the rehabilitation of South Capitol Street. Altman and his planners as well as those at the National Capital Planning Commission saw South Capitol Street as a grand urban boulevard and waterfront gateway. In his time, Pierre L'Enfant believed it would be one of the most important corridors into the city and connect the commerce of the waterfront with the political discourse of Capitol Hill. Sadly, South Capitol Street's history was less inspiring. By the end of the twentieth century it had become a thoroughfare of foul smelling empty lots, small fabricated establishments, a rubbish transfer site, abandoned businesses, and raffish gay night club crowds.

Planners hoped to change South Capitol's traffic flow by building a rotary with a five-acre park and viewpoint where the street ended at the Anacostia River. Along M Street, which intersected South Capitol, planners envisioned "mixed use cultural development"—federal office buildings, open space, and memorial sites. According to the National Capital Planning Commission, this area would be a new place for monuments and museums and relieve the "building pressure" on the Mall.[24] The street would remain 130 feet in width but would be landscaped with trees on both sides. A new bridge crossing the river at this point would connect two new major museum and commemoration areas and allow for park and memorial development of the seriously underutilized Poplar Point.[25] Further, a respected developer, Cleveland-based Forest City Enterprises, won the competition to develop forty-two acres of the Southeast Federal Center along the Anacostia River into offices, housing, and stores. The Forest City project was part of a larger effort to transform blighted commercial areas along the Anacostia into vibrant neighborhoods. A large part of that vision was the new headquarters of the U.S. Department of Transportation, which would move seven thousand employees to an adjacent waterfront building developed by JBG Corporation. According to one report, "the two projects at the Southeast Federal Center — Forest City's and JBG's — are expected to generate an estimated $30 million in tax revenue."[26]

Andrew Altman and D.C. Transportation Director Dan Tangherlini painted a picture in which both sides of the Anacostia would be transformed into a network of thriving neighborhoods, parks, and pedestrian-friendly boulevards. Altman believed that the Anacostia should rival the Potomac waterfront on the other side of town. "It's the same city," he claimed. "There should not be inequities in the same city."[27] Tangherlini echoed Altman's enthusiasm by imagining a time in the very near future when a family would take the subway to the Southwest waterfront and rent bicycles to ride for miles along the riverfront past the navy yard and on to Kingman Island and the National Arboretum. Those people out for a walk could board water taxis to parks, monuments, and other riverfront attractions. A pedestrian walkway, Tangherlini said, could connect the Anacostia waterfront with the Tidal Basin and Cherry Blossom Festival tourists.[28]

Seen from this perspective, the Anacostia Waterfront Initiative was a means to channel development into an area long overdue for improvement. It was an expensive proposition that would take at least thirty years and cost billions of dollars, but with the backing of the District and the federal government through grants and loan guarantees, developers were working to make the plan a reality. The only questions that seemed to go begging in the rush of enthusiasm was: Whose plan was it, and who would really benefit?

During Mayor Marion Barry's administration, District residents and environmentalists had seen the seamier side of urban planning. In 1997 the District negotiated a ninety-nine-year lease with private developers of the Island Development Corporation to construct a $150 million theme park on Kingman Island near RFK Stadium. The lease also gave the developers extensive rights to stadium parking. The city's deputy corporation counsel, Marian Holleran Rivera, found these provisions "extraordinary" and advised against the agreement. The deal also sparked determined community opposition from residents in Kingman Park and River Terrace, who argued that it was "environmentally inappropriate and would seriously damage local real estate values." Finally, D.C. Council member Sharon Ambrose of Ward 6, where the park would be located, exerted considerable pressure to have the project stopped. Residents breathed a sigh of relief that a potential Disneyland in their back yard had been scuttled. It also alerted the community to the fact that District "giveaways" to developers were not a thing of the past.[29]

As exhilarating as the prospects of Anacostia waterfront development were, the challenges were equally daunting. Along the western edge of the river near 1115 O Street, SE, were marinas and marine facilities that had the look of no man's land about them. For three miles along the eastern edge of the river, Anacostia Park offered splendid views of the Capitol. Unfortunately its facilities were in frequent disrepair and did not offer community members the quality swimming pool, skating pavilion, and playing fields available in other areas of the watershed. Further, the National Park Service over the years had turned Anacostia Park into a monotonous tree-deprived meadow.

Finally there was the river itself. While planners consulted their drawing boards, environmentalists like Robert Boone and Jim Connolly of the Anacostia Watershed Society looked out on a river plagued by combined sewage overflows and beset with the 70,000 tons of sediments, trash, and toxic substances that were annually dumped into the river. The Natural Resource Defense Council remarked that Andrew Altman and his planning staff were creating a modern "walkable and architecturally pleasant community on the banks of a floating cesspool." *Washington Post* architecture critic Benjamin Forgey chimed in that the river "calls attention to the fact that in the 21st century, a third of the city is still making do with a 133-year-old piping system that combines raw sewage with storm water during heavy or long rains. The Anacostia receives the bulk of this messy stuff—about three billion gallons in a typical year."[30] It was hard to visualize the riverfront's potential after a heavy rain, when the river was awash in sewage, Styrofoam, and assorted trash.

The Anacostia Waterfront Corporation nonetheless found itself instantly popular simply because it was doing something to counter the ugliness. Most people wished Mayor Williams, Andrew Altman, and the Anacostia Waterfront Initiative well, and the project sailed forth on the winds of favorable media coverage and impressive first starts at construction. The massive Department of Transportation building with its thousands of employees offered the prospect of transforming the economy of M Street and the South Capitol Street corridor. New condo units sprang up like mushrooms after a spring rain, and cityscape observers had to admit that Altman's project had "buzz." Mayor Williams was a dedicated conservationist and devout canoeist who loved to explore the Anacostia. While a candidate for office he began his campaign on Kingman Island and vowed to work to clean up the river. He prided himself on his environmental consciousness and went out of his way to secure $5 million for river improvements. In addition to Altman, the mayor had planners like Uwe Brandes, experienced in the difficulties of urban revitalization. He also had the National Capital Planning Commission and the Army Corps of Engineers, who could bring their own hard experience to the process.

In times past the District government had been relatively quiet about planning and developing the capital, but Anthony Williams exerted more forceful leadership. After briefly flirting with the idea of moving the University of the District of Columbia to Anacostia, an idea that had sparked resistance in northwest Washington, Williams and the District government settled on one very glamorous and visible solution—recruit a baseball team and build a new stadium on the banks of the Anacostia.[31] Baseball, the mayor proposed, was an excellent way to energize waterfront projects. If they built a stadium, developers and people would come.

Baseball: The Ecology and Economics of Stadium-building

Since the 1990s the United States has undergone a sports construction boom. New stadium facilities costing $200 million and more have sprung up or are underway in Baltimore, San Francisco, Pittsburgh, Cleveland, and Milwaukee. According to one report, "more than $7 billion was spent on new facilities for professional sports teams by 2006." Most of this money comes from public sources.[32] The popularity of sports in the general culture gives professional sports monopolies considerable leverage in getting cities to build the facilities for them with public funds.

Cities subsidize sports because there appears to be a strong rationale for them: Sports boost employment and instill civic pride. Proponents of professional baseball and football argue that building a stadium creates jobs in construction and elsewhere. People who attend games spend money in the community. Usually, stadium proponents say, a team attracts tourists and companies to the host city, further increasing local spending and jobs. All this new spending has a multiplier effect, as increased local income causes still more spending and job creation. Developers like to build next to a major growth site. The decision to recruit a professional baseball team, the Montreal Expos, and to build a new stadium looked like a win-win proposition to Washington's civic leaders.

Representatives of the D.C. Sports Entertainment Commission, the District's sports development agency, echoed the baseball mantra and claimed that the stadium would create jobs: 4,400 during construction, 360 full-time jobs annually, and 658 jobs outside the ball park, with an estimated $16.8 million in revenues collected from business franchise, payroll, and sales and use taxes.[33] A new stadium would be a showpiece of civic pride and indicate that the city had truly arrived. To the mayor of Washington, with its background of racism, poverty, urban blight, and riots, it was important to enter the big leagues.

Although the business community generally applauded the Williams administration's baseball plans as a way to increase the tax base, stimulate economic development, and foster civic pride, there were those who looked beyond the short-term baseball euphoria. Sportswriter Sally Jenkins thought the District was being sold a bill of goods. "It's lovely to have baseball in Washington again," she wrote in the *Post*. "But the deal that brings the Montreal Expos to Washington is an ugly baby. Let's be clear: The real and only benefit of a stadium is that people derive pleasure from it. It's not an especially wise financial thing for the city." Jenkins then cited a poll showing that more than 70 percent of D.C. residents objected to the public financing of a baseball stadium when the city had so many other pressing concerns.[34]

Economists entered the debate with studies showing that not one of the expensive new stadiums constructed across the country earned anything approaching a reasonable return on investment. In an open letter to Mayor Williams, ninety respected economists wrote that a baseball stadium in the District of Columbia "will not generate notable economic or fiscal benefits for the city."[35] Sports stadia attracted neither tourists nor new industry. Probably the most successful stadium has been the one at Oriole Park at Camden Yards, in Baltimore, whose games are exceptionally well-attended by residents and crowds from outside Baltimore. The net gain to Baltimore in terms of new jobs and additional tax revenues has been about $3 million a year, not much of a return on a $200 million public expenditure, argued Roger Noll and Andrew Zimbalist. Baltimore could have done better investing in savings bonds.[36]

Closer to home, the D.C. Fiscal Policy Institute examined all the familiar data and found that any stadium built for between $300 million and $500 million in public funds had no hope of paying for itself. Specifically its research found that sports stadia that are not in use most days of the year are not a catalyst for development in surrounding areas and do not contribute much to a city's revenue. To the extent that they are built with tax-exempt municipal bond funding, stadia do nothing to generate direct tax benefits for the city. Baseball teams create poor-quality jobs—dead-end concession, parking, and custodial positions—while highly paid ball players return to their home city immediately after the season's end.[37] Anyway, grumbled the *Washington Peace Letter*, "promises of job creation around sports complexes rarely pan out."[38] Furthermore, as soon as a city like Washington becomes proud of its team and comfortable at its new facility, it must worry that other localities will bid for the team and offer even larger subsidies for the easily transportable baseball franchise.[39] In their study of the economics of a new baseball stadium, Dennis Coates and Bard Humphreys of the University of Maryland, Baltimore County, offered the final economic word: "Attracting a professional sports franchise to a city and building that franchise a new stadium or arena will have no effect on the growth rate of real per capita income and may reduce the level of real per capita income in that city."[40] As of 2006, the District estimated construction costs of the new baseball stadium to be in the neighborhood of $611 million, the bulk of its cost to be covered by floating a bond issue on Wall Street.*

Eminent Domain

In the meantime, a few local property owners had to face a District government that used eminent domain to seize real estate in the Southeast as it put together packages of land for the ballpark. Court fights

---

* *D.C. Watch*, "Investments," November 17, 2004, voiced the strongest dissent: "The big boys want a stadium built at public expense because they will buy skyboxes there at their stockholders' expense, and then they will have a big shiny new toy at no expense to them. It's like Christmas, with the DC government playing their Santa Claus. Like all boys, however, they will tire of the shiny new toy very quickly, and that is another reason why the stadium is not an investment. The stadium advocates are talking now about how once the stadium bonds are fully paid for, in thirty or forty years or so, once we have come to the end of paying for all the underestimated costs and hidden costs and cost overruns, the city will make a profit from the stadium. You and I know, however, that in thirty years the brand-spanking, shiny new stadium will long since have been torn down as an old, ugly, undesirable antique."

over the real value of property as opposed to what the District was willing to pay for it brought back memories of how the city employed eminent domain to force the evacuation of Southwest Washington during its "revitalization" in the 1950s and 1960s. The city made offers totaling $97 million to twenty-three landowners, but many found the offer inadequate. A few sued, claiming that the city had no right to seize their land for municipal development despite a recent Supreme Court decision to the contrary in *Kelo v. New London* (2005).[41] Patricia Ghiglino and her husband Reinaldo Lopez had cast their life's work and investment into their art studio at 1338 Half Street, a stone's throw from the west bank of the Anacostia. They did not want to move and contested the District's seizure of their land and building in court. Property owners with their lawyers demanded in court the right to review the District's calculations in deciding the fair market values of seized properties. As the city moved onward in its suit to take their property, Patricia Ghiglino read a passage from Machiavelli's *The Prince:* "Above all he must abstain from taking the property of others, for men forget more easily the death of their father than the loss of their patrimony."[42]

Riverfront as Development

Andrew Altman and Uwe Brandes pointed out that the development of the Anacostia waterfront involved far more than construction of a baseball stadium. It was a blend of mixed-use residential space, parks, trails, recreation areas, and historic sites. The key to this initiative, according to Brandes, was its "live where you work" strategy. "It is geared to the sensible use of space in an age when the automobile is having such devastating effects on the countryside of metropolitan Washington." Our basic problem now, he said, is that "we have to get out of this mentality that development is bad. It is the type of development that is bad. Development is good for the environment if done properly."[43]

Although the baseball stadium gambit occupied center stage, little attention was being paid to the ecological consequences of locating a large sports facility at the water's edge. Once baseball on the river appeared to be a forgone conclusion, Robert Boone of the Anacostia Watershed Society testified before the District Council that he hoped that mayor and council could "close ranks behind a solid plan to tie clean water to the feverish building pitch for stadiums and new development along the river."[44]

The Natural Resources Defense Council called on the District to dedicate a percentage of stadium revenues to a trust fund to restore the river. An on-site wastewater treatment facility would minimize the stadium's pollution. Andy Fellows of Clean Air Action pointed out that the cost of building a "green stadium" would only be 2 percent greater than for a conventional one and would result in water savings, reduced waste, and lower maintenance costs.[45]

Meanwhile, many people championed waterfront development as the key to Washington's future. Benjamin Forgey of the *Washington Post* noted, "this is what smart cities do these days: Baltimore, Barcelona, Boston." The old downtown was full and with nowhere else to go by 2000, development flowed eastward. "Living near urban waterfronts is a proven global trend. Residential demand in the city is on the rise."[46]

The best part of the Anacostia Waterfront Initiative for Ann Breen and Dick Rigby was that it passed the "wake-up test." By this they meant that a plan of development can succeed "when there is a strong single-issue agency that gives us assurance that every day there is someone who wakes up and whose total focus is on the river — the river is his or her exclusive mission."[47] Andrew Altman and the Anacostia Waterfront Corporation was that agency. Its concept of waterfront revitalization emphasized Washington as an historic place rather than a tawdry waterfront town with a tourist center of monuments and federal buildings. Planning for a new riverine lifestyle in the national capital came at a time when cities, especially moderately sized cities of 500,000 like Washington, were enjoying a resurgence of popularity.

The magnet attracting young and old to these cities, say Breen and

Rigby, is "urbanity," i.e., walkability, density, diversity, hipness and public transit. By that standard, Washington scores high. Hip new bars
and eateries draw residents to restaurant row on 8th Street, SE, a short
distance from the navy yard. Pedestrian-friendly sidewalks and trails
along the river draw an educated and racially diverse population and
lend a vibrant pulse to nearby neighborhoods. The Metro subway and
bus system allows ease of movement throughout the city and the inner
suburbs. Fueling the Anacostia Waterfront Initiative is a human dimension based on people coming to the city in search of social contact
and a sense of community. Washington is a place with real buildings
and real history. Today's Americans seek authentic places that offered
street life, culture, and entertainment.[48]

By 2005 the construction of the Department of Transportation
building and the Southeast Federal Center as well as plans for an additional four thousand units of housing established the viability of the
planning process. Green space, parks, and an extended riverwalk would
soon become a reality along the Anacostia. Despite the controversy
over a baseball stadium, the Anacostia Waterfront Initiative was an important breakthrough in the city's urban planning. The single remaining
issue was the quality of the river.

Dr. Karimi's Anacostia Paradox

In a crowded office building on N Street, NE, analysts attempting
to chart the public health concerns of the city pored over data and sew-
er maps. Office signs carried disturbing appellations: "Rodent Control,"
"Toxics," "Hazardous Substances." In a spare corner office Dr. Hamid
Karimi held two jobs, that of Program Manager, Watershed Protection
Division and Interim Chief, Bureau of Hazardous Materials and Toxic
Substances. Sitting at his cluttered work table, he commented on the
current state of affairs.

"The Anacostia River is a paradoxical case," he began. "In our time it
is both improving and declining." It is improving in that everyone now

recognizes that it is severely afflicted. "Twenty years ago, that was not the case." Toxics and sewage have come to the forefront as regulatory issues, and the EPA has forced the District to examine the river in terms of fecal coliform and TMDLs. The heavy polluting incinerator, which the city used to dispose of trash, has been dismantled, and the open fires of the Kenilworth Dump are now history. "The city is now committed to a program of reducing combined sewage overflows into the river." Further, Dr. Karimi noted, "pollution of the river in the form of trash … is not as blatant as it used to be. Clearly there has been progress."

The Anacostia today is an issue that can no longer be ignored. "Environmental groups like Friends of the Earth, Earth Justice, the Natural Resources Defense Council and Anacostia Watershed Society have sued metropolitan governments over water issues and will continue to bring those issues to the attention of the courts and general public." And with Washington in the midst of major waterfront development, attention would remain focused on the river. "If you put up a $300 million building, do you want the stench of sewage in the river coming through your windows?" he asked.

The downside of the Anacostia's future is that many of its pollution issues are difficult to resolve. "To get tangible results is very expensive, and governments are more interested in public safety, fixing pot holes, and providing public schools." There are "very vocal constituencies on these issues," Karimi explained, and the Anacostia cannot match them. "Politicians regularly do a cost-benefit analysis on the way public money is going to be spent, and the Anacostia unfortunately doesn't have a high priority. The whole thing is about money. All the projects of pulling tires out of the river and shore-side projects won't amount to much if the river keeps on being a sewer. That is why groups like the Anacostia Watershed Society are filing lawsuits to force governments to do what they have little interest in doing."

The Anacostia is also declining insofar as there has been little environmental progress toward making the river fishable and swimmable as outlined in the Clean Water Act of 1972. But, Karimi added, the the Anacostia's pollution goes far beyond the city of Washington. "It involves policies upstream in Prince George's and Montgomery Counties. With the kind of tax-conscious middle-class income base in the watershed, raising taxes for expensive environmental retrofitting in either county is not a very attractive option. It doesn't pay political dividends." [49]

Lobbying the Anacostia

Many environmentalists continue to hope that incremental change can rehabilitate the river. Certainly, experts argue, if you remove the bacteria by building tunnels for combined sewer overflow and fix the leaky sewers in the suburbs, the river once again can be a place where people can swim, boat, and fish. This in turn can help to build a wider constituency on behalf of the river, though that will take perhaps twenty years to accomplish. Problems like those presented by the Anacostia are as much political as environmental. Groups like American Rivers, the Anacostia Watershed Society, and the Chesapeake Bay Foundation realized that in the twenty-first century they have to work the halls of Congress and the state legislatures to defend clean water and clean air.

Doug Siglin is an environmental lobbyist. The head of the Anacostia River Initiative and policy analyst for the Chesapeake Bay Foundation, Siglin is as comfortable in a business suit as he is in a kayak. All problems, he believes, have a technical and a political side, and he works well with scientists and with "friends" on Capitol Hill. Although the Anacostia became a ruined river in the nineteenth century, Siglin believes it is on the verge of becoming an "important economic and recreational amenity for the city's middle class." Two questions loom out of this development, he says. "How do we deal with the huge problematic infrastructures of waste elimination? And what do we do with poor people in the course of waterfront development? We need to make health and the issue of diversity key concerns." The task, Siglin believes, is to develop an effective political lobby for the Anacostia on Capitol Hill. [50]

In April 2002, the Anacostia Watershed Society embarked on a public lobbying effort of its own—a flagging project to alert users of the Potomac and Anacostia Rivers of pollution dangers. The flags were coded blue and yellow. A blue flag meant that fecal coliform levels were safe for boating (1,000/100 ml), and yellow was a warning that they were above the standard for boating and a potential health risk for people who made skin contact with the water. The flags were placed at key spots between the mouth of the river at Buzzard Point and the Bladensburg Waterfront Park. In recent years regional environmental groups have used the Clean Water Act of 1972 to sue polluters who were harming the Anacostia. In two major cases the defendants were sanitation authorities— the Washington, D.C., Water and Sewer Authority (WASA) and the Washington Suburban Sanitary Commission. (WSSC).

The suit against D.C. Water and Sewer filed in 2003 by Earth Justice, Anacostia Watershed Society, Sierra Club, Kingman Park Civic Association and the American Canoe Association rose out of the problem of combined sewer overflows to the Anacostia, Potomac, and Rock Creek. During storms the District allowed three billion gallons of overflows into the rivers with bacteria counts in the discharge often thousands of times above safe levels. In the settlement worked out in court, the District agreed to cut sewer overflows by 40 percent. WASA also agreed to fund $2 million in greening projects along the Anacostia designed to cleanse polluted storm water runoff from streets, industrial yards, and businesses. As part of its "Long Term Control Plan," the District pledged a billion-dollar construction project over the next decade to carve out ten miles of storage tunnels beneath the capital, with a sustained capacity of 119 million gallons, to serve as reservoirs during heavy rains. When the rains ceased, the water would be pumped out to sewage treatment. The proposal does not stop sewer overflows completely, and environmentalists like Hamid Karimi worry that without federal support the tunnels' cost will double the water bills of District residents.[51]

"Clearly some things are now in place that will greatly benefit the

Anacostia River," said Bill Matuszeski, a consultant and former director of the EPA's Chesapeake Bay Program. "The new Combined Sewer Overflow Plan for the District of Columbia will correct many of the District's sewage problems by ameliorating some of the major degrading of the water quality of the Anacostia River." Environmental activist Larry Silverman added that "given all the political and other issues affecting the District, it is remarkable that they have made the efforts they have to focus on the Anacostia and its storm water and sewage problems."[52]

In April 2004, Masaya Maeda, a water quality specialist for the Anacostia Watershed Society, found a cracked manhole stack on Sligo Creek with an exposed sewage pipe. The streambed was so eroded that the manhole stack was well into the stream. The following week, farther upstream, Maeda found a large sewer pipe with a crack in it. The area around the pipe smelled so strongly of sewage that Maeda became ill. These two events marked the beginning of a series of reports Maeda wrote on the watershed sewers of Montgomery and Prince George's Counties. They were dilapidated, leaked sewage, and constituted a serious public health threat to humans and wildlife in the watershed. A subsequent examination of public records showed that from January 2001 through July 2004, WSSC's sewer system experienced 445 overflows that together dumped ninety million gallons of raw sewage into streams and rivers in Montgomery and Prince George's Counties.[53]

On November 18, 2004, the Anacostia Watershed Society, the Natural Resources Defense Council, the Audubon Naturalist Society, and Friends of Sligo Creek joined the Environmental Protection Agency in a lawsuit against the Washington Suburban Sanitation Commission. The suit charged the commission with violating the Clean Water Act by illegally discharging raw sewage into the watershed. WSSC's system included approximately 640 pipe stream crossings and hundreds of miles of sewer pipes that ran along Maryland rivers and streams. Many of the pipes were over fifty years old, broken, decayed, and exposed. "The public is at risk," said Nancy Stoner, director of the Natural Resource Defense Council's Clean Water Project, "for contracting such water-borne illnesses such as gastroenteritis,"[54]

A little more than a year later, Baltimore and the WSSC negotiated a federal-state settlement worth $1 billion designed to inspect and fix 1,120 miles of sewer mains along the Anacostia, Patapsco, Patuxent, and Potomac Rivers in five years. The Anacostia portion of the settlement outlined a fourteen-year, $200 million plan to repair and upgrade its extensive system of pipes. The terms of the agreement required WSSC to develop "emergency response plans, for sanitary sewer overflows." The WSSC also paid a $1.1 million civil penalty to the State of Maryland.[55] At a press conference celebrating the settlement, Jim Connolly, executive director of the Anacostia Watershed Society, reflected: "It is not often in the environmental field that you can declare victory, but today let us rejoice in the fact that progress is being made in the Anacostia River basin on controlling sewage pollution in our waters!"[56]

Meanwhile, EPA officials were warning that bacteria and odors in urban rivers like the Anacostia could return to 1970 levels by 2016 if additional state and federal appropriations for new sewers were not forthcoming. They were not alone. "Riverfront redevelopment partnerships are part of a larger watershed picture," observed Betsy Otto, an ecologist at American Rivers Association. "Revitalization efforts won't be successful if we don't safeguard the water quality as well as the improvements that drew people back to their rivers in the first place. The nature of waste in our streams and rivers" suggests "serious front end problems." For example, in the first years of this century paper and plastic grew steadily as a percentage of solid municipal waste, and the chemical composition of these materials contributed more to the crisis than their huge quantities. In the old days, sewage systems were designed to deal with large amounts of organic matter. Plastic and Styrofoam pose more difficult environmental problems and demand more complex recycling methods than organic waste.[57]

It makes good sense for communities and developers to restore the river while rehabilitating properties along the bank, said Doug Siglin. "People spend time and money in attractive environments that emphasize natural beauty and wildlife. They avoid places where they smell sewage and see only concrete and pavement." Despite the economic advantages of a baseball stadium, "after a heavy rainfall, the river smells like sewage. Unless the baseball team wants to hand out air fresheners to every fan, we better do something to clean up the river."[58]

Waterfront Worries

Despite their enthusiasm for the future of development along the Anacostia, Ann Breen and Dick Rigby were concerned by what they deemed a "lack of enviro-philosophy" among those who were trying to deal with sewage and other issues. Breen and Rigby believed it imperative to get the universities and research institutions working with government agencies at the water's edge to solve these problems, something that had not taken place.[59] Real estate development along the Anacostia waterfront in 2005 also caused concern among local politicians, who wondered about the impact of thousands of new workers, consumers, and tourists on the sewers. "As we introduce more extensive economic development along the Anacostia," argued D.C. council member Jim Graham of Ward 1, " we have to be more mindful of the runoff." The District's system, he explained, was incomplete. "Many of our sewers don't lead to a treatment facility but lead right to the rivers and that's the problem." Noting that Washington's oldest sewers still carried both storm water and sewage that overflowed during torrential rains, Graham added that Anacostia waterfront development "increased the need for sewer-system improvements."

Council member-at-large Carol Schwartz and Congresswoman Eleanor Holmes Norton campaigned for an additional $150 million in federal funds to repair some of the construction flaws in the sewer system. The *Washington Times* quipped that people like Norton, Schwartz, and Graham saw the new waterfront development constructed on "a sewer system flushed with worry."[60]

At the same time African Americans in Anacostia were greatly concerned about the impact of waterfront development on their community. Life east of the river remained perilous in a community beset with not only a polluted river but social pollution in the form of chronic poverty, drugs, and violent crime. In April 2005, D.C. police reported that so far that year more than half the murders in Washington had been committed in Anacostia. As one young resident, David Smith, put it, "Anacostia's always been a haven for the poorest people. This is where they dump their trash and dump the people, who I guess the city didn't want to see." The Anacostia River and its communities are just a few blocks from the Capitol, says Smith. "But in reality. It's like 10 miles." The statistics on growing up black in this area and coming out alive before you are eighteen aren't very good, he added.[61]

Too many people in Ward 8 east of the river "feel like hostages in their own homes," observed Anacostia resident Malcolm H. Woodland. In a feisty newspaper essay, Woodland listed the many problems that continued east of the river in the age of the Anacostia Waterfront Initiative. "My community is overrun with halfway houses, homes for the mentally ill, homes for sex offenders, and methadone clinics. The dispersion of the city's neediest populations into this community is problematic because of the lack of resources in Ward 8." Drug addicts and alcoholics gather in front of the liquor stores from morning to night, Woodland complained. No stranger to urban policy, Woodland is a research fellow at the Center for Human Environment at the Graduate Center, City University of New York, and his words carried weight. Woodland believed that Washington officials "do not care and are willing to let my community die."[62]

In the unstable social and economic climate of 2005, two forces impinged on the residents of Anacostia: the ever-present criminal element and the ever-expanding development boom that was pushing affordable housing out of the District. On a hillside just east of Anacostia are garden apartments with stunning views of Washington. On clear nights residents like Kevin Jayson can see the National Cathedral, the Capitol and the Northern Virginia skyline across the Potomac. Despite the area's social problems, they fear gentrification more. Homes east of the river were exploding in value, and the land that ex-slaves settled and called Barry Farm and Uniontown was being marketed as prime future residential property. Homes that sold for $50,000 fifteen years ago were selling for $200,000, and had become unattainable to families with D.C.'s median resident family income of $40,000. Between 2000 and 2005, reported the *Washington Post*, "more new housing developments totaling nearly 8,000 units have been built in the area — which includes Anacostia, Barry Farms, Congress Heights, and Shipley Terrace — than anywhere else in the district except near downtown."[63] As Anacostia Advisory Neighborhood Commissioner Lendia Johnson put it, "I do worry that folks who lived here for so long will have to move if so much happens at once that they can't afford it."[64] With newer townhouses east of the river commanding prices upwards of $300,000, many African Americans complained they were being priced out of their community. In areas like Hillcrest upper-income blacks and whites were beginning to buy homes in significant numbers.

In the spring of 2005, D.C. officials reported that they expected to invest $200 million in downtown Anacostia over the next decade to renovate buildings and build a light rail system that would better connect the area with Capitol Hill and downtown Washington. New parks and pathways, monuments, and bridges coupled with high-priced condominiums may yet solve the conundrum of attracting the young white and black middle class to the city, but that still left many problems in the African American community unaddressed. Black activists and city leaders like Councilman Adrian Fenty complained that while the city prepared to spend $611 million on a baseball stadium, the D.C. school system remained dysfunctional and decrepit, the public library system was one of the worst in the nation, and the medical needs of the young and old who live along the Anacostia remained acute.[65] Further, they argued, the money spent on the stadium could be spent on the construction of homes and apartments to allow the city's police, firemen, nurses, teachers, and government workers to reside in the city rather than in some remote suburban subdivision.

The African American community has fought government policies that would have turned settled neighborhoods and park lands into amusement parks, monuments, and parking lots. Said civic leader Herbert Harris: "We have to keep a close watch on things at the local level if we want to protect our community from rampant growth and environmental degradation."[66] For Harris and residents of the Kingman Park neighborhood, the condition of the Anacostia had forced African Americans to become environmentalists because they were overburdened with the residue, debris, and decay of urban life in Washington. For example, Frazer Walton, president of the Kingman Park Civic Association near RFK stadium, "repeatedly sued the city, the Navy Yard, and the Environmental Protection Agency for polluting the river with PCBs and violating the Clean Water Act."[67] Theresa McDougald, a teacher at Anacostia High School, regularly used the river as a science laboratory to demonstrate the effects of pollution for her students. Norris McDonald, president of the local African American Environmentalists Association, helped to dramatize the environmental problems of blacks along the river. Even the briefest study of the Anacostia black community dispels the old canard that blacks have had little or no interest in environmental issues.

Today the descendants of slaves and free blacks live in the path of the Anacostia Waterfront Initiative. Developers like Louis S. Rizzo, president of Curtis Property Management Corporation and the largest landowner in Anacostia, anticipate changing the face of Barry Farm and Anacostia with new shops, restaurants, and condominiums. "I saw this coming a long time ago," says Anacostia resident Charles Scott. "This is the last frontier for Black folk who want to keep D.C. 'Chocolate City.'" African Americans fear their communities will be transformed out of existence. Said Angel Jones, owner of a local towing company: "It's going to be like Columbia Heights, Adams Morgan, Capitol Hill, and the rest of the city. The little people are going to be pushed out and the folks with money are going to come in. You see them lurking around here every day like vultures."[68]

Increasingly community leaders realize that the huge differences in economic growth in metropolitan Washington can no longer be ignored. The National Association to Restore Pride in America's Capital, a volunteer Internet think tank, recently published a report that documented the different growth patterns in Anacostia and Arlington, Virginia. Until the 1960s both communities had been similar in terms of income, education, and their share of federally owned parks and military facilities. NARPAC posed the question: Why had Arlington outpaced Anacostia in education, employment, housing values, and per capita income? It concluded that while the federal government from President Lyndon Johnson onward worked to enhance the economic value of federal properties in Arlington, it did not do so in Anacostia. The government was instrumental in building and expanding Reagan National Airport, a powerful economic stimulus to the Arlington community. In Anacostia the government chose to let its federal properties and parks lay fallow except those parcels currently in direct use. Although the military airfields that once occupied 1,300 acres have disappeared, the land remains under the control of the federal government—unused. In contrast "the seven hundred-acre Reagan National Airport on the Virginia side has grown into a major domestic regional airport and benefited both Alexandria and Arlington substantially." Until recently, argued NARPAC, "long-range planning east of the river has been woefully inadequate." With better land use and planning through concerted federal and municipal efforts, NARPAC believes that "statistically and economically, at least" Anacostia could become another Arlington.[69]

Two representatives to the Anacostia Waterfront Corporation from east of the river, Carl Cole and Loretta Tate, worked hard to ease local residents' suspicions. But the waterfront project received a lukewarm response anyway. Many residents had sharp memories of the destruction of Southwest Washington and the dispersal of Washington's black communities. Although Cole and Tate had excellent reputations in Ward 7 and Ward 8 where they resided, they battled widespread doubt about the future of African Americans east of the river. Tate agreed there was a lot of skepticism, but she recognized that "change is needed in my community." Carl Cole believed that the key to healthy development along the waterfront was to make blacks "key players in all of this."[70]

During the debates over the path development should take, Andrew Altman, the president of the Anacostia Waterfront Corporation and chief planner of the river initiative, resigned to take a new job outside the city. Arguments about the high cost of the baseball stadium and what it would do to Washington obscured the dilemma in which African Americans east of the river found themselves during the waterfront fever. Many black Anacostia residents therefore were left bewildered and adrift on the tides of change.

CHAPTER THIRTEEN

Currents of Hope, 2005

"We can have a much better Anacostia. It all begins with small
improvements in the streams of the upper watershed."
— Margaret Palmer, Scientist

A t the dawn of the twenty-first century scientists, planners, and Washington civic leaders hoped that the river had reached a critical turning point. It was improving, thanks largely to the actions of environmental organizations, litigation, and the Environmental Protection Agency. Certainly the Anacostia could no longer be dismissed as just another fetid waterway. District residents began to rediscover its beauty and splendor, and its recreational possibilities.

Rebuilding an Urban Watershed

Although urban development and environmental degradation have long been constants in the river's history, much newer are watershed approaches to achieving its rescue. In 2003 the Sierra Club listed Washington as the third most sprawl-threatened urban center in the nation, and environmentalists pointed out the danger sprawl posed to a significant migratory corridor for birds. The Audubon Society alerted citizens that the river and surrounding region were home to more than 170 rare or threatened bird species. Calling for better stewardship of the watershed and suggesting that homeowners try ground cover instead of grass and fertilizer, the Society for Ecological Restoration International announced that the time was at hand to rectify three centuries of mistreatment.[1]

Biologists, scientists and environmental planners are now at work learning more about the watershed and addressing the problems of the river by healing its tributaries. John Galli, an aquatic biologist who works for the Washington Council of Governments, believes that in order to restore the river "you have to understand the past to try to recreate as much as possible the basic physical conditions that existed prior to urbanization."[2] The Anacostia's problems are hardly unique. Today fewer than 2 percent of the rivers and streams in the contiguous forty-eight states remain in pristine condition, reports Mike Dombeck, chief of the U.S. Forest Service.[3] Near Wheaton, Maryland, and Sligo Creek, 55 percent of the watershed has been paved over. Many of the smaller streams are enclosed in pipe and buried underground. By 1990 nearly 70 percent of the entire watershed had been developed. Single-family houses, townhouses, and apartments constituted the single largest land use.

As streams lose their natural forest cover to development, they are increasingly unable to support aquatic habitat. The Maryland Biological Stream Survey found that streams flowing through developed areas where 25 percent of the surface is impervious, can support only the most pollution-tolerant species.[4] "During the initial building boom of the last forty years, people were not concerned about controlling storm water run off," adds Galli. But now that stream bank erosion threatens to undermine businesses and homes located near streams, people are becoming aware of how important it is to rebuild the watershed as a flood retention device. Every time it rains, the by-products of daily suburban life are collected and swept downstream. The runoff hits the streams at high velocity and gouges soil from the banks while it smothers benthic creatures. When it comes to dealing with the watershed, adds Robert Boone of the Anacostia Watershed Society, "a lot of us have been bad citizens. We built without thought of consequences. Now, for example, businesses along Paint Branch Creek as well as at least one dormitory of the University of Maryland at College Park may risk being undermined or flooded."

Anacostia's problems have made people come together to deal with a host of issues, from pollution to toxins and soil erosion. "We saw that the river was in trouble and we are taking real steps to turn it around," says Congressman Steny Hoyer (D-Md.). He points to successes like skimmer boats and floating booms that remove debris from the river, and environmental education in schools, which has brought about a change in public thinking. Additionally state, local, and federal agencies "are starting to put in storm water retrofits to make the streams act more like streams and less like storm water sluices." A cleaner watershed, he maintains, requires collaboration and collective effort. "If private landowners work in concert with local and state agencies, we can understand better the resource issues that confront us." The congressman has actively supported efforts of the Army Corps of Engineers to develop alternative strategies, like constructing riparian buffers and removing blockages that prevent the passage of herring upstream.[5] One of the most encouraging and useful recent developments has been the Anacostia Watershed Network's coordination of information. With the click of a computer mouse, a wide array of watershed data becomes available.[6]

Today scientists and planners are better equipped to study the many paths by which water finds its way into the river, and they more completely understand the toxins and other contaminants that have already arrived in the Anacostia. David Velinsky, of the National Academy of Natural Science in Philadelphia, is one of a number of scientists who have been tracking contaminants in the sediments and water column, measuring concentrations of PCBs (polychlorinated biphenyls), PAHs (polyaromatic hydrocarbons), and heavy metals, and charting their movement through food webs, their impact on fish, and ultimately their effect on human health. Velinsky has gathered a wealth of knowledge about contaminants, "hot spots," and sediment contamination in the watershed. This information provides today's environmentalists with the means to create models, or mathematical predictions, of pollution. The models in turn aid public officials and environmental planners. Jim Collier, a retired executive from the District Health Department agrees. "This allows for a better understanding of toxics in the river."[7]

Once the foundation of data and evidence has been established, science can point the way to a cleaner Anacostia. One successful application of science has been in locating toxic sediment spots in the river that can be covered by a "reactive cap," a material like sand or fabric that "captures" PCBs. According to Nick De Nardo a member of the Anacostia Toxic Watershed Alliance and an engineer at the Environmental Protection Agency, this is one of a number of new strategies being explored to repair the river. De Nardo adds that "if we did business as usual, we would never be able to completely characterize an area and therefore would never be able to begin any clean-up actions in the river."[8]

Alberta Paul, an executive with the Washington East Foundation, has been engaged with the environmental problems of the Anacostia for years. A native Washingtonian and graduate of Howard University, Paul has a pragmatic outlook on the future. "We have taken people by the busloads in caravans to see and study the Anacostia River—people from all walks of life. The Anacostia's future is an environmental issue," she says. "We need to put an end to all the studies of the river. . . . We have enough data. What we need to do is implement the process and begin attacking the problems. It will cost a lot of money. And insofar as the Anacostia is a national river that flows through the capital of the United States, we need Congress to fund a massive clean-up of the river." Paul is impatient with piecemeal programs. "In the District we have all of these $100K education and study grants from the Environmental Protection Agency. A $100K grant is not going to make much of a dent in the Anacostia's problems. . . . With grants like that, how can we get the community involved?"[9]

Mrs. Paul is very much aware that the city is changing demographically. "Nothing happens willy-nilly in life. Whether we think of change as part of a plan or not, we have to adapt. Regardless of the changes in racial diversity in the District, the environmental problems remain." She is nevertheless optimistic about Washington and the Anacostia River. As the city changes, people fed up with gridlock will want to live in the District. They will want amenities and a cleaner river. Businesses and homeowners will put pressure on the city government and Congress and change things for the better. Alberta Paul believes that native Washingtonians are not going to leave. "They love the city. They are working to improve their environment. It will be up to them to make sure that people in their community are educated on issues and show up and vote at the polls. Working-class folk and the poor can survive in this city if they are willing to work with community development agencies that have programs to serve them." The past five years have seen a positive swing in community attitudes east of the river. "They see the river as part of their future."[10]

Cameron Wiegand, the environmental manager for Montgomery County, is outspoken in his belief that the fate of America's water will be determined by what develops in its watersheds. Montgomery County, he believes, offers a successful model of how to improve wetland and storm water hydrology through environmental planning. Since 1997 Montgomery County has monitored twenty-three watersheds in its boundaries in order to identify healthy waters and improve unhealthy ones. "What we are proud of," says Wiegand, "is that we have raised the bar in terms of what we do with our streams." Wiegand's staff found that 75 percent of the sediment load in county streams came from stream bank erosion, so it was there that they concentrated their energies. Streams are constantly downcutting, destroying old channels, and eroding their banks. On upper Sligo Creek the county installed three storm water ponds that now prevent sediment runoff during storms. Ten species of fish have returned to Sligo Creek and other tributaries.

"We have a lot of tools in our box to help make our portion of the Anacostia watershed better," adds county environmental engineer Daniel Harper. A favored technique is careful placement of rock to resist bank erosion—riprap interspersed with willow planting. As the willows become established, roots invade and permeate the rock and underlying soil, binding them together into an erosion resistant mass. The willows also impart a more "natural" look to the shoreline. Restoration efforts can succeed, but they take work. "Finally you have to look at history," Wiegand concludes. "Here in Montgomery we have been working about fourteen years to repair these problems. It is not an overnight process."[11]

The Anacostia does not lack bold initiatives. In Bladensburg the Anacostia Watershed Society is working to develop, in concert with the EPA and the U.S. Army Corps of Engineers, wetland nursery projects. "Right now," says AWS President Robert Boone, "we are restoring wild rice in what is left of the Anacostia wetlands." The marshes were once full of wild rice (*Zizania aquatica*), which over the centuries has been a high energy food for Native Americans and migratory waterfowl. The wetlands nursery project "seeks to involve students and the public in helping revitalize the wetlands we've lost over hundreds of years. Wild rice is an amazing filtration device for nutrients. We call wild rice the river's kidneys." Bringing back this once dominant species will help the river regain its health. The Anacostia Watershed Society has also planted bulrush, pickerel weed, and arrow arum to improve plant and bird life in the new marshlands.

In 2005 the immediate need was to preserve along the river and wherever possible in the watershed the open landscape that makes the riverbanks attractive. Steve McKindley-Ward, a naturalist for the Anacostia Watershed Society, believes trees are the answer to many of the watershed's problems. Trees stabilize streams and perform a variety of functions essential to filtering carbon dioxide out of the urban atmosphere. A recent study from the Casey Trees Foundation in Washington reports that "healthy trees greater than 30 inches in diameter remove 70 times more pollution per year than small healthy trees that are 3 inches or less in diameter."[12]

McKindley-Ward maintains that one of the best things to have happened in the suburban counties was the development of "no mow zones" along the streams and river bank. By not cutting the grass, trees will "volunteer" there, provide resting places for kingfishers and other birds, and stabilize the soil. Every year after Christmas McKindley-Ward and a band of volunteers take hundreds of "used" Christmas trees and stake and tie them to the river and stream banks. This project has been remarkably successful on the Northwest Branch. "We have been able to rebuild an entire section of stream bank using four hundred Christmas trees that we have staked and cabled. The trees catch sand in stormwater overflows and build the toe of a stabilizing bank. Soon sand covers everything and erosion ceases." McKindley-Ward also has to reckon with pesky beaver who eat the young willow trees he plants along the stream banks. "We are planting sycamore and birch now. Beaver don't seem to like those trees"[13]

Today the restoration of wetlands proceeds apace, and with better storm water management the floods are now part of the past. Increasingly state authorities in Maryland recognize the value of the Anacostia watershed as part of its stream valley parkland system. Efforts to retrofit the river consist not of massive dykes and dredging operations but the restoration of marshlands and ponds that will offer habitat to a greater variety of aquatic and bird life.

As to pollution, members of the Anacostia Watershed Toxic Alliance point out that the river is no longer a "toxic soup." Both the District and Prince George's and Montgomery Counties have worked to reduce toxics in the watershed and to curb illicit discharges of dangerous chemicals into the Anacostia. Much remains to be done, concludes a recent report on the watershed's ecological progress, but the Anacostia Watershed Restoration Committee, a consortium of local government and environmental groups, hopes that by 2010 the goal of eliminating public health concerns and rebuilding the Anacostia habitat as a " living resource" will be achieved.[14] Alyssa Schuren Director of the Toxics Action Center in Boston believes that bottom-up pressure drives today's environmental progress. The grassroots, she believes "will act as catalysts and watchdogs, ensuring that new environmental laws are passed and that regulations are implemented and enforced."[15]

In July 2005, the Army Corps of Engineers drafted a comprehensive plan to improve the Anacostia watershed in concert with stakeholders like the Anacostia Watershed Society and the Natural Resources Defense Council. The corps' objectives included restoring one hundred acres of wetlands and twelve miles of forested riparian buffer, freeing stream passage for anadromous fish like shad and herring, restoring twenty miles of streams, and creating storm water controls for up to 30 percent of the watershed. One of the keystone projects incorporated into the plan is the restoration of a forty-two-acre marsh in upper Kingman Lake that began in 2000. The corps hopes to create a more diverse mix of habitats for fish, reptiles, and amphibians and make Kingman Island a showcase for environmental education.

The plan marked the beginning of new era of cooperation between the Corps of Engineers and communities in the watershed. In the words of the Anacostia Watershed Society's Robert Boone, this was a "most positive and hopeful sign" of interagency cooperation in rescuing the river and rebuilding the watershed. It marked the culmination of Army Corps of Engineers involvement on the Anacostia River that began with a survey of "the Eastern Branch of the Potomac" between the navy yard and Bladensburg in 1876.[16]

As army engineer Stacey Blersch has noted, determining the final shape of the restored Anacostia watershed has been a challenge. Many constituencies in the region have their own ideas about how the watershed can or should be restored. Although the debate is understandable, says Blersch, no one can predict how this ecosystem will evolve in terms of habitat and sustainability. Certainly the Anacostia will never be returned to the way it was before industrialism and urbanization. "Restored ecosystems take a long time to reach maturity and function properly."[17]

The Secrets of a Stone

Recently, the American ecological movement has seen a growing trend toward bringing ecology and natural science out of the rural hinterlands and into urban and suburban environments. "Instead of treating these areas as sacrifice zones and doing all our conservation in national parks and elsewhere, there is a growing appreciation of the need to incorporate conservation into urban planning," writes Dr. William Shaw, an expert in the study of renewable natural resources. Shaw believes that within metropolitan regions riparian areas have prime biologic importance and are logical places to focus attention.[18]

Stepping into the fast-moving waters of Paint Branch Creek, biologist Margaret Palmer lifts a stone and turns it to the light. On the bottom she spots a small brown bump of pebble and sand—a caddis fly case. She points out that although the caddis fly's winged life lasts but a few days, its waterborne larva can live from six months to two years, often beneath rocks and stones. The larvae also spin silky nets. "Some rifles," she says, "can be virtually covered with these filmy nets." Palmer has learned that the nets actually cause micro-turbulence in the stream, creating tiny eddies that help to entrain (hold) food, a phenomenon scientists have witnessed in marine organisms as well.

As a watershed ecologist, Margaret Palmer has been swimming upstream a long time. Her work as a biology professor at the University of Maryland, College Park, has centered on solving problems of streams and watershed tributaries in metropolitan areas. Often, those who work on watersheds employ scientific models based on the historical hydrology of streams and tributaries, but she speculated that there is little chance of restoring the hydrology of a watershed to its pristine state.

Instead, we must look at the watershed as a "process" in terms of nutrients and contaminants, while factoring in the consequences of public policies.

Palmer knows that it is hard to rebuild a watershed when people pursue maximum residential space with little thought of long-range consequences. Yet, like many other variables, property development has to be part of the scientific equation. "To work effectively in the Anacostia and other urbanized watersheds," she says, "we are going to need intensive collaboration among environmental professionals from diverse fields." Streams require all sorts of monitoring, from nitrogen studies, to toxic TMDLs, to landscape engineering.

Palmer also believes that in restoring watersheds it is frequently cheaper to restore previously drained wetlands (or even to build new ones from scratch) than to construct water filtration or sewage plants. Entrepreneurs will be attracted to watershed restoration if it becomes cost-effective. At the moment it costs about $130,000 to restore an acre of wetland, "far cheaper than building a filtration plant." Finally, Margaret Palmer insists that "all ecosystems must become fertile research ground, whether least impacted, managed, or highly degraded ecosystems."[19]

We can also have a "much better Anacostia." Palmer points to a Montgomery County stream in which a by-pass pipe redirected storm water from a surrounding subdivision. The pipe eliminated a thermal barrier to trout entering the stream by keeping the water cool and by reducing peak flows during storms. Decreasing the stream's temperatures by less than one degree allowed young trout to flourish in water that once was uninhabitable for them. "It all begins with small improvements in the streams of the upper watershed," she says. As we unlock the secrets of stones in a stream and change the hydrology, "we can have a watershed that is clean and cool enough for juvenile and adult trout to thrive. We all benefit from that in the long run."[20]

An Anacostia Prayer

Meanwhile, the Anacostia abides. Like anadromous fish in the spring, canoeists come upriver to Kenilworth marsh. A party of athletic Capitol Hill residents led by Susan Chapin paddle toward a lone man in a floppy hat who sits motionless in his kayak watching the fish jump. Robert Boone greets the canoeists and takes them into the marsh that can only be navigated at high tide. Here he points out the bird life. A kingfisher, beautiful, a good hunter, and tough as the river itself. Cormorants in the sycamore trees, looking like solemn members of a wedding waiting for the food to be served. The blue heron walking delicately on a log as if it were a gymnastic balance beam. In the stillness of Kenilworth marsh, Chapin and her canoe party glimpse a basic truth: the much abused river is still favored by nature. Here on the marsh the Anacostia is something greater than an EPA schema for pollution loadings, something greater than a scum-infested sewer. Here the Anacostia is a stunning mosaic of water, marsh, trees, birds, and today, crystal blue sky.

Robert Boone believes there is a spiritual dimension to defending this watershed. "This . . . is where we live. It is our home. And the whole idea of home is central to who we are as human beings." But the idea of home cannot last, Boone insists, unless we change the way we live and interact with our environment.

No doubt the Anacostia will experience significant challenges in the future, as it tries to deal with the legacies of the past. Changes in precipitation, temperature, and storm patterns combined with development and increases in population will profoundly affect water systems in this area, as elsewhere in the United States. The beautiful and the ugly live together here. Regardless, Boone cautions that we must exert our moral stewardship of our watersheds and we must do it now. "Any place can be beautiful if you take the trouble to discover what there is to love."

"The Creator created this river as a healthy system," says Doug Siglin, of the Chesapeake Bay Foundation. "But generations in the District and Maryland have *recreated* a very polluted river with only a fraction of the biota it once had." Boone and Siglin have both worked with ministers in developing an interfaith religious partnership to redeem the river. We need the power of religious endeavor, Boone maintains. "The Earth can't wait for some future generation to save the Anacostia."[21]

Throughout Maryland and in the District of Columbia, environmental stewardship is a growing presence in the churches. Currently organizations like the Maryland Presbyterian Congregation, the Unitarian Universalists, and Episcopal and Catholic Churches distribute information on how to save Maryland's rivers and the Chesapeake Bay. Church members ask how best to prevent runoff from large church parking lots and attend public meetings "to track environmental legislation" that affects them. "We want the churches to take action to protect God's gift of water in their own areas," says Cassandra Carmichael, director of the Eco-Justice Program at the National Council of Churches. "It's about justice for all God's creatures. Animals, plants, and people are all connected and you have to make sure that you are having right relationships with all of them."[22] Other religious leaders see rescuing the Anacostia as part of the effort to reconnect the secular with the sacred. "If we are going to be God's stewards," insists Reverend John Bryson Chane, bishop of the Episcopal Diocese of Washington, "with reclamation must come the realization that there is no such thing as a morally neutral choice when it comes to making decisions about how we treat the environment and its creatures." The Episcopal Diocese hosted boat trips to see first hand the pollution and its effect on surrounding communities.[23] Washington ministers of all faiths and races banded together in 2005 to form the Religious Partnership for the Anacostia with the assistance of environmental organizations like the Chesapeake Bay Foundation, the Anacostia Watershed Society, and Earth Conservation Corps. The purpose was to encourage churches and synagogues, as God's stewards, to become more active in programs of river restoration. Currently the

Partnership is involved in several long-range landscaping projects to improve water filtration by plants. It also builds biorentention islands in parking lots to prevent polluted water from entering the river, and works against what church leaders see as the general "abuse of Creation." Building faith in an environment as problematic and as polluted as the Anacostia has been a challenge so great it requires religion as well as science. "Churches are more aware that human health is fully dependent upon healthy ecosystems," says Mike Schut, co-director of the Seattle-based Earth Ministry Organization.

Many in this religion-based movement toward environmental stewardship are questioning the efficacy of the automobile. A 1992 report from the Metropolitan Council of Governments reported that 2,841,745 motor vehicles were registered in metropolitan Washington. Their exhaust amounted to 369 tons of hydrocarbons, 1,693 tons of carbon monoxide, and 161 tons of nitrogen oxides every day. By 2003 those automobile registration figures had soared to 3.5 million.[24] "What car would Jesus drive?" church stewards asked.

Along the Anacostia at St. Mark's Episcopal Church in southeast Washington, congregants translated their faith into action. On Earth Day 2005, twenty-three parishioners aged five to seventy-three donned waders and rubber gloves and, despite rain and nasty weather, installed emergent plants on the mudflats at low tide.[25] In the suburbs, Rabbi Fred Scherlinder and his Bethesda congregation, Adat Shalom, have practiced their commitment of "walking lightly on the earth" since 1997. They have used low impact materials in the construction of their synagogue, practiced energy conservation, and shaped their property with trees and creative landscaping rather than turning the land into a large asphalt parking lot. For their efforts, Adam Shalom became the second synagogue in the nation to receive an Energy Star Award from the Environmental Protection Agency.

George Fisher, a geology professor at the Johns Hopkins University, views religious environmental stewardship as a salutary development.

"Science alone is not enough," Fisher said. "All of our resource decisions, on any issue, will require deciding how to allocate resources. Who benefits, and who pays the price? That's a moral decision ultimately."[26]

African American churches, especially in urban areas, have always been involved with environmental issues that affect their quality of life. Reverend Roger Reed, pastor of the Campbell AME Church in southeast Washington, long ago recognized that both the river and its people needed the efficacy of prayer and environmental stewardship. "Anacostia once was a proud place," he reflected. Generations of pollution and misuse "brought the area down." People must pray, he said, because along the Anacostia "the whole community has devolved to a sense of nothingness, gone to seed." The river was once an important part of the community's life. Black people worked on the river and gained their livelihood from it. "Now the District continues to pour pollution into the river where the children can't go wading."[27]

Religious African Americans have always believed that "there is a testament of God's power in the Creation." In another time blacks came down to the Anacostia to be baptized and embrace the fullness of the Lord. "Every time I go on the river, I can feel the presence of God," says David Smith, Program Director of Earth Conservation Corps and a member of St. John's Baptist Church in Marshall Heights. Smith believes that "the river refuses to be defeated and somehow finds a way to support wildlife and vegetation." In church black people remembered the old poetic verses by Langston Hughes: "I've known rivers. Ancient, dusky rivers. My soul has grown deep like the rivers."[28] And now as they gathered at the river in prayer, they fervently hoped it was time for that testament of God's power to be applied to the Anacostia.

Carl Cole grew up in southwest Washington. He remembers picnics along the river, the vibrant waterfront life, "and how the whistle on the old Bay Line steamer to Norfolk would sound every night at 11 o'clock." As a boy he dove into the waters of the Anacostia off Buzzard Point. "The water was mesmerizing. The river pulled me there, and I have stayed there." As a consultant and community leader, Carl Cole has often been called upon to reflect on the Anacostia, and he offers a long-range view. "How did the river fall so far from grace? A lot of people who grew up loving the river moved out to the suburbs. . . . Ultimately people forgot what a true river could really be like."

"Rivers will get deep within you," Cole believes, "and they will never leave you. Most people would not believe the sereneness of this river. You can just close your eyes and know you're off some place else. You just sort of wrap yourself up in it and say, 'I'm home.'" [29]

On summer weekends the boat house of the Anacostia Rowing Club is awash with dozens of groups of rowers, young and old, who come to test their mettle on the river. Some are in a kayak or skull for the first time in their lives and are struck by the river's shimmering beauty. Occasionally a slender skull tips over and "baptizes" the rower. Upriver a pontoon launch piloted by Robert Boone of the Anacostia Watershed Society cruises down stream with a dozen college educators on board, eager to lean more about this intriguing environment. The boat drifts by what seems to be an anomaly on the Anacostia, a man in the water sitting in a truck inner tube lazily fishing for bass.

There is a lot of beauty left on the Anacostia River and it is becoming more widely appreciated. The river is a haven for bird watchers, recreational fishermen, and students of marsh and stream ecology. While there are not the vast fields of wild rice, dense forests, and wetlands that existed four centuries years ago when Captain John Smith sailed up the Anacostia, the river retains a kind of stark green lushness that refuses to submit totally to the forces of industrial and urban development. Despite the great losses of tidal and non-tidal wetlands, there is still so much along the river to delight the eye and stimulate the human imagination.

Today, signs of the river's return are everywhere. Within sight of the RFK Stadium, beaver ply the water intent on establishing their own habitat at water's edge. Osprey, eagles, and kingfishers call the river home; and black cormorants sit in the trees like dignified undertakers. Kenilworth Marsh is being restored and this singular project will go a long way to improving the tidal wetlands of the Anacostia. But the most important part of the river's evolution is that there are now no major fish kills on the Anacostia

With a slack tide and the current to your back you can paddle downstream in a canoe and see fish rippling the water, diving cormorants, and honking geese along the shoreline that offer a remarkable show. In the far distance one can hear the faint buzz of traffic, but on the water all is peaceful. As the sun sets, the sky explodes into vibrant colors that are reflected on the Anacostia. Along the shore a blue heron, that solitary aristocrat of the river, stands erect and watching.

Once the Anacostia seemed destined to die from a witches' hellbroth of toxins and sewage, and the river still suffers from a host of problems. But the Anacostia is no longer "the forgotten river." It is beginning to revive and show its splendor. It can be restored for the benefit of generations to come if only we have the will.

Epilogue

History, the Dutch scholar Peter Geyl once said, is an argument without end. The Anacostia River is now part of that ongoing and more than occasionally disruptive conversation. The history of the Anacostia is contentious simply because it is encumbered with heavy social, racial, and political freight that conditions our expectations for the region.

Over time the Anacostia has been a river formed and influenced by the energizing forces of racial slavery, economic change, urbanization, and pollution. The Anacostia's history has been one of constant change, and there can be no going back to that simpler time when the Anacostans harvested wild rice along its banks, celebrated the seasons, and placed the bones of their dead in ossuaries.

As Wendell Berry has explained in his *A Continuous Harmony*, our sense of place is historically conditioned, and without a sense of place, people are rootless and wont to drift. Our relationships with rivers like the Anacostia are relationships between environment and civic life. It concerns more than the physical defects of pollution, storm water runoff or sprawl. "The health and even the continuance of our life in America, in all regions, require that we enact in the most particular terms a responsible relationship to the land."[1]

Our organizational and technological skills far outstrip our moral and social development; the ethical costs of environmental change are not yet a part of our every day political and community life. We have yet to reach the point at which we can combine the ideas of ecological, social, and economic recovery into a single compelling vision of progressive change in America.

Ultimately we must recognize the fact that history will not go away. Neither will the Anacostia. Rivers have destinies of their own that do not always yield to human desires for economic and social development. Furthermore, controversies over the Anacostia were less economic and far more racial, aesthetic, and spiritual than we had supposed

We are just now beginning to understand the complex interplay between the city and the country and the role that technology has played in all of this. Over the past several centuries technology has been essential to the exploitation of nature, in the harvesting and extracting of resources like tobacco and timber and the transportation of raw and finished materials on the Anacostia waterway. William Cronon has referred to this process as people transforming "first nature" into "second nature"—a nature constructed by humans and subject to the whims of the national political economy, whether in energy, production or habitat.[2] Engineering efforts to manipulate and control nature have had a disastrous impact in the Anacostia watershed.

Currently in the United States we still function within a market economy that advances economic growth by depleting natural and social capital. Major aquatic habitats such as wetlands, floodplains, spawning and rearing grounds, and estuaries continue to be paved over, drained, filled, dammed, channeled, and otherwise altered by the onslaught of human activity.

The rapid metropolitan development of the Anacostia watershed poses challenges and limits to the potential restoration of the river. No single organization or government agency can restore the Anacostia. The work will always demand more money and more research on the state of the watershed. If the river is to survive, we may have to devise more creative approaches to dealing with our consumer economy. As public historian Jeffrey Stine has noted, "We ought to counter the all too common assertion that environmental laws and regulations needlessly impose economic hardship on businesses and the country as a whole."³

While it is impractical to approach this issue with a Huck Finn–like romanticism, it is possible to see in rivers like the Anacostia the key to environmental redemption. Rivers have not only been our source of water in America, they have conditioned our civic and social imagination. Today, every river in the United States is attracting population growth along its banks. In terms of amenities and recreation, rivers are part of the great urban redesign of America. Washington and other cities with long neglected river systems are discovering that rivers provide visually appealing environmental vistas that, in the words of Washington, D.C., mayor Anthony Williams, "offer repose, tranquility, and beauty. We love urban riverfronts because they provide a theater for human activity and because they offer a respite from urban stresses."⁴ Rivers, in other words, bring people together.

If we lose these water resources to pollution and development, we do so at great peril to the nation. Advances in scientific research and social planning, along with the will and commitment of government and citizen stakeholders, have made it possible to begin the rescue of the Anacostia and other urban rivers with broad-based initiatives to reconnect with history and make our urban waterways "swimmable and fishable" once more. If we return to our rivers and deal with them in a humane and historically sensitive manner, we can make the dream of civilized urban habitat a future reality.

Roberta Flack, the famous singer who began her career at "Mr. Henry's" restaurant on Capitol Hill once said, "There's a river somewhere that flows through the lives of everyone." Today many residents of metropolitan Washington have begun to recognize that the Anacostia flows through us.

References

Introduction

[1] Includes the entire population of the District of Columbia.

[2] Wilbur Zelinsky, "Landscapes," *Encyclopedia of American Social History* (New York: Scribner's, 1993), 2:1289. Richard Brewer, *Conservancy: The Land Trust Movement in America* (Hanover: Dartmouth College Press, 2003), 8.

[3] Libby Hill, *The Chicago River: A Natural and Unnatural History* (Chicago: Lake Clement Press, 2000); Blake Gumbrecht, *The Los Angeles River: Its Life, Death, and Possible Rebirth* (Baltimore: Johns Hopkins University Press, 1999).

[4] Louise Hutchinson, *The Anacostia Story, 1608-1930* (Washington: Smithsonian Institution Press, 1977).

[5] For good examples of this genre, see Frederic Gutheim, *The Potomac* (Baltimore: Johns Hopkins University Press, 1977) and Susan Q. Stranahan, *Susquehanna: River of Dreams* (Baltimore: Johns Hopkins University Press, 1993).

[6] David Schlosberg, *Environmental Justice and the New Pluralism* (New York: Oxford University Press, 1999).

Notes to Chapter One

[1] Richard J. Dent, Jr., *Chesapeake Prehistory: Old Traditions, New Directions* (New York: Plenum Press, 1995), 84–85. See also, K. Bruce Jones et al., *An Ecological Assessment of the United States Mid-Atlantic Region* (Washington, D.C.: Environmental Protection Agency, 1997), 1–104.

[2] C. W. Gilmore, "Fossil Animals in the District of Columbia," unpublished essay, 1933, Papers on Natural History, Box 37, Audubon Society Ms., Smithsonian Institution Archives.

[3] David B. Weishample and Luther O. Young, "Dinosaurs of the East Coast," *Johns Hopkins Magazine*, June 1996, electronic edition.

[4] Peter M. Kranz, *Dinosaurs of the District of Columbia* (Washington, D.C.: Dinosaur Fund, 2003), 13–21.

[5] J. D. MacDougall, *A Short History of the Planet Earth* (New York: John Wiley & Sons, 1998), 155–77.

[6] Grace S. Brush, "Forests Before and After the Colonial Encounter," in Philip Curtin, ed., *Discovering the Chesapeake: The History of an Ecosystem* (Baltimore: Johns Hopkins University Press, 2001), 1.

[7] Dent, *Chesapeake Prehistory*, 231.

[8] See Helen C. Rountree and Thomas E. Davidson, *Eastern Shore Indians of Virginia and Maryland* (Charlottesville: University Press of Virginia, 1997,) 1–46.

[9] Wayne E. Clark, "The Origin of the Piscataway and Related Indian Cultures," *Maryland Historical Magazine*, 75 (1980): 15.

[10] Thomas J. Cantwell, "Anacostia: Strength in Adversity," *Records of the Columbia Historical Society, 1973–1974,* 332,

[11] William Wallace Tooker, "On the Meaning of the Name Anacostia," *American Anthropologist,* vol. 7, October, 1894, 390.

[12] Jay F. Custer, *Prehistoric Cultures of the Delmarva Peninsula* (Newark: University of Delaware Press, 1989).

[13] Timothy Silver, *A New Face on the Countryside: Indians, Colonists, and Slaves in the South Atlantic Forests, 1500–1800* (Cambridge: Cambridge University Press, 1992), 49.

[14] Thomas Harriot, "A brief and true report of the new found land of Virginia" (1588), in Michael Alexander, ed., *Discovering the New World Based on the Books of Theodore DeBry* (New York: Harper and Row, 1976), 77, 79.

[15] Quoted in J. Thomas Scharf, *History of Maryland from the Earliest Period to the Present Day,* 3 vols. (Hatboro: Tradition Press, 1967), 1:10.

[16] P. L. Barbour, *The Complete Works of Captain John Smith,* 3 vols. (Chapel Hill: University of North Carolina Press, 1986), 2:167.

[17] See Dent, *Chesapeake Prehistory,* 271–85.

[18] Rountree and Davidson, *Eastern Shore Indians of Virginia and Maryland,* 85.

[19] "Narrative of Captain Henry Fleet," quoted in Scharf, *History of Maryland,* 1:13–20.

[20] A. J. Morison, "The Virginia Indian Trade to 1673," *William and Mary College Quarterly Historical Magazine,* series 2, vol. 1 (1921): 217–36.

[21] *Proceedings of the County Courts of Charles County, 1666–1674, Archives of Maryland,* vol. 60, preface, 45.

[22] Alfred Crosby, *Ecological Imperialism: The Biological Expansion of Europe* (Cambridge: Cambridge University Press, 1986), 210–13.

[23] Paul A. Shakel and Barbara J. Little, *Historical Archeology of the Chesapeake* (Washington D.C.: Smithsonian Institution Press, 1994), 31.

[24] For a radical critique of development in the New World, see Eduardo Galeano, *Open Veins of Latin America* (New York: Monthly Review Press, 1997).

Notes to Chapter Two

[1] "Narrative of Captain Henry Fleet," quoted in Scharf, *History of Maryland,* 1:13–20. See also Betsy Fleet, *Henry Fleete: Pioneer, Explorer, Trader, Planter* (Richmond: Privately printed, 1989).

[2] Rhys Isaac, *The Transformation of Virginia, 1749–1790* (Chapel Hill: University of North Carolina Press, 1982).

[3] J. Frederick Fausz, "Present at the Creation: The Chesapeake World that Greeted Maryland Colonists," *Maryland Historical Magazine,* 79 (1984): 12.

[4] The buffalo were marsh-dwelling animals in Maryland that ranged from the Anacostia to modern Garrett County. See Hamill Kenney, *The Placenames of Maryland: Their Origin and Meaning* (Baltimore: Maryland Historical Society, 1984), 49.

[5] Philip D. Morgan, *Slave Counterpoint: Black Culture in the Eighteenth-Century Chesapeake and Lowland* (Chapel Hill: University of North Carolina Press, 1998), 36.

[6] Bessie Gahn, *Original Patentees of Land at Washington Prior to 1770* (Silver Spring, Md.: Privately printed, 1936), 107.

[7] Agricultural report of Thomas Johnson, quoted in Wilhelmus Bogart Bryan, *History of the National Capital from Its Foundation Through the Period of the Adoption of the Organic Act*, 2 vols. (New York: The Macmillan Company, 1914–16), 1:171–72.

[8] For background see Allan Kulikoff, "The Colonial Chesapeake: Seedbed of Antebellum Southern Culture," *Journal of Southern History*, 45 (1979): 513–40.

[9] For background on the Notley family, see Harry Wright Newman, *To Maryland from Overseas* (Baltimore: Genealogical Publishing Company, 1986).

[10] Lois Green Carr and Lorena S. Walsh, "The Planter's Wife: The Experience of White Women in Seventeenth-Century Maryland," *William and Mary Quarterly*, 34 (1977): 564.

[11] Louise Daniel Hutchinson, *The Anacostia Story, 1608–1930* (Washington: Smithsonian Institution Press, 1977), 9.

[12] Ibid., 9.

[13] Prince George's County Court, Inventory of Thomas Addison, March 16, 1775, Prince George's Inventories, Recorded October 14, 1775.

[14] Ruth Beall Gelders, "Colonel Ninian Bell," File, Daughters of the American Revolution, Joseph Habersham Chapter, Atlanta, Georgia, 1976, www.geocities.com/Athens5568/Ninian1.HTML.

[15] For an exploration of planter wealth at this time see Jackson Turner Main, "The One Hundred," *William and Mary Quarterly*, 3rd series, 11 (1954): 354–84.

[16] Carson Gibb, "Captain Berry's Will: Debauchery, Miscegenation and Family Strife Among 18th Century Gentry," transcription, Record Group, SC 2221-28, Maryland State Archives, Annapolis.

[17] The land around Capitol Hill was part of a very large plantation estate put together in 1670 by Thomas Notley, who purchased the land from Thomas Gerrard and George Thompson. Notley united the earlier land grants into one manorial holding that he called Gerne Abbey Manor. Notley's godson, Notley Rozier, maintained the estate, which passed to his daughter Ann Rozier, who in 1727 married Daniel Carroll, uncle of Charles Carroll of Carrollton. Upon Carroll's death, his widow married Colonel Benjamin Young and became the stepmother of Notley Young.

[18] Frederick Tilp, *This Was Potomac River* (Alexandria, Va.: Privately printed, 1978), 159.

[19] Kulikoff, "Colonial Chesapeake," 535.

[20] Donald M. Sweig, "The Importation of African Slaves to the Potomac River, 1732–1772," *William and Mary Quarterly*, 42 (1985): 523.

[21] Ira Berlin, *Many Thousands Gone: The First Two Centuries of Slavery in North America* (Cambridge: Harvard University Press, 1998), 119, 117, 110. Berlin argues that after 1700 the Chesapeake replaced the Caribbean as the most profitable slave market in British North America.

[22] Allan Kulikoff, "The Origins of Afro-American Society in Tidewater Maryland and Virginia, 1700 to 1790," *William and Mary Quarterly*, 35 (1978): 239–40.

[23] John C. Pearson, "The Fish and Fisheries of Colonial Virginia," *William and Mary Quarterly*, series 2, vol. 22 (1943): 435–39 et passim.

[24] Morgan, *Slave Counterpoint*, 242–44.

[25] Quoted in Rev. John F. Biddle, "Bladensburg: An Early Trade Center," *Records of the Columbia Historical Society*, vols. 53–56 (1953–1956): 313.

[26] George D. Denny, *Proud Past Promising Future: A History of Prince George's Municipalities* (n.p., privately printed, 1994).

[27] The *Maryland Gazette* from 1749 through 1761 contains numerous references to the growth, development, and problems of the port of Bladensburg.

[28] Nelson R. Burr, "The Federal City Depicted, 1612–1801," *Library of Congress Quarterly Journal,* 8 (1950): 67 et passim.

[29] *Maryland Gazette,* January 21, 1761.

[30] Arthur Pierce Middleton, *Tobacco Coast: A Maritime History of Chesapeake Bay in the Colonial Era* (1953; repr., Baltimore: Johns Hopkins University Press, 1984), 58.

[31] See Jack Larkin, *The Reshaping of Everyday Life 1790–1840* (New York: Harper and Row, 1988), xv; Richard D. Brown, *Modernization: The Transformation of American Life, 1600–1865* (New York: McGraw-Hill, 1976), 107; E. L. Jones, "Creative Disruptions in American Agriculture, 1620–1820," *Agricultural History,* 48 (1974): 519.

[32] Brett Williams, "A River Runs Through Us," *American Anthropologist,* 103 (2001): 409.

Notes to Chapter Three

[1] Bryan, *History of the National Capital from Its Foundation . . .* , 1:68.

[2] See John Michael Vlach, "The Mysterious Mr. Jenkins of Jenkins Hill: The Early History of the Capital Site," *The Capital Dome,* U.S. Capitol Historical Society, Spring, 2004.

[3] Tobias Lear, *Observations on the River Potomak, the Country Adjacent and the City of Washington* (New York: Samuel Loudon, 1793). Reprinted in *Records of the Columbia History Society,* 8 (1905): 117–40.

[4] Carl Abbott, *Political Terrain: Washington, D.C. from Tidewater Town to Global Metropolis* (Chapel Hill: University of North Carolina Press, 1999), 41.

[5] Lucinda Prout Janke and Iris Miller, "Facilitating Transportation and Communication: The Prigs Map," in Iris Miller, *Washington in Maps, 1606–2000* (New York: Rizzoli International Publications, 2002), 32–33.

[6] Miller, *Washington in Maps, 1606–2000,* 44–45.

[7] Bob Arnebeck, *Through a Fiery Trial: Building Washington, 1790–1800* (Lanham, Md.: Madison Books, 1991), 3–4.

[8] Constance McLaughlin Green, *Washington: Village and Capital, 1800–1878* (Princeton: Princeton University Press, 1962), 5.

[9] Stephen H. Spurr, "George Washington, Surveyor and Ecological Observer," *Ecology,* 32 (1951): 544–49.

[10] See Margaret Brent Downing, "The Development of the Catholic Church in the District of Columbia from Colonial Times Until the Present," address before the Columbia Historical Society, February 21, 1911, Washington, D.C.

[11] See Margaret Brent Downing, "The American Capitoline Hill and Its Early Catholic Proprietors," *Catholic Historical Review,* 2 (1911): 269–82.

[12] See biography, Special Collections Register, William Prout Papers, 1783–1801, MS 216, Historical Society of Washington, D.C.

[13] According to local urban folklore, Stephen Girard, a French immigrant and the

richest man in Philadelphia, offered Daniel Carroll $200,000 for his Capitol Hill estate. Carroll refused the offer, saying the land was worth five times that price.

[14] Kenneth R. Bowling, *The Creation of Washington D.C.: The Idea and Location of the American Capital* (Fairfax: George Mason University Press, 1991), 213–21.

[15] C. M. Harris, "Washington's Gamble, L'Enfant's Dream: Politics, Design and the Founding of the National Capital," *William and Mary Quarterly*, 56 (1999): 536–57.

[16] Bryan, *A History of the National Capital*, 1:217. A full explanation of early real estate machinations in the capital can be found in Bob Arnebeck, *Through a Fiery Trial*, 147–89, et passim.

[17] Quoted in Arnebeck, *Through a Fiery Trial*, 65.

[18] See Kenneth Bowling, "The Other G.W.: George Walker and the Creation of the National Capital," *Washington History*, 3 (Fall/Winter 1991/1992): 5–21.

[19] Bryan, *A History of the National Capital*, 1:247.

[20] Significantly, in 1883, Benjamin Young, the great-grandson of Notley Young, sued in the courts to recover riverfront property between 7th and 11th Streets in the central part of the city that, he contended had been illegally transferred out of Notley's Young's estate into private and public ownership. His suit was unsuccessful. The U.S. Supreme Court ruled that with the founding of Washington all riparian rights accrued to the District of Columbia. See "A Claimant for the Riverfront," *Washington Post*, February 21, 1883, p. 4; "Riverfront Wharf Rights," ibid., January 8, 1884, p. 1.

[21] Bryan, *A History of the National Capital*, 1:304.

[22] See biographical summary, *Thomas Law Family Papers, 1791–1834*, MS 2386, Maryland Historical Society.

[23] John Williams Ward, ed., *Manners and Politics in the United States: Letters on North America* (Garden City, N.Y.: Anchor Books, 1961), 194–200.

[24] Robert Adam, "Naval Office on the Potomac," *William and Mary Quarterly*, 2nd series, vol. 2 (1922): 292–95.

[25] As early as 1795 the Maryland legislature authorized Congressman Daniel Carroll and Notley Young to hold two annual lotteries to raise $52,000 to cut a canal through Washington, D.C. The lottery, Young reported to the legislature, failed miserably in the sale of tickets.

[26] Constance McLaughlin Green, *Washington*, 2 vols. (Princeton: Princeton University Press, 1962–63), 1:28–29; Ira Berlin and Herbert G. Gutman, "Natives and Immigrants, Freemen and Slaves: Urban Workingmen in the Antebellum South," *American Historical Review*, 88 (1983): 1194–95, et passim. During the Civil War, Irish workers in Georgetown prospered, and many opened saloons and stores a short distance from the docks where they had worked like mules two decades earlier. See also Margaret H. McAleer, "The Green Streets of Washington: The Experience of Irish Mechanics in Antebellum Washington," in Francine Curro Carry, *Washington Odyssey: A Multicultural History of the Nation's Capital* (Washington: Smithsonian Books, 1996), 42–60.

[27] Quoted in Howard Gillette, *Between Justice and Beauty: Race, Planning and the Failure of Urban Policy in Washington, D.C.* (Baltimore: Johns Hopkins University Press, 1995), 17.

²⁸ See John Seeyle, *Beautiful Machine: Rivers and the Republican Plan, 1775–1825* (New York: Oxford University Press, 1991).

²⁹ James F. Duhamel, "Tiber Creek," *Records of the Columbia Historical Society,* 28 (1926): 203–25; William M. Franklin, "The Tidewater End of the Chesapeake and Ohio Canal," *Maryland Historical Magazine,* 81 (1986): 302–3.

³⁰ Taylor Peck, *Round-shot to Rockets: A History of the Washington Navy Yard and U.S. Naval Gun Factory* (Annapolis: United States Naval Institute Press, 1949), 10–69.

³¹ Edwin W. Beitzell, *Life on the Potomac River* (Abell, Md.: n.p., 1973), 27.

³² Letitia Woods Brown, "Residence Patterns of Negroes in the District of Columbia, 1800-1860," *Records of the Columbia Historical Society,* 69–70 (1969–70): 67–68.

³³ Green, *Washington,* 1:181–84.

³⁴ Diary of Michael Shiner, 1813–1865, Manuscript Division, Library of Congress.

³⁵ Harold Anderson, "Slavery, Freedom and the Chesapeake," *Maryland Marine Notes,* 16 (March/April, 1998).

³⁶ Quoted in Jeffrey Bolster, *Black Jacks: African-American Seamen in the Age of Sail* (Cambridge: Harvard University Press, 1997), 71.

³⁷ Robert J. Kapsch, "Building Liberty's Capital: Black Labor and the New Federal City," *American Visions* (February/March, 1995).

³⁸⁹ For an overview, see Bob Arnebeck, "Slaves in Early Washington," www.geocities.com/bobarnebeck/slaves.html.

³⁹ Letitia Woods Brown, *Free Negroes in the District of Columbia* (New York: Oxford University Press, 1972), 13.

⁴⁰ Constance McLaughlin Green, *Secret City: A History of Race Relations in the Nation's Capital* (Princeton: Princeton University Press, 1967), 13–34.

Notes to Chapter Four

¹ Ludwig Deppisch, "Andrew Jackson and American Medical Practice: Old Hickory and His Physicians," *Tennessee Historical Quarterly,* 63 (2003): 15–32.

² Betty L. Plummer, "A History of Public Health in Washington, D.C., 1800–1890," Ph.D. diss., University of Maryland, College Park, 1984.

³ Charles E. Rosenberg, *The Cholera Years: The United States in 1832, 1849, and 1866* (Chicago: University of Chicago Press, 1987), 2–3.

⁴ Plummer, "History of Public Health in Washington," 1:39–60.

⁵ Ibid.

⁶ Dr. Nathaniel P. Causin, "An Essay on the Autumnal Bilious Epidemic of the United States," *The American Medical Recorder,* January, 1824, 55–70, American Periodical Series Online.

⁷ Jones, "Creative Disruptions in American Agriculture, 1620–1820," 519; Lewis C. Gray, *History of Agriculture in the Southern States to 1860* (1933; repr., Gloucester, Mass.: Peter Smith, 1968), 1:126; George Anderson, "Growth, Civil War, and Change: The Montgomery County Agricultural Society, 1850–1876," *Maryland Historical Magazine,* 86 (1991): 396–406.

⁸ Harold T. Pinkett, "*The American Farmer*: A Pioneer Agricultural Journal, 1819–1834," *Agricultural History,* 24 (1950): 146–50.

⁹ "Charles Benedict Calvert," *Biographical Directory of the United States Congress, 1771 to the Present* (Washington, 1990).

¹⁰ *Washington Evening Star,* June 20, 1861.

¹¹ Garrett Power, *Chesapeake Bay in Legal Perspective* (Washington: U.S. Department of the Interior, 1970), 206.

¹² Michael A. Cooke, "Physical Environment and Sanitation in the District of Columbia, 1860–1868," *Records of the Columbia Historical Society of Washington, D.C.,* 52 (1989): 293.

¹³ For an overview of military camp life in the District see Michael A. Cooke, "The Health of the Union Military in the District of Columbia, 1861–1865, *Military Affairs,* 48 (1984): 194–99.

¹⁴ Ernest B. Ferguson, *Freedom Rising: Washington in the Civil War* (New York: Alfred A. Knopf, 2004), 301.

¹⁵ *Washington Evening Star,* May 16, 1864.

¹⁶ Franklin Cooling III, "Civil War Deterrent: Defenses of Washington," *Military Affairs,* 29 (Winter, 1965–1966): 164–78.

¹⁷ Dorothy Provine, "The Economic Position of the Free Blacks in the District of Columbia, 1800–1860," *The Journal of Negro History,* 58 (1973): 61–72.

¹⁸ Benjamin Henry Latrobe, *The Journal of Latrobe. Being the Notes and Sketches of an Architect, Naturalist and Traveler in the United States from 1796 to 1820* (New York: D. Appleton and Company, 1905), 131.

¹⁹ Green, *Washington,* 1:234–35.

²⁰ Plummer, "History of Public Health in Washington," 1:108.

²¹ Ferguson, *Freedom Rising,* 256–57.

Note to Chapter Five

¹ Mary Clemmer Ames, *Ten Years in Washington: Life and Scenes in the National Capital* (Hartford, Conn.: Worthington and Company, 1873), 69.

² Quoted in Green, *Washington,* 1:83.

³ Plummer, "History of Public Health in Washington, D.C. 1800–1890," 1:184.

⁴ Alfred Thayer Mahan, *The Influence of Seapower Upon History, 1660–1783* (repr.; New York: Sagamore Press, 1957).

⁵ Peck, *Round-shot to Rockets,* 188.

⁶ George E. Waring Jr., *Report on the Social Statistics of Cities,* Part II (Washington: Government Printing Office, 1887), 51–52.

⁷ David R. Goldfield, "The Business of Health Planning: Disease Prevention in the Old South," *Journal of Southern History,* 42 (1976): 559–63.

⁸ D.C. Water and Sewer Authority, *History of Our Sewerage System,* www.dcwasa.com.

⁹ For an overview of the problem see, Stanley K. Schultz and Clay McShane, "To Engineer the Metropolis: Sewers, Sanitation and City Planning in Late Nineteenth-Century America," *Journal of American History,* 65 (1978): 389–411.

¹⁰ "Valuation of Real Property," *City of Washington Statistical Maps, 1880.* For an overview, see Green, *Washington,* 2:42–46.

¹¹ For a good overview of Washington at this time see William L. Gillette, *Between Justice and Beauty.*

[12] Plummer, "History of Public Health in Washington, D.C.," 2:9.

[13] James Maskalyk, "Typhoid," *Canadian Medical Association Journal*, vol. 169 (July 22, 2003): 132.

[14] Werner Troesken, "Race, Disease and the Provision of Water in American cities, 1889–1921," unpublished paper, Department of History, University of Pittsburgh, December, 2000.

[15] H. F. Mills, "Typhoid Fever in Relation to Water Supplies," *Journal of the New England Waterworks Association*, 5 (1891): 149–61.

[16] Plummer, "History of Public Health in Washington, D.C.," 2:212.

[17] Plummer, "History of Public Health in Washington," 2:222.

[18] Martin V. Melosi, *Garbage in the Cities: Refuse, Reform and the Environment, 1880–1930* (New York: Dorsey Press, 1981), 79–104.

[19] Alvah H. Doty, M.D. "Cholera from a Modern Standpoint," *The American Journal of Medical Sciences*, vol. 141, January 11, 1911.

[20] John Duffy, *The Sanitarians, A History of American Public Health* (Urbana: University of Illinois Press, 1990), 316.

[21] Plummer, "History of Public Health in Washington." 2:182.

[22] Fred Mather, "Poisoning and Obstructing the Waters," *Forest and Stream—A Journal of Outdoor Life*, vol. 4, February 18, 1875.

[23] "The Purification of Rivers," *Appleton's Journal of Literature, Science and Art*, vol. 12, October 17, 1874.

[24] "What is Bad Water?" *Scientific American*, vol. 34, June 10, 1876.

[25] Professor John Darby, "The Disposal of Sewage," *Scientific American*, vol. 23, July 9, 1870,

[26] Alan Lessoff, *The Nation and Its City: Politics, "Corruption" and Progress in Washington, D.C., 1861–1902* (Baltimore: The Johns Hopkins University Press, 1994), 90–94.

[27] Waring, *Report on the Social Statistics of Cities*, Part II, 27–52.

[28] Green, *Washington*, 2:45.

[29] Michael Farquhar, "The City's Pretty New Face, Boss Shepherd Got the Job Done—at a Steep Price," *Washington Post*, November 28, 2000.

[39] "Bathing Old Habit While Sanitation Is Recent Practice," *Washington Post*, April 3, 1927, F 10.

[31] Martin V. Melosi, *The Sanitary City: Urban Infrastructure from Colonial Times to the Present* (Baltimore: Johns Hopkins University Press, 2000), 19.

[32] Waring, *Report on the Social Statistics of Cities*, Part II, 45.

[33] Melosi, *The Sanitary City*, 46–60.

[34] Lt. F. V. Green for the Commissioners of Washington, D.C., *City of Washington Statistical Maps*, Map No. 7, Sewers, 1880.

[35] "Sewer Districts and Sewer Lines, Washington, 1880," in Waring, *Report on the Social Statistics of Cities*, Part II, 41.

[36] "The Tiber Creek Flushing Gates, Washington, D.C.," *Engineering News and Railway Journal*, February 8, 1994.

[37] George W. Rafter and M. N. Baker, *Sewage Disposal in the United States* (New York: Van Nostrand and Company, 1894), 125.

[38] Ibid.

[39] "Washington's Greatest Need: A Better Sewage System," *Washington Post,* January 11, 1896, p. 4.

[40] "New Sewage Pumping Plant," *Washington Post,* August 4, 1901, p.12

[41] "Rush Sewage System," *Washington Post,* November 4, 1906, R6.

[42] United States House of Representatives, 51st Congress Document 445, *Report Upon the Sewerage of the District of Columbia* (Washington: Government Printing Office, 1890).

[43] "New Sewage Pumping Plant," *Washington Post,* August 4, 1901, p. 12; "Rush Sewage System," ibid., November 4, 1906, R6.

[44] *Report of the Potomac River Oyster Pollution Commission* (Washington, D.C., 1912).

[45] Rudolph Hering and Samuel A. Greeley, *Collection and Disposal of Municipal Refuse* (New York: 1921), 13, 28; Washington D.C. Health Department, *Report of Health Officer,* 1889, 31.

[46] F. H. Newell, "Pollution of the Potomac River," *National Geographic,* 8 (1897): 351.

[47] "Stop River Pollution," *Washington Post,* February 28, 1906, p. 2.

[48] "Scrutiny of the Potomac," *Washington Post,* November 29, 1904, p. 12; "Report on Potomac River pollution," " ibid., February 14, 1905, p. 10; "The New Consulting Hydrographer" ibid., May 11, 1907, p. 4.

Notes to Chapter Six

[1] "Striped Bass Fishing," *Forest and Stream: A Journal of Outdoor Life,* October 21, 1886, 6.

[2] Henry Talbott, "Fishing Up and Down the Eastern Branch of the Potomac," ibid., March 12, 1898, 210.

[3] John Burroughs, *Wake Robin* (Boston: Houghton Mifflin, 1899), 139, 56–233.

[4] J. V. Glumer, "Map of the Anacostia River or Eastern Branch Region," Geography and Maps Division, Library of Congress, 1880.

[5] "Hunting Season Begins," *Washington Post,* September 1, 1914, p. 10.

[6] "Reed Bird and Ortolan, A Busy Day for Sportsmen in the Eastern Branch Marshes," *Washington Post,* September 2, 1884, p. 4.

[7] "Farms of a Few Acres," *Washington Post,* November 29, 1889, p. 8.

[8] For background on the rural character of Anacostia at this time, see Louise Daniel Hutchinson, *The Anacostia Story, 1608–1930* (Washington, D.C.: Smithsonian Institution Press, 1977).

[9] "Three Groups Immersed," *Washington Post,* May 4, 1896.

[10] "District Audubon Society," *Washington Star,* February 11, 1905, Clip File, Audubon Records, Box 1, Record Unit 7294, Smithsonian Institution Archives. See also "Obituary: Paul Bartsch," *Journal of Conchology,* 25 (July 1961).

[11] Paul Bartsch, "Notes on the Herons of the District of Columbia," Smithsonian Miscellaneous Collections, vol. XLV, No. 1419, 1904, pp. 104–11.

[12] Christine E. Seidenschnur, "The Botanical Activities of Paul Bartsch (1870–1960)," *Proceedings of the Biological Society of Washington,* 78 (1961: 272–92; Irston Barnes, "Paul Bartsch, Smithsonian Curator," *Atlantic Naturalist,* January–February, 1953, 124–39; Irston Barnes, "Paul Bartsch, Biologist and Naturalist," *Atlantic Naturalist,* May–August, 1952, 217–29.

¹³ *Annual Report, Chief of Engineers*, 1889, vol. 2, 994.

¹⁴ "Another Aquatic Mecca is Due in Near Future," *Washington Post*, July 30, 1916, p. S2.

¹⁵ "Formal Start Made for Anacostia Park," *Washington Post*, August 3, 1923, p. 13.

¹⁶ "Southeast Capital Developed through Growth of Navy Yard," *Washington Post*, March 10, 1929, p. M22. For an historic overview of the "Aquatic Mecca," see *Report of the Chief of Engineers*, vol. 1, 1927, 1926–33.

¹⁷ "Anacostia Project Assessments Plan Assailed as Unfair," *Washington Post*, February 29, 1924; "Would Develop Anacostia Flats," ibid., January 17, 1924.

¹⁸ "Anacostia Park Plan Progressing." *Washington Post*, August 1, 1924, p. 7.

¹⁹ National Capital Planning Commission, Frederick Gutheim, consultant, *Worthy of the Nation: The History of Planning for the National Capital* (Washington, D.C.: Smithsonian Institution Press, 1977), 142.

²⁰ "River Commerce Less at Capital," *Washington Post*, August 5, 1919, p. 13.

²¹ Audubon Society to General Lansing Beach, Chief of Engineers, Washington, D.C., November 9, 1923, Box 2, 1916–1925, Audubon Records, Smithsonian Institution Archives.

²² "Park Developments," *Washington Post*, January 14, 1925, p. 6.

²³ "Condemns Site for Park," *Washington Post*, April. 21, 1920, p. 1.

²⁴ "Southeast to Unite in Fight for Water Main Extensions." *Washington Post*, December 29, 1925. p. 8; "Anacostia's Water Situation Held Acute," ibid., August 30, 1925.

²⁵ "Anacostia Reality Boom," *Washington Post*, January 1, 1926.`

²⁶ "Anacostia Reality Boom," *Washington Post*, January 1, 1926.

²⁷ George C. Havenner, "The Old and the New Anacostia," *Washington Post*, January 24, 1926.

²⁸ "The Polluted Potomac," *Washington Post*, September 5, 1925, p. 6.

²⁹ Lisa Bentley, *Historic Significance of Takoma Park*, www.takoma.org.

³⁰ Robert J. Brugger, *Maryland: A Middle Temperament, 1634–1980* (Baltimore: Johns Hopkins University Press in association with the Maryland Historical Society, 1988), 442.

³¹ "Sewers for Suburbs," *Washington Post*, March 15, 1916.

³² *Report of the Chief of Engineers, US Army*, vol. 2, 1914, 1892–93.

³³ *Report of the Chief of Engineers, U.S. Army*, vol. 3, 1914, 3399–3401.

³⁴ *Report of the Chief of Engineers, U.S. Army*, vol. 1, 1921, 2027–2029.

³⁵ "Anacostia Flats Reclamation Plan Would Fill 6 Years," *Washington Post*, February 21, 1926, p. 10.

³⁶ Flooding of Anacostia Due to Erosion," *Washington Post*, August 13, 1945, p. 4.

Notes to Chapter Seven

¹ *Annual Report of the Chief of Engineers, 1878* (Washington, D.C.: Government Printing Office), 1:503.

² Washington Engineer Commissioner, "Map of the City of Washington, D.C.," 1883. Geography and Print Division, Library of Congress.

³ Topographical Map of the District of Columbia and a Portion of Virginia, U.S. Army Corps of Engineers, 1884, Geography and Maps Division, Library of Congress.

[4] *Annual Report of the Chief of Engineers*, vol. 2, 1878, 506.

[5] Martin K. Gordon, "The Origins of the Anacostia River Improvement Project," *Soundings: A Journal of the Writings and Studies of the Potomac River Basin Consortium*, Spring 1987.

[6] "Examination of the East Branch of Potomac River from the Navy Yard to Bladensburg," *Annual Report of the Chief of Engineers*, 1876, 1:355–58.

[7] "Urges Ship Canal to Bay," *Washington Post*, May 24, 1910, p. 4.

[8] Ibid. 505–6.

[9] "The Malaria at the Jail," *Washington Post*, November 10, 1881, p. 2.

[10] Gordon, "Origins of the Anacostia River Improvement Project," 12.

[11] "Reclaiming the River Flats" *Washington Post*, June 4, 1880, p. 4.

[12] "Work on the River Flats," ibid., July 7, 1888.

[13] "Reclamation of Flats," *Washington Post*, December 17, 1898, p. 12; "Big Sums for Sewers, ibid., October 10, 1895, p.10.

[14] "Anacostans Are Aroused," *Washington Post*, November 12, 1909, p. 5.

[15] Betty Plummer, "History of Public Health in Washington," 2:149.

[16] Gordon, "Origins of the Anacostia River Improvement Project," 13.

[17] "Urge Reclamation," *Washington Post*, October 14, 1909.

[18] Hugh T. Taggart, *Public and Private Rights on the Anacostia River* (Washington: 62nd Congress, 1911).

[19] Map of Anacostia River in the District of Columbia and Maryland, surveyed Under the direction of Lt. Colonel Peter C. Haines, 1880. Geography and Map Division, Library of Congress.

[20] "Urge Reclamation," *Washington Post*, October 14, 1909.

[21] "To Ask Aid for Flats," ibid., October 19, 1909.

[22] Gutheim, *Worthy of the Nation*, 142–43; "Favors New River Park," *Washington Post*, June 25, 1912, p. 16.

[23] Gutheim, *Worthy of the Nation*, 141–46.

[24] See *Baist Insurance Atlas of Washington, D.C., 1903*, vol. 2 and *Sanborn Insurance Map of Washington, D.C., 1927*, Plate 935, Geography and Prints Division, Library of Congress.

[25] Baist Real Estate Surveys of Washington. D.C. (1903–1909), G1275.B2, Geography and Prints Division, Library of Congress.

[26] Gillette, *Between Justice and Beauty*, 73.

[27] Ruth Ann Overbeck, "Capitol Hill: The Capitol is Just Up the Street," the Ruth Ann Overbeck Capitol Hill Project, CapitolHistory.org.

[28] John A. Carpenter, *Sword and Olive Branch: Oliver Otis Howard* (Pittsburgh: University of Pittsburgh Press, 1964), 188.

[29] Such developments must have irritated George Washington Talbert, a former slave-owner, who was still one of the wealthiest men in the Anacostia and owned 327 acres overlooking Washington, where the Anacostia community museum is now located.

[30] Hutchinson, *The Anacostia Story*, 136.

[31] For background see Hutchinson, *The Anacostia Story*.

[32] "It Was a Mighty Rain," *Washington Post*, June 1, 1889, p. 2.

[33] "Need of a Sewerage System," *Washington Post*, February 15, 1899, p. 11.

[34] "Big Sewer Now in Construction Near the Capitol," ibid., September 26, 1898.

Notes to Chapter Eight
[1] John Dos Passos, "Anacostia Flats," *New Republic*, June 1932.
[2] Quoted in Paul Dickson and Thomas B. Allen, *The Bonus Army: An American Epic* (New York: Walker and Company, 2004), 151.
[3] Quoted in Jennifer D. Keene, *Doughboys, the Great War, and the Remaking of America* (Baltimore: Johns Hopkins University Press, 2001), 191.
[4] "Bonus Army to Erect Own Camp Near City," *Washington Post*, May 28, 1932, p. 1.
[5] John W. Killigrew, "The Army and the Bonus Incident," *Military Affairs*, 26 (1962): 59.
[6] Linda Wheeler, "Routing a Ragtag American Army," *Washington Post*, April 12, 1999, p. A01
[7] Quoted in Wyatt Kingseed, "A Promise Denied: The Bonus Expeditionary Force," *American History*, 39 (2004): 28 ff.
[8] See Paul Dickson and Thomas B. Allen, "Marching on History," *Smithsonian Magazine*, February 2005.
[9] Killigrew, "The Army and the Bonus Incident," 64.
[10] "Old D.C. Law Invoked in War Upon Abattoir," *Washington Post*, July 21, 1937, p. 1.
[11] Ibid.
[12] "Projects Advance in Northeast Area," ibid., April 26, 1938, B3,
[13] "Board Probes Polluted Water in Anacostia," *Washington Post*, September 2, 1943, p. 1
[14] Senator James McMillan was chairman of the Federal District Committee and a major power in the Congress in 1901.
[15] Quoted in Gillette, *Between Justice and Beauty*, 137.
[16] Ibid., 139
[17] Ibid., 142.
[18] *Washington Star*, January 19, 1942.
[19] Elaine B. Todd, "Urban Renewal in the Nation's Capital: A History of the Redevelopment Land Agency in Washington, D.C.," Ph.D. diss., 1987, Howard University, 493.
[20] Quoted in Gillette, *Between Justice and Beauty*, 163.
[21] An engineering officer in the U.S. Army, Grant parlayed on his District and family connections and rarely left Washington save for short assignments.
[22] David L. Lewis, *District of Columbia: A Bicentennial History* (New York: Norton, 1976), 78.
[23] Todd, "Urban Renewal in the Nation's Capital," 178.
[24] Gutheim, *Worthy of the Nation*, 157–85.
[25] *Washington Daily News*, July 8, 1946; H. Paul Kaemmerer, "Washington After the War," *The Journal of the Society of Architectural Historians*, 6 (1947): 31.
[26] "Segregated Swimming," *Washington Post*, August 8, 1949.
[27] Quoted in Harry S. Jaffe and Dean Sherwood, *Dream City: Race, Power and the Decline of Washington* (New York: Simon and Schuster, 1994), 28.

[28] Quoted in Gutheim, *Worthy of the Nation*, 233; Arthur Goodwillie, *The Rehabilitation of Southwest Washington as a War Housing Measure: A Memorandum to the Federal Home Loan Bank* (Washington, D.C.: Government Printing Office, 1942).

[29] *Washington Star*, May 11, 1952.

[30] Louis Justement, *New Cities for Old* (New York: McGraw-Hill Book Co., 1946), 3, 6, 8.

[31] *Washington Post*, July 12, 1954.

[32] Todd," Urban Renewal in the Nation's Capital," 65.

[33] *Washington Post*, June 30, 1956, Vertical File, Martin Luther King Library, Washington D.C.

[34] Jessica I. Elfenbein, *Civics, Commerce, and Community: The History of the Greater Washington Board of Trade, 1889–1989* (Dubuque: Kendall/Hunt Publishing Company, 1989), 96.

[35] Todd, "Urban Renewal in the Nation's Capital." 143.

[36] *Washington Post*, June 21, 1959.

[37] Quoted in Linda Wheeler, "Broken Ground, Broken Hearts—Urban Renewal Cost Homes," *Washington Post*, June 21, 1999.

[38] "Move to Halt Southwest Program Fails," *Washington Post*, January 1, 1953, p. 15; "Clear Track for RLA." *Washington Post*, November 7, 1953, p. 10.

[39] Compared to the wreckage of Southwest Washington by eminent domain in the 1950s under *Berman v. Parker*, the recent Supreme Court case of *Kelo v. New London* (2005) involved only 115 houses. One thing both cases had in common, though, is that under the current interpretation of eminent domain by the federal courts, no person's home is safe from an urban renewal program.

[40] Justice Douglas, Opinion of the Court, Supreme Court of the United States, *Berman v. Parker*, 348 U.S. 26, November 22, 1954.

[41] Sam Smith, *Captive Capital: Colonial Life in Modern Washington* (Bloomington: Indiana University Press, 1974), 217–18.

[42] *Washington D.C. Courier*, April 2, 1955; *Washington Star*, July 11, 1955.

[43] Todd, "Urban Renewal in the Nation's Capital," 167–78.

[44] Jane Jacobs, *The Life and Death of Great American Cities* (New York: Vintage, 1961).

[45] *Washington Star*, June 23, 1963.

[46] Ibid., May 11, 1976.

[47] Jon C. Teaford, "Urban Renewal and Its Aftermath," in *Housing Policy Debate* (Washington, D.C.: Fannie Mae Foundation), vol. 11, No. 2, 443.

[48] Charlotte Allen, "A Wreck of a Plan" *Washington Post*, July 17, 2005, B4.

[49] Quoted in Williams, "A River Runs Through Us," 421.

[50] "Anacostia: Housings City Dump," *Washington Post*, January 19, 1968, B1.

[51] "Anacostia's Schools Bulging," ibid., February 17, 1969, B1.

[52] "Public Housing: No Cure All for the Ghetto," *Washington Post*, January 10, 1967, B1.

[53] "The Armies of the Anacostia," *Washington Post*, August 14, 1966, E7.

[54] Kathryn J. Oberdeck, "From Model Town to Edge City: Piety, Paternalism and the Politics of Urban Planning in the United States," *Journal of Urban History*, 26 (2000): 508.

Notes to Chapter Nine

[1] For an analysis of how indiscriminate highway construction atomized and isolated black communities see John McWhorter, *Winning the Race: Beyond the Crisis in Black America* (New York: Gotham Books, 2006).

[2] "The Thirsty Capital," *Science News*, vol. 108, August 9, 1975.

[3] Washington Suburban Sanitary Commission, "About WSSC: A Thumbnail History," www.wssc.dst.md.us.

[4] "District Ready to Begin Work on Sewer Plan," *Washington Post*, August 23, 1933, p. 9.

[5] "PWA Believed About to Act on Pollution," ibid., September 11, 1938, p. 10.

[6] "U.S. to Attack Pollution of Streams Here," *Washington Post*, September 18, 1938, p. 1.

[7] "Walton League Maps Campaign to Purify River," ibid., November 10, 1938, p. 5.

[8] "Commissioners Veto Suburban Sewage Plan," *Washington Post*, December 18, 1938.

[9] "Potomac Basin Antipollution Plan Outlined," ibid., December 13, 1946. p. 6; "Bids Sought on Clean-Up of Anacostia and Potomac," ibid., December 25, 1949, M1.

[10] John Griffin, "The WSSC—A Thumbnail History," Washington Suburban Sanitary Commission pamphlet.

[11] Thomas J. Cantwell, "Anacostia: Strength in Diversity," *Records of the Columbia Historical Society of Washington, D.C.* (1973–1974): 366–67.

[12] "River Tests Inaugurated for Checkup on Pollution," *Washington Post*, August 21, 1952.

[13] "Sewage and Health," ibid., July 28, 1952, p. 6.

[14] "Officials Warn of Possible Polio Infection in Polluted Potomac and Anacostia Rivers," ibid., September 12, 1952, p. 1.

[15] Norris McDonald, *Our Unfair Share: Race and Pollution in Washington, D.C.* (Washington D.C.: African American Environmentalist Association, 2000).

[16] D.C. Scrapbooks, "Washington Floods," Washington Collection, MLK Library, "Floods of the Eighties," *Washington Post*, December 6, 1927.

[17] "Four Feet of Water at Bladensburg," *Washington Post*, August 3, 1906.

[18] *Washington Star*, April 29, 1923; "Towns Near City Flooded," *Washington Post*, March 30, 1924.

[19] "Floods Swirl Over Wharves," *Washington Post*, August 24, 1933, p. 17.

[20] *Washington Star*, April 27, 1937; *Washington Daily News*, April 26, 1937; *Washington Herald*, December 17, 1937.

[21] *Washington Star*, November 27, 1937.

[22] "$75,000 Flood Plan Asked for Anacostia," *Washington Post*, June 17, 1952.

[23] Chief of Engineers, U.S. Army, *Annual Report*, Part One, 1883, 776–77.

[24] The flooding of the Northwest Branch of the Anacostia in Maryland increased from once or twice a year in the 1940s and 1950s to as much as six times annually in the 1990s, according to a recent study. The District has experienced record rainfalls in recent years, like that of February 1984, when six inches of rain fell in the mountains above the District. In September 1996 rains from Hurricane Fran brought high

water to the falls of the Potomac. In recent times uncontrolled housing development in the watersheds has been a principal factor in flooding. C. P. Conrad, "Effects of Urban Development on Floods," *U.S. Geological Survey Fact Sheet 076-03.*

[25] "Record Flood Crest Passes, Water Level Falls Rapidly," *Washington Post*, October 18, 1942, p. 1.

[26] *Washington Post*, October 17, 1942; *Washington Daily News*, October 16, 1942.

[27] *Washington Post*, May 29, 1968.

[28] M, Gordon Wolman, "A Cycle of Sedimentation and Erosion in Urban River Channels," *Physical Geography*, 49 (1967): 385–95.

[29] Ellis L. Armstrong, ed., *History of Public Works in the United States* (Chicago: American Public Works Association, 1976), 279.

[30] *Annual Report of the Corps of Engineers*, FY 1977, vol. 1, 7.

[31] *Washington Star*, February 1, 1981.

[32] Frederic M. Miller and Howard Gillette Jr., *Washington Seen: A Photographic History, 1875–1965* (Baltimore: Johns Hopkins University Press, 1995), 160.

[33] See Zachary M. Schrag, "The Freeway Fight in Washington, D.C.," *Journal of Urban History*, 30 (2004): 648–73.

[34] For automobile statistics see "Registered Automobiles by State, 1976 and 1993," *Research and Markets*, www.researchandmarkets.com. Every day in 2005 people in the DC metropolitan area drove over three million cars for work and leisure, causing problems that ranged from asthma to skin cancer. U.S. Bureau of the Census, *Statistical Abstracts of the United States.*

[35] U.S. Geological Survey, *Hydrogeology and Ground-Water Quality of the Anacostia River Watershed*, August 10, 2004. Project Summary.

Notes to Chapter 10

[1] George Middendorf and Bruce Grant, "The Challenge of Environmental Justice," *Frontiers in Ecology*, 1 (2003): 154–60.

[2] "New Civil Rights Battlegrounds," *Blue Ridge Press*, November 25, 2002.

[3] "Out of Breath," Clean Air Task Force Report (Boston: U.S. PIRG), www.pirg.org, October 1999). See Robert D. Bullard, *Dumping in Dixie: Race Class and Environmental Quality* (Boulder: Westview Press, 1990), chap. 2.

[4] Vicki Been and Francis Gupta, "Coming to the Nuisance or Going to the Barrio? A Longitudinal Analysis of Environmental Justice Claims," *Ecology Law Quarterly*, 24 (1997): 30–35.

[5] Ryan Holifield, "Defining Environmental Justice and Environmental Racism," *Urban Geography*, 22 (2001): 86.

[6] For background see Linda Goldstein, et al., "A Tale of Two Cities," *Legal Times*, February 14, 2005.

[7] "A Washington District That's a World Apart," *New York Times*, October 8, 1992.

[8] Interview with Carl Cole, January 17, 2006.

[9] Interview with George Gurley, November 15, 2005.

[10] *D. C. Ward 8 Profile, NeighborhoodInfo DC*, Urban Institute, Washington, D.C.

[11] For Marion Barry's political career in Washington, see Jonetta Rose Barras, *The Last of the Black Emperors: The Hollow Comeback of Marion Barry in a New Age of Black*

Leaders (Baltimore: Bancroft Press, 1998). Also see Michael Powell, "D.C.'s Dema-gogue-in-Chief," *Washington Monthly*, September, 1998; "The Barry Years: 40 Years of Committed Public Service," *DC Watch*, May 21, 1998; and endorsement articles: *Washington Post*, December 16, 1979 and September 10, 1982.

12 *Washington Post*, June 18, 1961.

13 Ibid., December 4, 1963.

14 See "Daily Dump Fires Cloud City Skies," ibid., November 17, 1965.

15 Ibid., February 17, 1968.

16 The dump had an acrimonious history. Citizens picketed it in 1966 in an attempt to close it, but the District government refused to halt the burning of refuse. Nothing was done until Kelvin Mock's death. See "25 Pickets Block Trucks at Kenilworth Dump," *Washington Post*, December 18, 1966, and "Court Won't Halt Burning at Dump," ibid., June 15, 1967.

17 "The City Dump: A Park in the Making," ibid., October 13, 1968.

18 Ibid., December 31, 1972.

19 *Washington Post*, December 6, 1979.

20 *Washington Post*, April 7 and 10, 1970.

21 U.S. General Accounting Office, Report, *Siting of Hazardous Waste Landfills and their Correlation with Racial and Economic Status of Surrounding Communities* (Washington: GAO, 1983), 1.

22 Bullard, *Dumping in Dixie*, chap. 2.

23 McDonald, *Our Unfair Share*, chap. 2.

24 Ibid., 34.

25 Michael L. Kronthol, "Local Residents, the Anacostia River and Community," Contract Study for the EPA, Society for Applied Anthropology, 1995, 34 ff.

26 "Poor Communities Entrusted with Natural Resources Flourish," *Environmental News Service*, August 31, 2005.

27 Williams, "A River Runs Through Us," 422.

28 Norris McDonald, *Our Unfair Share*, 3.

29 Gurley Interview, November 15, 2005.

30 Public Health Activities, Agency for Toxic Substances and Disease Registry, Atlanta, Ga., 1997–2004 Survey. www.atsdr.cdc.gov. Public criticism of local government environmental policy continues at River Terrace. George Gurley organized "Urban Protectors" to publicize and draw attention to the continuing high rate of cancer in River Terrace. See "Environmental Justice," *Capital Sierran*, Fall, 2005, 10.

31 District of Columbia, *District of Columbia Healthy People 2010 Plan*, September, 2000, 20.

32 Interview with George Gurley, November 15, 2005.

33 Linda Fennel, "East of the River Foundation Launches Program for Areas East of the Anacostia," *Capital Sierran*, November, 2004.

34 "Black Neighbors Know U.S. Still Ignores Environmental Justice," *Pacific News Service*, October 23, 2003.

35 Interview with Carl Cole, January 16, 2006.

36 "Executive Summary," Office of the Inspector General, United States Environmental Protection Agency, Evaluation Report, "EPA Needs to Consistently

Implement the Intent of the Executive Order on Environmental Justice," *Report No. 2004-P-0007*, March 1, 2004.

[37] McDonald, *Our Fair Share*, 3, 4.

[38] Ibid., 7.

[39] CH2MHill, "Rock Creek Conservation Study," U.S. Department of the Interior, 1979.

[40] EPA, *An Environmental Characterization of the District of Columbia: A Scientific Foundation for Setting and Environmental Agenda* (Washington, D.C.: EPA, 2003), chap. 5.

[41] Pamela Wood, "Growths Found on 30 Catfish," *The Capital* [Annapolis], March 30, 2005.

[42] "Health Effects of PCBs," U.S. Environmental Protection Agency, September 8, 2004, www.epa.gov/pcb/effects.

[43] Agency for Toxic Substances and Disease Registry, *Managing Hazardous Materials Incidents*, vol. 3, "Chlordane," Public Health Service, 1995.

[44] Environmental Protection Agency, *Health Consultation on Fish as a Public Health Hazard*. During this period the EPA had meetings and issued public reports that were organized by Anacostia River Initiative, a coalition of local government and environmental groups in Washington, D.C., 1991. See also, Barry L. Johnson, et al., *Public Health Implications of Exposure to Polychlorinated Biphenyls (PCBs)*, Agency for Toxic Substances and Disease Registry, n.d., 1–39.

[45] Paige Doelling Brown, "Trophic Transfer of Polychlorinated Biphenyls (PCBs) in the Food Web of the Anacostia River," PhD. diss., George Mason University, 2001. Summary.

[46] Harriet Phelps, "Sources of Bioavailable Toxic Pollutants in the Anacostia," Report to the DC Water Resources Research Center, May 30, 2002.

[47] Brown, "Trophic Transfer of Polychlorinated Biphenyls."

[48] Rita R. Colwell, "Global Climate and Infectious Disease: The Cholera Paradigm," *Science*, 274 (December, 1996), 2027.

[49] Raymond J. Seidler, et al., "Isolation, Enumeration, and Characterization of Aeronomas from Polluted Waters Encountered in Diving Operations," *Applied Environmental Microbiology*, 39 (1980): 1010–18.

[50] "Aging U.S. Sewer System Threatens Public Health," press release, Natural Resources Defense Council, February 19, 2004.

[51] Chesapeake Bay Foundation, *The State of the Anacostia River: A Health Index, 2003–2004* (Annapolis: The Foundation, 2004).

[52] "Policy News: Americans Are Swimming in Sewage," *Environmental Science and Technology*, November 17, 2004. News Release, ES&T Online News. For one of the most comprehensive and insightful studies on this subject, see Mark Dorfman, *Swimming in Sewage: The Growing Problem of Sewage Pollution and How the Bush Administration Is Putting Our Health and Environment at Risk* (Washington: Natural Resource Defense Council, February, 2004).

[53] American Rivers, "1993 Most Endangered Rivers in the United States," americanrivers.org.

Notes to Chapter Eleven

[1] Sen. Gaylord Nelson, "How the First Earth Day Came About," earthday.envirolink.org/history.html.

[2] Marcus Hall, "Looking Back at American Wilderness Troubles," Carnegie Council on Ethics and Human Affairs, 2004, www.cceia.org.

[3] "Environmental Contaminants," U.S. Fish and Wildlife Service, October 1, 2005.

[4] Environmental Protection Agency, "Clean Water Act History," Laws and Regulations, www.epa.gov.

[5] Robert W. Adler, Jessica C. Landman, and Diane M. Cameron, *The Clean Water Act 20 Years Later* (Washington, D.C.: Island Press, 1993), 8.

[6] Washington Council of Governments, *Natural History of the Anacostia Watershed: Hydrology*, Anacostia Watershed Restoration Committee, *Annual Reports*, 1987–1990.

[7] Interviews with Robert Boone and James Connolly at the AWS headquarters, June–November 2005. For a biographical essay on Robert Boone see "Robert E. Boone," in Ann E. Dorbin and Richard A. Dorbin, *Saving the Bay: People Working for the Future of the Chesapeake* (Baltimore: Johns Hopkins University Press, 2001), 78–81.

[8] Interviews with Robert Boone, September–October, 2004.

[9] *Annual Reports* for 2002–2005, Anacostia Watershed Society, Bladensburg, Maryland.

[10] Interviews with Jim Connolly, November–December, 2005.

[11] Interviews with Robert Boone, September–October, 2004.

[12] *United States Navy Environmental Investigation Report*, Washington Navy Yard, Washington, D.C., November 1997. Executive Summary and Recommendations.

[13] Harold Kennedy, "Navy's Oldest Base Gets Clean Sweep, Fore and Aft," *National Defense*, August, 2001.

[14] "Navy and General Services Administration Agree to Clean Up Pollution at Navy Yard and Southeast Federal Center," *Earth Justice News Bulletin*, March 27, 1998.

[15] Ibid.

[16] Jane Sims Podesta, "River of Dreams," *People Magazine*, August 1, 2005. This is a summary of material found in "Endangered Species," a documentary film about the travail of Earth Conservation Corps in Washington, D.C., produced and distributed in 2005.

[17] This sketch of the watershed is based on reports and overviews of the Maryland Department of Natural Resources summarized in its 1984 document, *Maryland's Scenic Rivers: The Anacostia* (Annapolis: Maryland Department of Natural Resources, 1984), 1–35.

[18] Professor George H. Callcott, an historian at the University of Maryland, recalled that in the plantation economy of the nineteenth century, boats loaded with tobacco sailed from docks on Paint Branch Creek to Bladensburg.

[19] EPA, *Progress Under the Anacostia Ecosystem Initiative, RPA #903 B-99-003*, April 1999.

[20] *Anacostia Watershed Restoration Highlights, 1987–Present*," Publication of the Anacostia Watershed Restoration Committee (AWRC).

[21] "Analysis: Scat squad; finding pollution's sources," NPR Radio Text for *All Things Considered*, August 25, 2005.

[22] John R. Wennersten, "Recovering the Anacostia: An Urban Watershed and Its Future," *Chesapeake Quarterly*, vol. 2, no. 2, 2003, p. 9.

[23] Interviews with Tom Schuler, Neil Weinstein, and Larry Coffman, spring, 2003. See also Wennersten, "Recovering the Anacostia," 1–9.

[24] Interview with Jon Capacasa, EPA Water Director, Division III, November 15, 2005.

[25] See EPA, *Solid Waste and Emergency Response* (Washington, D.C.: Anacostia Watershed Toxics Alliance, 1999), updated April 11, 2003.

[26] Interview with Jonathan Essoka, EPA Division III Environmental Engineer and Anacostia Specialist, November 15, 2005.

[27] Capacasa interview, EPA, November 15, 2005.

[28] Interviews with Robert Boone, December 2005.

[29] EPA, Capacasa Interview, November 15, 2005

[30] Ibid.

[31] For a critical perspective on the limitations and disappointments of the EPA, see William A. Shutkin, *The Land That Could Be: Environmentalism and Democracy in the Twenty-First Century* (Cambridge: MIT Press, 2000), 63–105.

[32] For example, between 1987 and 2000 the *Washington Post* and the *New York Times* carried more than fifty lengthy stories on the condition of the Anacostia River, a body of water that most Americans had never heard of. Other articles appeared in *American Forests, NRDC Journal, Audubon Magazine, Sierra Magazine* and *E-Magazine*.

Notes to Chapter 12

[1] Most of the bridges crossing the Anacostia are old and in desperate need of repair. They were designed to serve less than half the number of automobiles now using them. The Benning Road Bridge, for example, carries 68,400 vehicles daily. See Arlo Wagner, "Many Bridges in Need of Repair, Nearly a Third Outdated," *Washington Times*, April 8, 2003.

[2] Interview with Jim Connolly, January 3, 2003.

[3] "Anthropology and the Anacostia River: Seafarer's Yacht Club," American University, Department of Anthropology, 2001, http://www.american.edu/academic.depts/cas/anthro/anacostia_watershed_society. html. See also, "Focus on a Forgotten River," *Boat/US Magazine*, September 2000.

[4] American University, Department of Anthropology, "Anthropology and the Anacostia River: Seafarer's Yacht Club."

[5] Interviews with Carl Cole, May, 2005. See also "Carl Cole Leads River Walk," *East of the River*, October, 2005.

[6] Quoted in Jack Greer, "Child of the Urban Wilderness," *Chesapeake Quarterly*, vol. 2, no.2, p.12.

[7] Ann Breen and Dick Rigby, *The New Waterfront: A Worldwide Urban Success Story* (New York: McGraw-Hill, 1996), 11.

[8] C. M. Harris, "Washington's Gamble," 536–57.

[9] John R. Wennersten, "A Capital Waterfront: Maritime Washington, D.C.,

1790–1880," paper presented to the 32nd Annual Conference on Washington, D.C., Historical Studies, November 4–5, 2005.

[10] "Two Miles of Rail and River Terminal Facilities Mapped," *Washington Post*, August 8, 1928.

[11] "Army Engineers to Lift the Potomac's Face," *Washington Post*, August 16, 1936.

[12] "This Morning Without Shirley Povich," *Washington Post*, February 4, 1939.

[13] "Trade Board Adopts Water Front Agenda." *Washington Post*, March 7, 1945.

[14] Brett Williams, "Gentrifying Water and Selling Jim Crow," *Urban Anthropology and Studies of Cultural Systems and World Economic Development*, 31 (Spring 2002): 93ff.

[15] National Capital Planning Commission, *Waterfront Development in Washington, D.C.*, 1972, p. 17.

[16] National Capital Planning Commission, 1972 Report, "Impact of the Suggested Improvements Program."

[17] See National Capital Planning Commission, *Extending the Legacy: Planning America's Capital for the 21st Century*, 1997.

[18] Mark Seasons, "Plan Reviews: Planning America's Capital," Canadian Institute of Planners, 1996.

[19] "Developing the Waterfront," *New York Times*, October 16, 1988; "A Master Plan for River Site," ibid., March 8, 1992.

[20] "A Vision for Buzzard Point," *Washington Post*, August 20, 1988,

[21] National Capital Planning Commission, "Washington's Waterfronts," 1996.

[22] *Washington Post*, January 19, 2004.

[23] Fred A. Bernstein, "Revitalizing the Banks of Washington's Forgotten River," *New York Times*, March 27, 2005.

[24] See National Capital Planning Commission, *Memorials and Museum Master Plan*, December 2001, 33–104. From South Capitol Street to the river, the NCPC envisioned a "Waterfront Crescent" and a "Memorial Corridor extending to Arlington, Virginia, to the south and eastward towards the Anacostia at the current area of RFK Stadium, Kingman Island and Anacostia Park."

[25] National Capital Planning Commission, "South Capitol Street," unpublished planning document, 2005.

[26] *Washington Post*, January 30, 2004.

[27] Altman quoted in Debbi Wilgoren, "Lively—Costly—Area Envisioned Along Anacostia," *Washington Post*, September 9, 2001.

[28] Ibid.

[29] For background, see "Theme Park Troubles City Lawyer," *Washington Post*, October 19, 1997.

[30] Benjamin Forgey, "Coming Clean About the Future," *Washington Post*, July 13, 2004.

[31] A look at a chronology of development on the Anacostia waterfront shows that a number of projects were underway to transform the benighted neighborhood long before the District began having dreams of hosting major league baseball there.

[32] Roger G. Noll and Andrew Zimbalist, "Sports, Jobs and Taxes: Are New Stadiums Worth the Cost?" *The Brookings Review*, 15 (Summer, 1997): 35–39.

[33] D.C. Sports and Entertainment Commission, DC Ballpark Community Meeting Information Packet, public meeting agenda, November 1, 2005, p. 7.

[34] Sally Jenkins, "Is the District Being Sold a Bill of Goods?" *Washington Post*, September 30, 2004.

[35] "An Open Letter to Mayor Anthony Williams and the DC Council from 90 Economists on the Likely Impact of a Taxpayer-Financed Baseball Stadium in the District of Columbia," October 21, 2004, Letters, National Taxpayers Union Foundation.

[36] Roger G. Noll and Andrew Zimbalist, *Sports, Jobs and Taxes: The Economic Impact of Sports Teams and Stadiums* (Washington: Brookings Institution, 1997), especially chapters 1 and 2.

[37] Ed Lezere, "Would a Publicly Financed Baseball Stadium Pay Off for DC?" unpublished paper, DC Fiscal Policy Institute, June 9, 2003.

[38] Steve Donkin, "Book Review: Big League Rip-Off," *Washington Peace Letter*, vol. 36, no. 3, April, 1999.

[39] See Noll and Zimbalist, *Sports, Jobs and Taxes,* op. cit.

[40] Dennis Coates and Brad R. Humphreys, "The Stadium Gambit and Local Economic Development," *Journal of Economic Development*, 23 (2000): 20.

[41] *Washington Times*, October 6, 2005.

[42] Quoted in David Nakamura, "Landowners in Stadium's Path Fight to Stay Put," *Washington Post, District Magazine*, February 2, 2006.

[43] "The Anacostia Waterfront Initiative: Development and the Environment," press release, May 2004.

[44] Testimony of Robert E. Boone before the city council, April 18, 2005.

[45] "Baseball Stadium on the Anacostia Should be Green Conservationists Say," press release, Natural Resources Defense Council, October 28, 2004.

[46] Benjamin Forgey, "The Ripple Effect: An $8 Billion Development Plan Promises Payoffs Far Beyond the High-Water Mark," *Washington Post*, July 12, 2004.

[47] Interview with Ann Breen and Dick Rigby, June 12, 2005.

[48] See Ann Breen and Dick Rigby, *Intown Living: A Different American Dream* (Washington, D.C.: Island Press, 2004), 1–39.

[49] Interviews with Dr. Hamid Karimi, October 11–18, 2005, January 18, 2006.

[50] Interview with Doug Siglin, April 12, 2005.

[51] "Settlement Promises Cleaner Waters Around Washington D.C.," Earthjustice press release, June 25, 2003.

[52] Interviews with Larry Silverman and Bill Matuszeski, September 2003. Also quoted in *Chesapeake Quarterly*, vol. 2, No.2, p. 10.

[53] *Natural Resources Defense Council,* press release, November 18, 2004.

[54] "EPA Files Suit to Keep Anacostia River Free of Raw Sewage," *Environmental News Service*, November 22, 2004.

[55] "WSSC Reaches Agreement with EPA and Conservationists on Sewer Overflows," *Natural Resources Defense Council,* press release, July 26, 2005.

[56] "Major Sewage Victory for the Upper Anacostia," *Voice of the River* [Anacostia Watershed Society], Winter 2006.

[57] Interview with Betsy Otto, December 28, 2005; "Report: Waterfront Development, river restoration best done together," American Rivers, press release, July 7, 2004.

[58] Statement in NRDC press release, October 28, 2004.

[59] Interview with Breen and Rigby, November 1, 2004.

[60] *Washington Times*, March 11, 2005.

[61] Television interview. *60 Minutes*, CBS News, April 24, 2005.

[62] Malcolm H. Woodland, "Dismissed and Disdained, Ward 8 Drowns in Appalling Neglect," *Washington Post District Magazine,* February 2, 2006.

[63] "Housing Surge and Resurgence," *Washington Post*, November 7, 2005.

[64] Quoted in *Washington Informer*, April 1, 2005.

[65] The *Washington Post*, a booster of waterfront development and the new baseball stadium, carried little adverse commentary from the black community. But that comment could be found in black newspapers, internet blog sites, church sermons, and on the pages of the *Common Denominator* and the *City Paper,* which cast a hard, critical eye on the whole waterfront development scheme.

[66] Interview with Herbert Harris, September 2003.

[67] Williams, "A River Runs Through Us," 427.

[68] Quoted in Bruce Branch, "New Ballpark Causes Fears that Gentrification is Headed for Anacostia," *The Washington Informer,* April 1, 2005, p. 1.

[69] National Association to Restore Pride in America's Capital, *In-Depth Analysis: East of the Anacostia, West of the Potomac, October 5, 2002.* www.NARPAC.org. What NARPAC did not mention was the way in which the National Capital Planning Commission, the most powerful land use organization in the capital, has treated communities east of the Anacostia River. We have noted elsewhere in this study the demonstrations by blacks to have parcels of land from Bolling Air Base turned over to community economic and residential development.

[70] "Checking in: Carl Cole and Loretta Tate," *East of the River*, November 2005.

Notes to Chapter 13

[1] "Topics for Consideration in Urban restoration," *Society for Ecological Restoration Online*, www.ser.org/abstracts. Because of heavy fertilizer application and nitrogen runoff, grass yards in the suburbs are a significant threat to the vitality of watersheds,

[2] "The Anacostia Watershed: Rescuing a Lost Treasure," in Region, Metropolitan Washington Council of Governments, *Annual Report on the Anacostia River,* December 1993, 3–6.

[3] Michael P. Dombeck, et al., "Restoring Watersheds, Rebuilding Communities," *American Forests*, 103 (Winter, 1998).

[4] Karl Blankenship, "Developing a Better Watershed," *Bay Journal*, 11 (January–February, 2002).

[5] See Media Releases, Metropolitan Washington Council of Governments, 1993–2005. MWCOG.org.; news release, "Hoyer Secures Funds Vital to Prince George's County," September 9. 2005.

[6] www.Anacostia.net.

[7] Interview with Jim Collier at Citizens Advisory Council, D.C. Department of the Environment, April, 11, 2006.

[8] Quoted in John R. Wennersten, "Recovering the Anacostia: An Urban Watershed and Its Future," *Chesapeake Quarterly*, vol. 2, No.3 (2003): 8.

[9] Interview with Alberta Paul, April 11, 2006.

[10] Ibid.

[11] Interviews with Cameron Wiegand and Daniel Harper, September 2003. See also Wennersten, "Recovering the Anacostia," 10.

[12] Casey Trees Endowment, "Assessing Urban Forest Effects and Values: Washington, DC," August, 2005.

[13] Interviews with Steve McKindley-Ward, January, 13–20, 2006.

[14] Anacostia Watershed Restoration Committee, *Anacostia Watershed Restoration Highlights, 1987–Present* (Washington D.C. Council of Governments, 2005).

[15] "Forum," *Frontiers in Ecology and the Environment*, 4 (2006): 51.

[16] U.S. Army Corps of Engineers, Baltimore District, "Anacostia River and Tributaries, Maryland and the District of Columbia Comprehensive Watershed Plan," Section 905b (WRDA) Analysis, July 2005.

[17] Stacey Sloan Blersch, "The Anacostia River of the 21st Century: Restoring an Estuary in the Nation's Capital," *National Wetlands Newsletter*, vol. 24, November–December, 2002, 7–10.

[18] "Urban Ecology: Nature in an Urban Setting," *Arizona Water Resource*, vol. 9, March–April, 2000, p. 6.

[19] "Restoration Drama," *The Economist*, August 8, 2002; John R. Wennersten, "An Ecologist on the Anacostia Watershed," *Chesapeake Quarterly*, vol. 2, No.2, pp. 7–8; H. Hassett, M. A. Palmer, E. S. Bernhardt, S. Smith, J. Carr, and D. Hart, "Status Trends of River and Stream Restoration in the Chesapeake Bay Watershed," *Frontiers in Ecology and the Environment*, 3 (2005): 259–67.

[20] Interview with Dr. Margaret Palmer, Department of Biology, University of Maryland, College Park March 10, 2003.

[21] Interview with Robert Boone, January 12, 2003.

[22] "Environmental Stewardship Growing Presence in Churches," *Bay Journal*, vol. 15, February 2006, 1–16.

[23] Episcopal Diocese of Washington, "Report of the Commission on Peace," January 2005.

[24] Metropolitan Washington Council of Governments, "Vehicular Wastes in the Metropolitan Washington Area," 1992; "The Air," *Washingtonian Magazine*, May 2003.

[25] Nancy Anne Dawe, "Building Faith in the Environment," *American Forests Magazine*, Summer 2005.

[26] "Environmental Stewardship," op. cit.

[27] "Undoing the Damage to Sacred Banks," *Washington Post*, October 30, 2004.

[28] Langston Hughes, *The Negro Speaks of Rivers* (1926).

[29] Interview with Carl Cole, January 17, 2006. Also quoted in Vernon Loeb, "Currents of Change," *Washington Post*, December 1, 1996.

Epilogue

[1] Wendell Berry, *A Continuous Harmony: Essays Cultural and Agricultural* (New York: Harcourt Brace Jovanovich, 1970), 66.

[2] William Cronon, *Nature's Metropolis: Chicago and the Great West* (New York: 1991), introduction.

[3] Jeffrey Stine, "Placing Environmental History on Display," *Environmental History*, 7 (October, 2002): 567, 571.

[4] Quoted in John R. Wennersten, "D.C. Builds: The Anacostia Waterfront Exhibition," *The Public Historian: A Journal of Public History*, 26 (Summer, 2004): 96.

Bibliography

Manuscripts
Audubon Records, Box 1, Record Unit 7294, Smithsonian Institution Archives.
Carson Gibb, "Captain Berry's Will: Debauchery, Miscegenation and Family Strife Among 18th Century Gentry," transcription, Record Group, SC 2221-28, Maryland State Archives, Annapolis.
Diary of Michael Shiner, 1813–1865, Manuscript Division, Library of Congress.
"Map of Anacostia River in the District of Columbia and Maryland," surveyed Under the direction of Lt. Colonel Peter C. Haines, 1880. Geography and Map Division, Library of Congress.
Thomas Law Family Papers, 1791–1834, MS 2386, Maryland Historical Society.
Washington Engineer Commissioner, "Map of the City of Washington, D.C.," 1883. Geography and Print Division, Library of Congress.
William Prout Papers, 1783–1801, MS 216, Historical Society of Washington, D.C.

Newspapers

Capital Sierran	*Washington Daily News*
DC Watch	*Washington Evening Star*
Environmental News Service	*Washington Herald*
Maryland Gazette	*Washington Monthly*
New York Times	*Washington Post*
The Capital	*Washington Star*
Washington D.C. Courier	*Washington Times*

Institutional Web Sites
D.C. Water and Sewer Authority, *History of Our Sewerage System*, www.dcwasa.com.
Public Health Activities, Agency for Toxic Substances and Disease Registry, Atlanta, Ga., 1997–2004 Survey. www.atsdr.cdc.gov.
"Health Effects of PCBs," U.S. Environmental Protection Agency, September 8, 2004, www.epa.gov/pcb/effects.
American Rivers, "1993 Most Endangered Rivers in the United States," Americanrivers.org.
Environmental Protection Agency, "Clean Water Act History," Laws and Regulations, www.epa.gov.
"Anthropology and the Anacostia River: Seafarer's Yacht Club," American University, Department of Anthropology, 2001, http://www.american.edu/academic.depts/cas/anthro/anacostia_watershed_society.html.
National Association to Restore Pride in America's Capital, "In-Depth Analysis: East of the Anacostia, West of the Potomac, October 5, 2002." www.NARPAC.org.
"Out of Breath," Clean Air Task Force Report. (Boston: U.S. PIRG), www.pirg.org, October 1999.

"Topics for Consideration in Urban restoration," *Society for Ecological Restoration Online*, www.ser.org/abstracts.

Washington Suburban Sanitary Commission, "About WSSC: A Thumbnail History," www.wssc.dst,md.us.

"Working Together to Restore the Anacostia," Anacostia Watershed Partnership, www. Anacostia.net.

Government Reports & Documents

"Environmental Contaminants," U.S. Fish and Wildlife Service, October 1, 2005.

"Executive Summary," Office of the Inspector General, United States Environmental Protection Agency, Evaluation Report, "EPA Needs to Consistently Implement the Intent of the Executive Order on Environmental Justice," *Report No. 2004-P-0007*, March 1, 2004.

Annual Report, Chief of Engineers, U.S. Army.

District of Columbia, *District of Columbia Healthy People 2010 Plan*, September, 2000.

Environmental Protection Agency, *Health Consultation on Fish as a Public Health Hazard.*

Environmental Protection Agency, *Progress Under the Anacostia Ecosystem Initiative, RPA #903 B-99-003*, April 1999.

Environmental Protection Agency, *An Environmental Characterization of the District of Columbia: A Scientific Foundation for Setting and Environmental Agenda.* Washington, D.C.: EPA, 2003.

Environmental Protection Agency, *Solid Waste and Emergency Response.* Washington, D.C.: Anacostia Watershed Toxics Alliance, 1999, updated April 11, 2003.

Kronthol, Michael L. "Local Residents, the Anacostia River and Community," Contract Study for the EPA, Society for Applied Anthropology, 1995.

Maryland Department of Natural Resources, *Maryland's Scenic Rivers: The Anacostia.* Annapolis, 1984.

National Capital Planning Commission, "Washington's Waterfronts," 1996.

National Capital Planning Commission, 1972 Report, "Impact of the Suggested Improvements Program."

National Capital Planning Commission, *Extending the Legacy: Planning America's Capital for the 2ist Century*, 1997.

National Capital Planning Commission, *Waterfront Development in Washington, D.C.*, 1972.

National Capital Planning Commission. *Memorials and Museum Master Plan*, December 2001, 33–104. [25] National Capital Planning Commission, "South Capitol Street," unpublished planning document, 2005.

Seasons, Mark. "Plan Reviews: Planning America's Capital," Canadian Institute of Planners, 1996.

U.S. Army Corps of Engineers, Baltimore District, "Anacostia River and Tributaries, Maryland and the District of Columbia Comprehensive Watershed Plan," Section 905b (WRDA) Analysis, July 2005.

U.S. General Accounting Office, Report, *Siting of Hazardous Waste Landfills and their Correlation with Racial and Economic Status of Surrounding Communities.* Washington: GAO, 1983.

U.S. Geological Survey, *Hydrogeology and Ground-Water Quality of the Anacostia River Watershed*, August 10, 2004. Project Summary.

United States Navy Environmental Investigation Report, Washington Navy Yard, Washington, D.C., November 1997. Executive Summary and Recommendations.

Washington D.C. Health Department. *Report of Health Officer*, 1889.

Secondary Sources

Abbott, Carl. *Political Terrain: Washington, D.C. from Tidewater Town to Global Metropolis.* Chapel Hill: University of North Carolina Press, 1999.

Adam, Robert. "Naval Office on the Potomac," *William and Mary Quarterly*, 2nd series, vol. 2 (1922): 292–95.

Adler, Robert W., Jessica C. Landman, and Diane M. Cameron. *The Clean Water Act 20 Years Later.* Washington, D.C.: Island Press, 1993.

Agency for Toxic Substances and Disease Registry, *Managing Hazardous Materials Incidents*, vol. 3, "Chlordane," Public Health Service, 1995.

"Aging U.S. Sewer System Threatens Public Health," Press Release, Natural Resources Defense Council, February 19, 2004.

"The Air," *Washingtonian Magazine*, May 2003.

Allen, Charlotte. "A Wreck of a Plan" *Washington Post*, July 17, 2005, B4.

Ames, Mary Clemmer. *Ten Years in Washington: Life and Scenes in the National Capital.* Hartford, Conn.: Worthington and Company, 1873.

Anacostia Watershed Restoration Committee, *Anacostia Watershed Restoration Highlights, 1987–Present.* Washington D.C. Council of Governments, 2005.

Anacostia Watershed Restoration Highlights, 1987–Present," Publication of the Anacostia Watershed Restoration Committee (AWRC).

Anacostia Watershed Society. *Annual Reports* for 2002–2005. Bladensburg, Maryland.

Anderson, George. "Growth, Civil War, and Change: The Montgomery County Agricultural Society, 1850–1876," *Maryland Historical Magazine*, 86 (1991): 396–406.

Anderson, Harold. "Slavery, Freedom and the Chesapeake," *Maryland Marine Notes*, 16 (March/April, 1998).

Armstrong, Ellis L., ed., *History of Public Works in the United States.* Chicago: American Public Works Association, 1976.

Arnebeck, Bob. "Slaves in Early Washington," www.geocities.com/bobarnebeck/slaves.html.

———. *Through a Fiery Trial: Building Washington, 1790–1800.* Lanham, Md.: Madison Books, 1991.

Barbour, P. L. *The Complete Works of Captain John Smith*, 3 vols. Chapel Hill: University of North Carolina Press, 1986.

Barnes, Irston. "Paul Bartsch, Biologist and Naturalist," *Atlantic Naturalist,* May–August, 1952, 217–29.

———. "Paul Bartsch, Smithsonian Curator," *Atlantic Naturalist,* January–February, 1953, 124–39.

Barras, Jonetta Rose. *The Last of the Black Emperors: The Hollow Comeback of Marion Barry in a New Age of Black Leaders.* Baltimore: Bancroft Press, 1998.

"Bathing Old Habit While Sanitation Is Recent Practice," *Washington Post*, April 3, 1927.

Been, Vicki and Francis Gupta. "Coming to the Nuisance or Going to the Barrio? A Longitudinal Analysis of Environmental Justice Claims," *Ecology Law Quarterly*, 24 (1997): 30–35.

Beitzell, Edwin W. *Life on the Potomac River*. Abell, Md.: n.p., 1973.

Berlin, Ira and Herbert G. Gutman. "Natives and Immigrants, Freemen and Slaves: Urban Workingmen in the Antebellum South," *American Historical Review*, 88 (1983).

Berlin, Ira. *Many Thousands Gone: The First Two Centuries of Slavery in North America*. Cambridge: Harvard University Press, 1998.

Berry, Wendell. *A Continuous Harmony: Essays Cultural and Agricultural*. New York: Harcourt Brace Jovanovich, 1970.

Biddle, Rev. John F. "Bladensburg: An Early Trade Center," *Records of the Columbia Historical Society*, vols.53–56 (1953–1956).

Blankenship, Karl. "Developing a Better Watershed," *Bay Journal*, 11 (January–February, 2002).

Blersch, Stacey Sloan. "The Anacostia River of the 21st Century: Restoring an Estuary in the Nation's Capital," *National Wetlands Newsletter*, vol. 24, November–December, 2002, 7–10.

Bolster, Jeffrey. *Black Jacks: African-American Seamen in the Age of Sail*. Cambridge: Harvard University Press, 1997.

Bowling, Kenneth R. *The Creation of Washington D.C.: The Idea and Location of the American Capital*. Fairfax: George Mason University Press, 1991.

Breen, Ann and Dick Rigby. *Intown Living: A Different American Dream*. Washington, D.C.: Island Press, 2004.

———. *The New Waterfront: A Worldwide Urban Success Story*. New York: McGraw-Hill, 1996.

Brewer, Richard, *Conservancy: The Land Trust Movement in America*. Hanover: Dartmouth College Press, 2003.

Brown, Letitia Woods. "Residence Patterns of Negroes in the District of Columbia, 1800-1860," *Records of the Columbia Historical Society*, 69–70 (1969–70).

———. *Free Negroes in the District of Columbia*. New York: Oxford University Press, 1972.

Brown, Paige Doelling. "Trophic Transfer of Polychlorinated Biphenyls (PCBs) in the Food Web of the Anacostia River," PhD. diss., George Mason University, 2001. Summary.

Brown, Richard D. *Modernization: The Transformation of American Life, 1600–1865*. New York: McGraw-Hill, 1976.

Brush, Grace S. "Forests Before and After the Colonial Encounter," in Philip Curtin, ed., *Discovering the Chesapeake: The History of an Ecosystem*. Baltimore: Johns Hopkins University Press.

Bryan, Wilhelmus Bogart. *History of the National Capital from Its Foundation Through the Period of the Adoption of the Organic Act*, 2 vols.. New York: The Macmillan Company, 1914–16.

Bullard, Robert D. *Dumping in Dixie: Race Class and Environmental Quality*. Boulder: Westview Press, 1990), chap. 2.

Burr, Nelson R. "The Federal City Depicted, 1612–1801," *Library of Congress Quarterly Journal*, 8 (1950).

Burroughs, John. *Wake Robin*. Boston: Houghton Mifflin, 1899.

Cantwell, Thomas J. "Anacostia: Strength in Diversity," *Records of the Columbia Historical Society of Washington, D.C.* (1973–1974): 366–67.

Capital Planning Commission, 1972 Report, "Impact of the Suggested Improvements Program."

"Carl Cole Leads River Walk," *East of the River*, October 2005.

Carpenter, John A. *Sword and Olive Branch: Oliver Otis Howard*. Pittsburgh: University of Pittsburgh Press, 1964.

Carr, Lois Green and Lorena S. Walsh. "The Planter's Wife: The Experience of White Women in Seventeenth-Century Maryland," *William and Mary Quarterly*, 34 (1977).

Causin, Dr. Nathaniel P. "An Essay on the Autumnal Bilious Epidemic of the United States," *The American Medical Recorder*, January, 1824, 55–70, American Periodical Series Online.

CH2MHill, "Rock Creek Conservation Study," U.S. Department of the Interior, 1979.

"Charles Benedict Calvert," *Biographical Directory of the United States Congress, 1771 to the Present*. Washington, 1990.

Chesapeake Bay Foundation, *The State of the Anacostia River: A Health Index, 2003–2004*. Annapolis: The Foundation, 2004.

Clark, Wayne E. "The Origin of the Piscataway and Related Indian Cultures," *Maryland Historical Magazine*, 75 (1980).

Coates, Dennis and Brad R. Humphreys. "The Stadium Gambit and Local Economic Development," *Journal of Economic Development*, 23 (2000).

Colwell, Rita R. "Global Climate and Infectious Disease: The Cholera Paradigm," *Science*, 274 (December, 1996), 2027.

Conrad, C. P. "Effects of Urban Development on Floods," *U.S. Geological Survey Fact Sheet 076-03*.

Cooke, Michael A. "Physical Environment and Sanitation in the District of Columbia, 1860–1868," *Records of the Columbia Historical Society of Washington, D.C.*, 52 (1989).

———. "The Health of the Union Military in the District of Columbia, 1861–1865, *Military Affairs*, 48 (1984): 194–99.

Cooling, Franklin III. "Civil War Deterrent: Defenses of Washington," *Military Affairs*, 29 (Winter, 1965–1966): 164–78.

Cronon, William. *Nature's Metropolis: Chicago and the Great West*. New York: Norton, 1991.

Crosby, Alfred. *Ecological Imperialism: The Biological Expansion of Europe*. Cambridge: Cambridge University Press, 1986.

Custer, Jay F. *Prehistoric Cultures of the Delmarva Peninsula*. Newark: University of Delaware Press, 1989.

D.C. Ward 8 Profile, Neighborhood Info DC, Urban Institute, Washington, D.C.

Darby, John. "The Disposal of Sewage," *Scientific American*, vol. 23, July 9, 1870,

Dawe, Nancy Anne. "Building Faith in the Environment," *American Forests Magazine*, Summer 2005.

Denny, George D. *Proud Past Promising Future: A History of Prince George's Municipalities*. n.p., privately printed, 1994.

Dent, Richard J. Jr., *Chesapeake Prehistory: Old Traditions, New Directions*. New York: Plenum Press, 1995.

Deppisch, Ludwig. "Andrew Jackson and American Medical Practice: Old Hickory and His Physicians," *Tennessee Historical Quarterly*, 63 (2003): 15–32.

Dickson, Paul and Thomas B. Allen, "Marching on History," *Smithsonian Magazine*, February 2005.

———. *The Bonus Army: An American Epic*. New York: Walker and Company, 2004.

Dombeck, Michael P. et al. "Restoring Watersheds, Rebuilding Communities," *American Forests*, 103 (Winter 1998).

Dorbin Ann E. and Richard A. Dorbin, *Saving the Bay: People Working for the Future of the Chesapeake*. Baltimore: Johns Hopkins University Press, 2001.

Dorfman, Mark. *Swimming in Sewage: The Growing Problem of Sewage Pollution and How the Bush Administration Is Putting Our Health and Environment at Risk.* Washington: Natural Resource Defense Council, February, 2004.

Doty, Alvah H., M.D. "Cholera from a Modern Standpoint," *The American Journal of Medical Sciences*, vol. 141, January 11, 1911.

Downing, Margaret Brent. "The American Capitoline Hill and Its Early Catholic Proprietors," *Catholic Historical Review*, 2 (1911).

———. "The Development of the Catholic Church in the District of Columbia from Colonial Times Until the Present," address before the Columbia Historical Society, February 21, 1911, Washington, D.C.

Duffy, John. *The Sanitarians, A History of American Public Health.* Urbana: University of Illinois Press, 1990.

Duhamel, James F. "Tiber Creek," *Records of the Columbia Historical Society,* 28 (1926): 203–25.

Elfenbein, Jessica I. *Civics, Commerce, and Community: The History of the Greater Washington Board of Trade, 1889–1989.* Dubuque: Kendall/Hunt Publishing Company, 1989.

"Environmental Stewardship Growing Presence in Churches," *Bay Journal*, vol. 15, February 2006, 1–16.

Farquhar, Michael. "The City's Pretty New Face, Boss Shepherd Got the Job Done—at a Steep Price," *Washington Post*, November 28, 2000.

Fausz, J. Frederick. "Present at the Creation: The Chesapeake World that Greeted Maryland Colonists," *Maryland Historical Magazine*, 79 (1984).

Ferguson, Ernest B. *Freedom Rising: Washington in the Civil War.* New York: Alfred A. Knopf, 2004.

Fleet, Betsy. *Henry Fleete: Pioneer, Explorer, Trader, Planter.* Richmond: Privately printed, 1989.

"Focus on a Forgotten River," *Boat/US Magazine*, September 2000.

Franklin, William M. "The Tidewater End of the Chesapeake and Ohio Canal," *Maryland Historical Magazine*, 81 (1986).

Gahn, Bessie. *Original Patentees of Land at Washington Prior to 1770.* Silver Spring, Md.: Privately printed, 1936.

Galeano, Eduardo. *Open Veins of Latin America.* New York: Monthly Review Press, 1997.

Gillette, Howard. *Between Justice and Beauty: Race, Planning and the Failure of Urban Policy in Washington, D.C.* Baltimore: Johns Hopkins University Press.

Gilmore, C. W. "Fossil Animals in the District of Columbia," unpublished essay, 1933, Papers on Natural History, Box 37, Audubon Society Ms., Smithsonian Institution Archives.

Glumer, J. V. "Map of the Anacostia River or Eastern Branch Region," Geography and Maps Division, Library of Congress, 1880.

Goldfield, David R. "The Business of Health Planning: Disease Prevention in the Old South," *Journal of Southern History*, 42 (1976): 559–63.

Goldstein, Linda et al., "A Tale of Two Cities," *Legal Times*, February 14, 2005.

Goodwillie, Arthur. *The Rehabilitation of Southwest Washington as a War Housing Measure: A Memorandum to the Federal Home Loan Bank.* Washington, D.C.: Government Printing Office, 1942.

Gordon, Martin K. "The Origins of the Anacostia River Improvement Project," *Soundings: A Journal of the Writings and Studies of the Potomac River Basin Consortium*, Spring 1987.

Gray, Lewis C. *History of Agriculture in the Southern States to 1860*. 1933. repr., Gloucester, Mass.: Peter Smith, 1968.

Green, Constance McLaughlin. *Secret City: A History of Race Relations in the Nation's Capital*. Princeton: Princeton University Press, 1967.

———. *Washington*, 2 vols. Princeton: Princeton University Press, 1962–63.

Green, Lt. F. V. for the Commissioners of Washington, D.C., *City of Washington Statistical Maps*, Map No. 7, Sewers, 1880.

Griffin, John. "The WSSC—A Thumbnail History," Washington Suburban Sanitary Commission Pamphlet.

Gutheim, Frederic. *The Potomac*. Baltimore: Johns Hopkins University Press, 1977.

Hall, Marcus "Looking Back at American Wilderness Troubles," Carnegie Council on Ethics and Human Affairs, 2004, www.cceia.org.

Harriot, Thomas. "A brief and true report of the new found land of Virginia" (1588). In Michael Alexander, ed., *Discovering the New World Based on the Books of Theodore DeBry*. New York: Harper and Row, 1976.

Harris, C. M. "Washington's Gamble, L'Enfant's Dream: Politics, Design, and the Founding of the National Capital," *William and Mary Quarterly*, 56 (1999): 536–57.

Harris, G. M. "Washington's Gamble, L'Enfant's Dream: Politics, Design and the Founding of the National Capital," *William and Mary Quarterly*, 56 (1999).

Hassett, H., M. A. Palmer, E. S. Bernhardt, S. Smith, J. Carr, and D. Hart, "Status Trends of River and Stream Restoration in the Chesapeake Bay Watershed," *Frontiers in Ecology and the Environment*, 3 (2005): 259–67.

Hering, Rudolph and Samuel A. Greeley. *Collection and Disposal of Municipal Refuse*. New York: 1921.

Hill, Libby. *The Chicago River: A Natural and Unnatural History*. Chicago: Lake Clement Press, 2000. Blake Gumbrecht, *The Los Angeles River: Its Life, Death, and Possible Rebirth*. Baltimore: Johns Hopkins University Press, 1999.

Holifield, Ryan. "Defining Environmental Justice and Environmental Racism," *Urban Geography*, 22 (2001).

Hutchinson, Louise Daniel. *The Anacostia Story, 1608–1930*. Washington: Smithsonian Institution Press, 1977.

Isaac, Rhys. *The Transformation of Virginia, 1749–1790*. Chapel Hill: University of North Carolina Press, 1982.

Jacobs, Jane. *The Life and Death of Great American Cities*. New York: Vintage, 1961.

Jaffe, Harry S. and Dean Sherwood. *Dream City: Race, Power and the Decline of Washington*. New York: Simon and Schuster, 1994), 28.

Janke, Lucinda Prout and Iris Miller. "Facilitating Transportation and Communication: The Prigs Map," in Iris Miller, *Washington in Maps, 1606–2000*. New York: Rizzoli International Publications, 2002.

Johnson, Barry L. et al. *Public Health Implications of Exposure to Polychlorinated Biphenyls (PCBs)*. Agency for Toxic Substances and Disease Registry, n.d., 1–39.

Jones, E. L. "Creative Disruptions in American Agriculture, 1620–1820," *Agricultural History*, 48 (1974).

Jones, K. Bruce et al. *An Ecological Assessment of the United States Mid-Atlantic Region*. Washington, D.C.: Environmental Protection Agency, 1997.

Justement Louis. *New Cities for Old*. New York: McGraw-Hill Book Co., 1946.

Kaemmerer, H. Paul. "Washington After the War," *The Journal of the Society of Architectural Historians*, 6 (1947).

Kapsch, Robert J. "Building Liberty's Capital: Black Labor and the New Federal City," *American Visions* (February/March, 1995).

Keene, Jennifer D. *Doughboys, the Great War, and the Remaking of America.* Baltimore: Johns Hopkins University Press, 2001.

Kennedy, Harold. "Navy's Oldest Base Gets Clean Sweep, Fore and Aft," *National Defense*, August, 2001.

Kenneth Bowling, "The Other G. W.: George Walker and the Creation of the National Capital," *Washington History*, 3 (Fall/Winter 1991/1992): 5–21.

Killigrew, John W. "The Army and the Bonus Incident," *Military Affairs*, 26 (1962).

Kingseed, Wyatt. "A Promise Denied: The Bonus Expeditionary Force,"*American History*, 39 (2004).

Kranz, Peter M. *Dinosaurs of the District of Columbia.* Washington, D.C.: Dinosaur Fund, 2003.

Kulikoff, Allan. "The Colonial Chesapeake: Seedbed of Antebellum Southern Culture," *Journal of Southern History*, 45 (1979).

Kulikoff, Allan. "The Origins of Afro-American Society in Tidewater Maryland and Virginia, 1700 to 1790," *William and Mary Quarterly*, 35 (1978).

Larkin, Jack. *The Reshaping of Everyday Life 1790–1840.* New York: Harper and Row, 1988.

Latrobe, Benjamin Henry. *The Journal of Latrobe. Being the Notes and Sketches of an Architect, Naturalist and Traveler in the United States from 1796 to 1820.* New York: D. Appleton and Company, 1905.

Lear, Tobias. *Observations on the River Potomak, the Country Adjacent and the City of Washington.* New York: Samuel Loudon, 1793. Reprinted in *Records of the Columbia History Society*, 8 (1905): 117–40.

Lessoff, Alan. *The Nation and Its City: Politics, "Corruption" and Progress in Washington, D.C. 1861–1902.* Baltimore: The Johns Hopkins University Press, 1994.

Lewis, David L. *District of Columbia: A Bicentennial History.* New York: W. W. Norton, 1976.

Lezere, Ed. "Would a Publicly Financed Baseball Stadium Pay Off for DC?" unpublished paper, DC Fiscal Policy Institute, June 9, 2003.

MacDougall, J. D. *A Short History of the Planet Earth.* New York: John Wiley & Sons.

Maskalyk, James. "Typhoid," *Canadian Medical Association Journal*, vol. 169 (July 22, 2003): 132.

Mather, Fred. "Poisoning and Obstructing the Waters," *Forest and Stream—A Journal of Outdoor Life*, vol. 4, February 18, 1875.

McAleer, Margaret H. "The Green Streets of Washington: The Experience of Irish Mechanics in Antebellum Washington," in Francine Curro Carry, *Washington Odyssey: A Multicultural History of the Nation's Capital.* Washington: Smithsonian Books, 1996.

McDonald, Norris. *Our Unfair Share 3: Race and Pollution in Washington. D.C.*. Washington: African-American Environmentalist Association, 2000.

McWhorter, John. *Winning the Race: Beyond the Crisis in Black America.* New York: Gotham Books, 2006.

Melosi, Martin V. *Garbage in the Cities: Refuse, Reform and the Environment, 1880–1930.* New York: Dorsey Press, 1981.

———. *The Sanitary City: Urban Infrastructure from Colonial Times to the Present.* Baltimore: Johns Hopkins University Press, 2000.

Metropolitan Washington Council of Governments, "Vehicular Wastes in the Metropolitan Washington Area," 1992.

Middendorf, George and Bruce Grant. "The Challenge of Environmental Justice," *Frontiers in Ecology,* 1 (2003): 154–60.

Middleton, Arthur Pierce. *Tobacco Coast: A Maritime History of Chesapeake Bay in the Colonial Era.* 1953. repr., Baltimore: Johns Hopkins University Press, 1984.

Miller, Frederic M. and Howard Gillette Jr. *Washington Seen: A Photographic History, 1875–1965.* Baltimore: Johns Hopkins University Press, 1995.

Mills, H. F. "Typhoid Fever in Relation to Water Supplies, "*Journal of the New England Waterworks Association,* 5 (1891): 149–61.

Morgan, Philip D. *Slave Counterpoint: Black Culture in the Eighteenth-Century Chesapeake and Lowland.* Chapel Hill: University of North Carolina Press, 1998.

Morison, A. J. "The Virginia Indian Trade to 1673," *William and Mary College Quarterly Historical Magazine,* series 2, vol. 1 (1921).

"Navy and General Services Administration Agree to Clean Up Pollution at Navy Yard and Southeast Federal Center," *Earth Justice News Bulletin,* March 27, 1998.

Nelson, Gaylord. "How the First Earth Day Came About," earthday.envirolink.org/history.html.

Newell, F. H. "Pollution of the Potomac River," *National Geographic,* 8 (1897).

Newman, Harry Wright. *To Maryland from Overseas.* Baltimore: Genealogical Publishing Company, 1986.

Noll, Roger G. and Andrew Zimbalist. "Sports, Jobs and Taxes: Are New Stadiums Worth the Cost?" *The Brookings Review,* 15 (Summer, 1997): 35–39.

———. *Sports, Jobs and Taxes: The Economic Impact of Sports Teams and Stadiums.* Washington: Brookings Institution, 1997.

Oberdeck, Kathryn J. "From Model Town to Edge City: Piety, Paternalism and the Politics of Urban Planning in the United States," *Journal of Urban History,* 26 (2000).

Overbeck, Ruth Ann. "Capitol Hill: The Capitol is Just Up the Street," the Ruth Ann Overbeck Capitol Hill Project, CapitolHistory.org.

Passos, John Dos. "Anacostia Flats," *New Republic,* June 1932.

Pearson, John C. "The Fish and Fisheries of Colonial Virginia," *William and Mary Quarterly,* series 2, vol. 22 (1943).

Peck, Taylor. *Round-shot To Rockets: A History of the Washington Navy Yard and U.S. Naval Gun Factory.* Annapolis: United States Naval Institute Press, 1949.

Phelps, Harriet "Sources of Bioavailable Toxic Pollutants in the Anacostia," Report to the DC Water Resources Research Center, May 30, 2002.

Pinkett, Harold T. "*The American Farmer*: A Pioneer Agricultural Journal, 1819–1834," *Agricultural History,* 24 (1950): 146–50.

Plummer, Betty L. "A History of Public Health in Washington, D.C., 1800–1890," Ph.D. diss., University of Maryland, College Park, 1984.

Podesta, Jane Sims "River of Dreams," *People Magazine,* August 1, 2005.

"Policy News: Americans Are Swimming in Sewage," *Environmental Science and Technology,* November 17, 2004.

Power, Garrett. *Chesapeake Bay in Legal Perspective.* Washington: U.S. Department of the Interior, 1970..

Proceedings of the County Courts of Charles County, 1666–1674, Archives of Maryland, vol. 60.

Provine, Dorothy. "The Economic Position of the Free Blacks in the District of Columbia, 1800–1860," *The Journal of Negro History,* 58 (1973): 61–72.

"The Purification of Rivers," *Appleton's Journal of Literature, Science and Art,* vol. 12, October 17, 1874.

Rafter, George W. and M. N. Baker, *Sewage Disposal in the United States*. New York: Van Nostrand and Company, 1894.

Report of the Potomac River Oyster Pollution Commission. Washington, D.C., 1912.

"Restoration Drama," *The Economist*, August 8, 2002.

Rosenberg, Charles E. *The Cholera Years: The United States in 1832, 1849, and 1866*. Chicago: University of Chicago Press, 1987.

Rountree, Helen C. and Thomas E. Davidson, *Eastern Shore Indians of Virginia and Maryland*. Charlottesville: University Press of Virginia, 1997.

Scharf, J. Thomas. *History of Maryland from the Earliest Period to the Present Day*, 3 vols. Hatboro: Tradition Press, 1967.

Schlosberg, David. *Environmental Justice and the New Pluralism*. New York: Oxford University Press, 1999.

Schrag, Zachary M. "The Freeway Fight in Washington, D.C.," *Journal of Urban History*, 30 (2004): 648–73.

Schultz, Stanley K. and Clay McShane, "To Engineer the Metropolis: Sewers, Sanitation and City Planning in Late-Nineteenth Century America," *Journal of American History*, 65 (1978): 389–411.

Seasons, Mark. "Plan Reviews: Planning America's Capital," Canadian Institute of Planners, 1996.

Seeyle, John. *Beautiful Machine: Rivers and the Republican Plan, 1775–1825*. New York: Oxford University Press, 1991.

Seidenschnur, Christine E. "The Botanical Activities of Paul Bartsch (1870–1960)," *Proceedings of the Biological Society of Washington*, 78 (1961): 272–92.

Seidler, Raymond J. et al. "Isolation, Enumeration, and Characterization of Aeronomas from Polluted Waters Encountered in Diving Operations," *Applied Environmental Microbiology*, 39 (1980): 1010–18.

Shakel, Paul A. and Barbara J. Little. *Historical Archeology of the Chesapeake*. Washington D.C.: Smithsonian Institution Press, 1994.

Shutkin, William A. *The Land That Could Be: Environmentalism and Democracy in the Twenty-First Century*. Cambridge: MIT Press, 2000.

Silver, Timothy. *A New Face on the Countryside: Indians, Colonists, and Slaves in the South Atlantic Forests, 1500-1800*. Cambridge: Cambridge University Press, 1992.

Smith, Sam. *Captive Capital: Colonial Life in Modern Washington*. Bloomington: Indiana University Press, 1974.

Spurr, Stephen H. "George Washington, Surveyor and Ecological Observer," *Ecology*, 32 (1951).

Stine, Jeffrey. "Placing Environmental History on Display," *Environmental History*, 7 (October, 2002).

Stranahan, Susan Q. *Susquehanna: River of Dreams*. Baltimore: Johns Hopkins University Press, 1993.

Sweig, Donald M. "The Importation of African Slaves to the Potomac River, 1732–1772," *William and Mary Quarterly*, 42 (1985).

Taggart, Hugh T. *Public and Private Rights on the Anacostia River*. Washington: 62nd Congress, 1911.

Talbott, Henry. "Fishing Up and Down the Eastern Branch of the Potomac," *Forest and Stream, A Journal of Outdoor Life*, March 12, 1898.

Teaford, Jon C. "Urban Renewal and Its Aftermath," in *Housing Policy Debate*. Washington, D.C.: Fannie Mae Foundation, vol. 11, No. 2.

"The Thirsty Capital," *Science News*, vol. 108, August 9, 1975.

"The Tiber Creek Flushing Gates, Washington, D.C.," *Engineering News and Railway Journal*, February 8, 1994.

Tilp, Frederick. *This Was Potomac River*. Alexandria, Va.: Privately printed, 1978.

Todd, Elaine. "Urban Renewal in the Nation's Capital: A History of the Redevelopment Land Agency in Washington, D.C.," Ph.D. diss., 1987, Howard University, 493.

Tooker, William Wallace. "On the Meaning of the Name Anacostia," *American Anthropologist*, vol. 7, October, 1894.

Troesken, Werner. "Race, Disease and the Provision of Water in American cities, 1889–1921," Unpublished paper, Department of History, University of Pittsburgh, December, 2000.

U.S. Geological Survey, *Hydrogeology and Ground-Water Quality of the Anacostia River Watershed*, August 10, 2004. Project Summary.

United States House of Representatives, 51st Congress Document 445, *Report Upon the Sewerage of the District of Columbia*. Washington: Government Printing Office, 1890.

Vlach, John Michael. "The Mysterious Mr. Jenkins of Jenkins Hill: The Early History of the Capital Site," *The Capital Dome*, U.S. Capitol Historical Society, Spring, 2004.

Ward, John Williams, ed., *Manners and Politics in the United States: Letters on North America*. Garden City, N.Y.: Anchor Books, 1961.

Waring, George E. Jr. *Report on the Social Statistics of Cities*, Part II. Washington: Government Printing Office, 1887.

Washington Council of Governments, *Natural History of the Anacostia Watershed: Hydrology*, Anacostia Watershed Restoration Committee, Annual Reports, 1987–1990.

Weishample, David B. and Luther O. Young. "Dinosaurs of the East Coast," *Johns Hopkins Magazine*, June 1996, electronic edition.

Wennersten, John R. "A Capital Waterfront: Maritime Washington, D.C., 1790–1880," paper presented to the 32nd Annual Conference on Washington, D.C., Historical Studies, November 4–5, 2005.

———. "An Ecologist on the Anacostia Watershed," *Chesapeake Quarterly*, vol. 2, No.2, pp. 7–8.

———. "D.C. Builds: The Anacostia Waterfront Exhibition," *The Public Historian: A Journal of Public History*, 26 (Summer, 2004).

———. "Recovering the Anacostia: An Urban Watershed and Its Future," *Chesapeake Quarterly*, vol. 2, no. 2, 2003, p. 9.

"What is Bad Water?" *Scientific American*, vol. 34, June 10, 1876.

Wheeler, Linda. "Routing a Ragtag American Army," *Washington Post*, April 12, 1999, p. A01

Williams, Brett. "A River Runs Through Us," *American Anthropologist*, 103 (2001).

———. "Gentrifying Water and Selling Jim Crow," *Urban Anthropology and Studies of Cultural Systems and World Economic Development*, 31 (Spring 2002).

Wolman, M, Gordon. "A Cycle of Sedimentation and Erosion in Urban River Channels," *Physical Geography*, 49 (1967): 385–95.

Woodland, Malcolm H. "Dismissed and Disdained, Ward 8 Drowns in Appalling Neglect," *Washington Post District Magazine*, February 2, 2006.

Zelinsky, Wilbur. "Landscapes." *Encyclopedia of American Social History*. New York: Scribner's, 1993.

Chronology

	conduit. By 1873 underground sewers empty into the Anacostia and Rock Creek
1887	Construction of Brentwood, a suburb for U.S. Colored Troops
1896	Case of *Plessy v. Ferguson* institutionalizes racial segregation
1898	Regional trolley lines connect the District with the suburbs
1890–1898	Col. Peter C. Haines plans to reclaim the Anacostia mudflats
1902	Army Corps of Engineers dredges the Anacostia to the Washington Navy Yard plus a smaller channel to the District line
1917–1945	Automobiles in Maryland increase from 55,000 to 375,000
1918	Washington Suburban Sanitary Commission organizes to investigate a typhoid epidemic and to ensure pure water for Montgomery and Prince George's Counties
1930s	Evolution of land use in the watershed from agriculture to urbanization.
1932	Bonus March in Washington. First major public scare from untreated waste in the Potomac. Bacterial contamination closes the Anacostia from Three Sisters bridge to Fort Washington
1934–1941	CCC and WPA in Anacostia
1938	Wastewater treatment plant at Blue Plains opens
1938–1996	District of Columbia Water and Sewer Utility Administration is part of the District government
1948	Water Pollution Control Act of 1948 provides the first federal funds for state water pollution control programs. Details are left to the states and its provisions are not enforced
1950s	Army Corps of Engineers completes the Anacostia River Flood Control and Navigation Project
1950–2000	Prince George's County experiences rapid population growth
1954	*Brown v. Board of Education of Topeka, Kansas*
1965	President Lyndon B. Johnson calls the Potomac "a national disgrace"
1969	Cuyahoga River in Cleveland catches fire
1971	DC Council prohibits water contact sports in the Potomac, Rock Creek, and the Anacostia
1972	Anacostia River experiences major fish kills. Federal Clean Water Act passes
1980	50 percent of the Anacostia watershed is urbanized. Population reaches 569,000

1980–1991 Environmental Protection Agency begins to use biological wter quality criteria and the Index of Biotic Integrity.

1985 State and local governments issue advisories on fishing. PCBs and chlordane contaminate fish.

1987 98 percent of the tidal wetlands and 75 percent of the basin's freshwater wetlands lost or destroyed by this date; Congress creates section 319 of the Clean Water Act to get states to identify waters damaged or threatened by runoff and reduce or eliminate pollution from land-based sources.

1987 Anacostia Watershed Restoration Agreement involves the District and Maryland's Prince George's and Montgomery Counties. Six Point Action Plan in 1991

1988–1995 260 spills of hazardous substances totaling nearly 60,000 gallons in the Anacostia

1988 U.S. Army Corps of Engineers conducts a study of the Anacostia River

1991 Federal Water Quality Study of the Anacostia River; District of Columbia hires its first urban forester

1993 Maryland Department of Natural Resources appoints an Anacostia forester; Potomac Conservancy incorporated in Maryland.

1996 Creation of the district of Columbia Water and Sewer Authority, a semi-autonomous regional entity

1999 Founding of the Anacostia Watershed Toxic Alliance. Anacostia Summit. Maryland and the District of Columbia reaffirm their commitment to: 1) dramatically reduce pollution loads; 2) protect and restore the ecological integrity of the Anacostia River and its streams; 3) restore the natural range of resident and anadromous fish; 4) increase the filtering capacity and habitat diversity of the watershed by increasing tidal and non-tidal wetlands; 5) protect and expand forest cover throughout the watershed and create a riparian forest buffer adjacent to streams, wetlands, and the river; 6) increase citizen and business awareness of their role in the cleanup and revitalization of the watershed.

2000 Potomac Watershed Partnership

2002 Rainscaping Initiative launched by Potomac Conservancy in partnership with Montgomery County, Md.

2003 Anacostia Watershed Initiative of 2003, federal law.

Index

economic growth and destruction of
  wetlands, 272
and health of communities, 186
history of
  and early development, 49
  as the Eastern Branch, 36, 39
  and link to plantation culture, xi
  and persistence of plantation
    heritage, 56
  and Pierre L'Enfant's design of
    Washington, D.C., xii
  as political and social chronicle, xv
  as shaper of Washington social
    identity, xiv
  and slavery, 3
  social, racial, and political elements,
    271
industrial waste, 73
and industry, 75
land issues and eminent domain,
  240–41
land use
  and local government, 64
  and riparian rights, 120
land use issues, 83
  as dumping ground, xi
  and riverfront development,
    241–43
  and waterfront development,
    226–31
navigation hindered by silting, 115
politics and environment linked, 245
and pollution
  efforts to address, 200
pollution of
  navy yard and industrial waste, 74
and pollution problems, 244
as product of historical and political
  events, 3, xiv
and racial issues, xii
reclamation of, 120–21, 270
and sanitation, 119
science applied to rescue of, 257–58
sewage, 117, 181, 193, 194, 236, 237
  delays in addressing, 199–200
  dumping of untreated sewage into
    streams, 247
  increase in, 199

issue overlooked by environmental
  groups, 203
pollution of associated with child
  mortality, 61
settlement to fix sewer mains, 248
sewer problems, 94
sewer systems
  plans to end overflow, 246–47
of social and racial oppression, xi
and social issues, 16, xv
storm water runoff, 213
upper region
  silting hinders commercial naviga-
    tion, 125
waste, 92
water, pollution of
  and bacteria levels, xii
  construction of sewage disposal
    plant, 122
  contamination and decline in fish
    species, 190, 192
  continued presence of disease
    microbes, 109
  presence of toxins, 74, 181, 189–91
  as public health threat, 57
and wildlife
  fish unsafe, 186
  wildlife of, 269–70
Anacostia River Flats
  and Bonus March, 131–37
  serves as encampment for U.S. Colored
    troops during Civil War, 132
  as site of first freedmen's camps, 132
Anacostia River region
  abundant fish stocks of, 13, 14
  climate and terrain
    effect on early communities, 17–18
  deforestation of, 67
  developers and conservationists, 129
  diversity of population, 94
  early inhabitants of, 5, 6, 7
  growth outpaces infrastructure, 107
  Indian settlements in, 7
  and lack of dredged channel for com-
    merce, 127
  landscape and topography of, xiii
  ongoing problem of flooding and
    storm water management, 127–28